OPERATIONAL ECONOMICS OF ELECTRIC UTILITIES

OPERATIONAL ECONOMICS OF ELECTRIC UTILITIES

by CONSTANTINE W. BARY

COLUMBIA UNIVERSITY PRESS

New York and London   1 9 6 3

About the Author

B.S.E.E., Massachusetts Institute of Technology

Fellow and Member for life, American Institute of Electrical Engineers

Member, Load Research Committee Association of Edison Illuminating
    Companies (its past chairman and also of its predecessor the Special
    Committee on Load Studies)

Director, Economic, Cost and Rate Analysis, Philadelphia Electric
    Company

Member, Economics Committee, Atomic Power Development Associ-
    ates, Inc.

Chairman, Steering Committee Heat Storage Research Project, Edison
    Electric Institute
        Formerly:

Consultant, Executive Office of the President of the United States

Consultant, Defense Electric Power Administration, U.S. Department of
    the Interior

Advisor, Office of Energy and Utilities, National Security Resources
    Board

Chairman, Committee on Public Utility Reports of the Advisory Council
    on Federal Reports to the U. S. Bureau of the Budget

Guest Lecturer at the Industrial College of the Armed Forces

Consultant: Office of War Utilities, War Production Board, Office of
    Production Management

Author of numerous monographs, papers, and discussions presented at
        local, regional, national, and international meetings of profes-
        sional, technical, and business societies and organizations

Copyright © 1963 Columbia University Press
Library of Congress Catalog Card Number: 63-9807
Manufactured in the United States of America

*Dedicated to my wife, Kay,
and to our son, David*

PREFACE

In this book I have set forth my views on the operational economics of modern electric utilities. Having written on individual and specific aspects of this subject, I am now combining
and expanding them into a comprehensive whole by describing
and illustrating conceptual models, methods, principles, and
procedures which I developed over the years in the study of the
most probable incidence of costs for electric utility services
and in designing equitable and compensatory rates therefor,
under a consistent general and unified theory. This book also
covers my views on a general appraisal of the probable economic impacts of now foreseeable developments in the fields of
production, transmission, and distribution of electric services
by utilities; and includes a description of the more important
techniques that can be used in evaluating the economic significance of alternative plans or actions in the operations of
such enterprises. Also provided in the Appendix are six sets
of tables of numerical data which should facilitate the computations in such evaluations.

The decision to write this book came to me a few months
after my conversation in December, 1960, with Walker L. Cisler,
President of The Detroit Edison Company and a distinguished
leader in the electric utility industry, and my subsequent discussions with J. A. Thielman, a close associate and then Assistant Director, Economic and Rate Analysis Division of
Philadelphia Electric Company. Thus this work was under-

taken to fill a void in the literature previously available on an important subject of an important industry which has contributed so much to so many in the progress of man.

I consider myself fortunate in having been able to develop my theories and concepts of this subject in an atmosphere of scientific objectivity, away from the heat of controversy in defending an established position. Throughout the years of studying this subject, my aim has been to discover and then to apply in a practical manner the probable effects of complex forces, phenomena, and trends which are present in the operational economics of electric utilities in the United States, as they have existed over the past third of a century, and as I visualize they will exist in the foreseeable future. I have written this book to provide, what appears to me and to many thoughtful people in and out of the industry with whom I discussed this subject, a very much needed exposition of the fundamental principles which would bridge the existing gap between theories of academic economists and the concepts well suited for, and employed in, the practical direction and administration of the affairs of electric utility enterprises.

The techniques for effectuating the methodology set forth in this book have had a test of over thirty years' experience. Grateful acknowledgment is due for this to the foresightedness of the managements of the Philadelphia Electric Company over these years, especially to such distinguished men as H. P. Liversidge, its former President and later Chairman of the Board of Directors; and to N. E. Funk, a former Executive Vice President; more recently also to R. G. Rincliffe, now Chairman of its Board of Directors and chief executive officer. They provided the organization, the environmental conditions and incentives which were conducive over the years to a systematic development and application of this methodology, and the use of its results in the operations of the enterprise. Like any other worthwhile activity, this one too requires an organizational set-up and an expenditure of effort, money, and time to reach a systematic functioning, not unlike that of other activities required in an effective conduct of the business of an electric utility. For best results this activity too must be continuous, and should be guided by technical personnel experienced in utility operations, dedicated to scientific objectivity, always searching for facts, inquiring into the causes of the observed effects, and interpreting results with clear and sound judgment.

I cannot close this preface without expressing my deep sense of gratitude to many distinguished men in the electric utility industry, who over the years through correspondence and personal discussions with me, have enlarged, strengthened, and clarified many aspects of my views on the subject matter of this book. I can only name here a few who have been most helpful: H. A. Snow, former Controller of The Detroit Edison Company; P. H. Chase, former Assistant to Vice President, Engineering, Philadelphia Electric Company; F. M. Terry, former Rate Engineer of the Consolidated Edison Company of New York, Inc.; W. R. Waggoner and James A. Zobel, former Rate Advisors of Southern Services, Inc.; P. H. Jeynes, Engineering Economist, Public Service Electric and Gas Company; F. W. Brooks, Vice President, The Cleveland Electric Illuminating Company; Nelson Dezendorf, Vice President, General Motors Corporation; G. B. Warren, Vice President, General Electric Company, now retired; R. E. Ginna, now Chairman of the Board of Directors, Rochester Gas and Electric Corporation; Edwin Vennard, Vice President and Managing Director of the Edison Electric Institute; James C. Bonbright, Professor Emeritus of Finance of the Graduate School of Business at Columbia University; and P. Schiller, Utilization Research Engineer, the Electricity Council of Great Britain, now retired.

To my colleagues A. Abramovitz, E. H. Bromer (retired) and W. T. Brown, engineers in charge of responsible aspects of the Economic, Cost and Rate Analysis division of the Philadelphia Electric Company, and to A. H. Kidder, Assistant to Vice President, Engineering and Research, of that Company, I record here my appreciation for their skillful analytical work and many excellent ideas and suggestions over the years. To many other members of that organization, but especially to the personnel of its Testing Section and to Helen H. Neill, my secretarial assistant, I express here my sincerest thanks for devotion to duty in the preparation, computation, compilation and setting-up of the extensive data produced over the years, and which have formed the foundation for the material set forth in this work.

To F. M. Hunter, Esquire, a distinguished lawyer and an outstanding counsel of much experience in matters of public utility law, I record here my profound gratitude for his valuable suggestions on the original manuscript; and to F. S. Walters, Rate Engineer of Potomac Electric Power Company, I express my sincerest thanks for a thorough review and thoughtful comments on the original draft of this book.

Constantine W. Bary

"Four Views"
Whitemarsh, Pennsylvania
November, 1962.

CONTENTS

FIGURES

OPERATIONAL
ECONOMICS
OF ELECTRIC
UTILITIES

1. GENERAL CONCEPTS

By far the largest portion of electric utility service in the United States of America is now being rendered by corporate enterprises whose ownership is held directly or indirectly by a vast number of individuals. These enterprises have been granted certain rights and privileges in connection with the supply of their services in specified geographic areas. By reason of the inherent nature of these businesses they are under regulation by duly authorized government bodies on many phases of their activities, rights, and responsibilities. Among them, regulation of earnings, through rates charged for service rendered, is one of the most important features. The basic principles of such rate regulation rest upon administrative and juridical concepts of justness and reasonableness, and avoidance of unfair and unreasonable discrimination or prejudice. Within such regulatory framework, managements of these enterprises may exercise judgment to an extent not too dissimilar from the unregulated enterprises.

There are other distinguishing features of these enterprises; the major ones are:

1. Electricity, now in general use, cannot be stored. The supply of electric service responds instantly to the demands for it. It involves continuous and relatively long-term relationships between the enterprise and each of its individual customers through continuous and repetitive business dealings, and through physical ties between the service-rendering facilities of the enterprise and service-utilization equipment of its customers.

2. The supply of electric service is a public necessity, its continuity is essential to the welfare of the public, its administration is vested with a high public responsibility, and its operational economics cause a slow turnover of the investment in its plant facilities.

3. By far the largest portion of electric service by utilities is made available for use by customers at all hours of the day and on all days of the year. It may be used by a customer for any legitimate purpose without a direct knowledge of the enterprise supplying it, and under widely varying conditions as to its quantity, rate, and time of use. It must be supplied to anyone meeting the availability requirements for the service within the territory of the enterprise.

The economic significance of such distinguishing features finds expression, in one way or another, in the day-to-day operating practices of these enterprises; in the thoughts, attitudes, and actions of their managements, employees, and regulatory agencies; in the planning for future requirements; in the cost-keeping techniques; in rate structures, rules, regulations and conditions under which service is, or is offered to be, supplied——in short, in the over-all operational economics of supplying electric utility service. Some of these features are created by physical phenomena which are susceptible of apprehension by human senses; others are conceptual in nature established by the brain of man as a result of his observations, experience, study of phenomena, and imaginative thought.

Concepts are the product of the thinking process. Their creation depends upon the establishment by the human brain of a theory which tries to link the observed facts together by either qualitative or quantitative relationships, the basic aim being to permit us to predict events in the future. In this process we endeavor to understand the behavior of complex phenomena and workings of complex mechanisms, and to perceive the nature of forces which act on them. But our brain cannot do that without simplifying, without reducing things to component elements, and without establishing for us and within us conceptual models of the thing we are trying to understand. Obviously, all such simplifications are arbitrary. They are relative and reflect the scale of observation our brain is capable of at the time. Every time such scale of observation is changed, new phenomena will be encountered which are likely to lead the brain to promulgate a new theory to conform to the new scale of observation.[1]   However, without any theory and without any model we cannot proceed.

So it is, in our attempts to understand the complex interrelationships of electric supply facilities, loads, and costs-to-serve of a modern electric utility, the quantitative and qualitative relationships which exist within and between them, and the manner in which they behave over a wide range of electric service requirements. Such understanding is a prerequisite to a proper determination of the operational economics of rendering such services, and, what is even more important, to our ability of foreseeing and predicting the effects of changing conditions on the physical, operational and economic features of such service supply. To accomplish this, we too must establish concepts and theories of their behavior, which cannot be capricious and unstable in day-to-day operations, but which must conform to general standards of consistency throughout their range of application, be enduringly stable, and be harmonious with the basic juridical-economic principles so that their application will produce results which are proper, equitable, and void of unfair discrimination.

Operational economics is a term which is being used in this book to describe collectively those functions of a modern electric utility which deal with the economic aspects of: its cost (used in its broadest sense) of rendering service, which shall be called "cost-to-serve," over a wide range of requirements; the revenues derived from the services rendered through a scheme of prices reflected in rate schedules; and the techniques of evaluating alternative plans, or actions, to satisfy economically the requirements of service supply.

There are many considerations which underly the formulation of the rate function of such operational economics; but, notwithstanding anything to the contrary, the major ones are: the cost (used in its broadest sense) to the utility enterprise of rendering service, and the load characteristics of the service supplied. But, since practically all cost elements of a modern electric utility system are jointly created by more than one customer

[1]From the standpoint of man, it is the scale of observation which creates the phenomenon. This fundamental fact was first pointed out by the Swiss physicist, Professor Charles Eugene Guye.   Lecomte duNoüy, *Human Destiny* (New York, Longmans, Green and Co., 1947).

and since the economic effects of individual customers' loads upon the system are greatly affected by their relationships to the loads of other customers, each of these two major features per se has no absolute base of reckoning. They are basically abstractions, products of the human brain which has codified the observed phenomena into concepts and theories of behavior under an established scale of observation.

COST-TO-SERVE

One of the objects in this book is to set forth a description of the concepts, principles, practices, and procedures reflected in the system of determining cost-to-serve developed by me, with the assistance of a number of associates, over many years of studies and application. We have employed this system, with only minor modifications, for over one-third of a century. It, thus, has had the benefit of time-test and has yielded consistent results and sound indications on all operational economic phases of rendering electric service with which we have been confronted over this period of time.

The significance of this system rests on five basic features: 1) the establishment of a conceptual independence of the incidence of costs-to-serve and the prices charged for the service; 2) the use of a conceptual cost formula composed of four parametric components, forming the major cost parameters of rendering electric service (see Chapter 2); 3) the creation of a conceptual cost model of an electric supply system by physical-functional subdivisions, (see Chapter 3); 4) the establishment of a conceptual model of an electric utility's load structure, (see Chapters 4 and 5); and, 5) the blending of these features into a composite whole under a general unified theory, (see Chapters 6, 7, and 8).

Conceptual Models. A modern electric utility system is a complex structure, or mechanism. It functions continuously, not unlike a living organism, and performs simultaneously the functions of production, transportation, and delivery of its services, for a concurrent utilization by its customers. By far the largest portion of its physical plant is used jointly by its customers, and similarly almost all of its expenses in supplying the service are incurred jointly for its customers. The industry has experienced a rapid and continuous growth since its inception about three-quarters of a century ago, and all indications point to a continuation of the growth into the foreseeable future.

In order to enable the human brain to understand and grasp the physical and economic significance of operation of this mechanism for the purpose of understanding its operational economic behavior, it is necessary to simplify its complex phenomena by reducing them to component elements. This will be done through the establishment of conceptual models which could serve as bases for the observation of the behavior of cost-to-serve. Such models for individual electric utility systems may differ in many details from those described in this book. It is impossible and impractical to set forth one single conceptual interpretation which may be applicable without some modification to all utilities. The actual significance of such models as applied to each enterprise can be appraised only through a study and full knowledge of the individual enterprise's conditions, and the practices peculiar to its own operations; and similarly, any interpretations of details must be made by taking into account existing local conditions. It is possible, however, to offer certain general concepts, in the broader aspects of their significance, which are believed to be of fundamental nature.

What Kind of Cost-to-Serve. Before proceeding with such descriptions, let us reflect on what kind of cost-to-serve we are after. Do we want to know the cost to serve each and every individual customer of the enterprise? Are we after the cost to serve every conceivable appliance or each individual application? Obviously, the answer is "no." Knowledge of such costs-to-serve is impractical, economically infeasible, and of little, if any, significance in the day-to-day operations of a modern utility system. It would make no more sense than for a physicist, in studying the behavior of gases, to attempt to draw conclusions from a study of behavior of each and every molecule of the gas he is studying. But, how then does he succeed in foretelling and in expressing the laws governing the behavior of the gas? The general method employed is the statistical method, that is, a method based upon the behavior of the *average* of a great number of active elements. Since the physicist is confronted with a mass made up of an immense number of minute particles, he can apply the statistical methods, provided that on the average each element can be considered as obeying the laws of chance; that is, can act without any artificial restrictions, and simply in accord with its own ebb-and-flow requirements. It is only in this case that the statistical laws are valid.

In the case of our problem,—the study of the cost-to-serve on a modern electric utility system—we too are confronted with a large mass made up of a large number of individual elements: of property, of customers, and of loads; and we too have to direct our attention toward developing a method which would permit us to foretell qualitatively and quantitatively the most probable behavior of such costs on the average, over a wide range of customers' unrestricted service requirements. The general method we have to follow is thus one through which we will endeavor to determine the behavior for the average of the elements comprising the mass.

Averages. There are a number of ways of obtaining averages. They range from a simple arithmetic averaging of all the elements of a mass to a refined and complex subdivision of a heterogeneous mass into more or less homogeneous classes, strata, or groups, as the particular conditions or objectives dictate. Experience has demonstrated that for modern electric utilities a simple averaging of all the elements of the entire mass of property or of customers or of loads, for cost-to-serve determinations, will not provide the necessary means to foretell reliably the probable behavior of such costs over a wide range of service conditions, nor to assign them in an equitable manner among the various classes or groups. Thus, we have to resort to subdividing the mass into classes, strata, or groups of sufficient homogeneity to form relatively stable averages throughout the subdivision. Any such subdivisions require a classification or sorting of individual cases on the basis of their *functional* nature or of their *controlling* characteristic, the selection of which has to be based upon good judgment and care to insure that such sorting faithfully reproduces the desired *functional* nature or the desired *controlling* characteristic, as the case may be, of the whole. Mathematical technique is no substitute for such judgment. Once established, they become the dominant principles upon which the determination of cost behavior must proceed.

This latter statement may need amplification. Suppose, for example, the established practice, like that in the United States of America, is to bill residential customers for electric service on the basis of their monthly use of energy, irrespective of any other distinguishing characteristic. Of what practical application would it be to obtain averages for "costing" purposes by stratifying the entire mass of these customers using some other controlling feature such as, for example, the number in the family or the occupations of heads of families or physical size of premises or family income, or the like? Or of what use would it be to establish "costing units" in terms of averages for energy usage of customers within specified periods of time, such as at night, in the daytime, and in the evening? This latter feature would be essential if the practice were to bill customers for energy used during a number of specified daily periods, as is the case in some parts of Europe. Thus, for meaningful comparisons there must be a compatibility between the principles of averaging employed in the pricing of electric service and in the techniques of costing it.

The process of obtaining stratified averages of the cost-to-serve, in actual practice, must be confined to the controlling characteristic under which the particular class or stratum is expected to be administered in the day-to-day operations. But, insofar as individual elements are concerned, the averages obtained under one method of stratification, employing one controlling characteristic, will not necessarily produce the same results as under another method of stratification, employing another controlling characteristic.

The necessity of breaking up a mass into its parts, and the parts into elements, and so forth, causes us to create conceptual models of that mass, just as science creates them of the universe and of matter. The propriety of such models lasts only so long as they are able to provide us with the means of explaining the behavior of that which we study under a unified theory which we have conceived. A change in the level of our observation usually causes us to alter the theory, which in turn compels us to seek the establishment of new models or structures that would fit better in explaining the newly observed phenomena under a new unified theory of the whole.

RATE STRUCTURE

"The art of rate making is an art of wise compromise," so states Professor James C. Bonbright in his distinguished work on public utility rates. He further states after analyzing a number of rate standards, that "Nevertheless, one standard of reasonable rates can be said to outrank all others in the im-

portance attached to it by experts and by public opinion alike—
the standard of cost of service...."[2]

A. C. Marshall and H. A. Snow, former president and controller, respectively, of The Detroit Edison Company, in a paper
before the annual meeting of NELA state that "Man's inborn
sense of fairness and equity seems strangely satisfied if he be
assured that he is paying for a unit of energy only what it has
cost to generate and deliver it. Furthermore, business is most
stable, and progress most sure-footed when each part of the
business earns its own cost; that is, when the charges made to
each group of customers are adjusted to the costs of serving
them. These two considerations urge the exact adjustment of
rates to costs."[3]

Chief Justice Stone, speaking for the U. S. Supreme Court said:
"The establishment of a rate for a regulated industry often involves two steps of different character, one of which may appropriately precede the other. The first is the adjustment of a
general revenue level to the demands of a fair return. The
second is the adjustment of a rate schedule conforming to that
level, so as to eliminate discriminations and unfairness from its
details." [4] And Justice Jackson, dissenting, in another case
said: "I must admit that I possess no instinct by which to know
the 'reasonable' from the 'unreasonable' in prices and must
seek some conscious design for decision." [5]

It is my basic premise that modern rate schedules applicable
to the unrestricted services of the general classes of the mass
of customers of an electric utility should conform reasonably
well to the most probable cost-to-serve trends determined under
a general unified theory of cost and load behavior which reflects, at the existing level of observation, fairly and reasonably: the incidence of the costs, their causation, or the manner
in which they are incurred in the supply of service. A rate
structure designed in accordance with this basic premise should

[2]James C. Bonbright, *Principles of Public Utility Rates* (New York,
Columbia University Press, 1961), pp. 38 and 67.

[3]A. C. Marshall and H. A. Snow, "Distribution Costs—Residential
Service," *Proceedings*, 54 Conference (New York, National Electric
Light Association, 1931) LXXXVIII, 106.

[4]Federal Power Commission v. Natural Gas Pipeline Co., 315 U.S.
575 (1941).

[5]Federal Power Commission v. Hope Natural Gas Co., 320 U.S.
591 (1944).

be equitable to the utility supplying the service and to the customers using that service. Based on my lengthy experience, chances are very good that, from long-range considerations, it should be economically sound for all new and additional volumes of business in relation to existing ones.

Rate schedules are in themselves statements of differential prices over a wide range of requirements of existing and prospective users of service of a utility enterprise. While I firmly believe that good judgment is a fundamental prerequisite in their formulation, I am also of the opinion that the quality of such judgment will be enhanced through a well-rounded knowledge of the most probable cost-to-serve relationships. No one expects a captain to sail a ship on a predetermined narrow course no matter what the conditions; but no good captain will sail a ship without knowledge of that course. It seems to me that in the electric utility business, be it investor-owned or a government enterprise, cost-to-serve relationships reflecting most probable conditions indicated under existing level of our observations, are the charts of the course rate designs must take for the unrestricted services of electricity supply to the general classes of customers; thus the second objective of this book is to provide information on this subject.

ALTERNATIVE PLANS

The third objective of this book is found in the third function of operational economics, as previously defined. It is the principles which underly the evaluations of the significance of alternative plans or actions or of changes in environmental conditions, to satisfy economically the requirements of service supply. The basic mathematical techniques for such evaluations are not new; their general features have been covered over the years in the technical literature; but some of the more important aspects are included in the closing chapters of this book, as they seemed to me to be pertinent to the general theme of this work, especially since some of them, in my opinion, have not received adequate attention in the past, and others have an important and interrelated bearing on the first two functions of the operational economics, that is, to foresee the trends in the cost-to-serve for an adequate design of rates, which are to be effective in the future.

2. COST CONCEPTS

The word *cost* is ambiguous. Unless accompanied by a definition as to the purpose or kind, it can have different meanings to different people or, in its use, for different purposes. In a classical economic sense, it means: "that which is sacrificed to obtain anything;"[1] or, "the sum total of labor expended and wealth consumed in producing anything."[2] However, even with these definitions the term remains ambiguous in day-to-day use because in general it can cover a multitude of different meanings. There are different kinds of cost, different problems require different types of cost information, and different people inherently view or understand them in a different manner.

There are *private* costs and *public* costs, *absolute* and *relative, average* and *incremental, long-term* and *short-term, direct* and *indirect, constant* and *variable, sliding* and *levelized, special* and *joint, investment* and *operating.* It is beyond the scope of this book to go into their detailed explanation. They are mentioned here only as illustrations of the kinds of cost that economists and laymen speak about.

People concerned with the study of costs, but viewing them from different levels, backgrounds, and objectives are: engineers, financiers, accountants, statisticians, economists—to name just a few, who come first to mind.

Problems encountered in the operational economics of a modern electric utility which require information on costs, range

[1]Webster's New International Dictionary, 2d Edition, Unabridged.
[2]Encyclopaedia Britannica, VI, 508.

from determining economic effects of alternative plans or actions or of changing environmental conditions, to the substantiation of the reasonableness of a rate structure, the promulgation of new rates for heretofore non-existent loads, or the economical scheduling and loading of production facilities.

The comprehensiveness of the coverage of cost elements pertaining to a specified problem will differ depending upon the objectives, the accuracy, and the attitude of the individuals concerned with the problem. For example, the problem of determining cost of meter-reading could cover either the direct cost of labor and supplies incurred by the personnel performing this function; or it could, in addition, reflect the indirect cost of general administration of such personnel, the applicable pension expenses and social security taxes; or it could, in addition, comprehend some or all elements of cost of the equipment needed to perform this function.

The foregoing statement should give the reader a general idea of the wide variety of concepts possible when pronouncing the word *cost*. It thus behooves us to be careful in conveying the meaning we intend this word to have in our analysis of operational economics of electric utilities.

Classes of Cost. Generally, in our analyses we will encounter three major classes of cost:

1. Investment, which comprises the cost to the enterprise of land and facilities constituting the physical plant devoted to the supply of electric service. In accordance with existing requirements of the Uniform System of Accounts for electric utilities, the dollar values of such plant must represent the original cost of it when first devoted to public service. Being a balance sheet entry it reflects conditions *as of a given time.*

2. Revenue Deductions, which comprise recurring operating expenditures for labor and supplies and appropriations for such requirements as pensions, depreciation and taxes, made by the enterprise in the course of its operations pertaining to the supply of electric service. Being entries of the income statement they reflect conditions *for a stated period*, such as a month or a year.

3. Costs, which comprise the sum of revenue deductions and the needed compensation of investors for the capital provided by them. This is an entry *peculiar to operational economics*, and is related to conditions *of a stated period* such as a month,

or a year. It is in effect synonymous with the concept of revenue needed to cover the labor expended, wealth consumed,
taxes incurred and compensation provided to investors, in the
supply of electric service under specified conditions of the
supply.

Thus, the study of the cost-to-serve on an electric utility
system can be expressed by the following equation:

$$C = D_R + M_i \tag{2.01}$$

where

C = the cost for a specified period, such as a year
D_R = revenue deductions for such specified period
M_i = requirements over such specified period for compensation on capital provided by investors

Both terms, D_R and M_i, can be subdivided into a number of
subitems, and then these subitems can be recombined along the
lines suitable to a particular problem. However, in general in
most problems of operational economics of electric utilities
such recombining takes either of the following forms:

It can be expressed as:

$$C = C_0 + C_r \tag{2.02}$$

where

C_0 = the portion of revenue deductions incurred at a zero
return on investment, including that portion of taxes not
dependent on return
C_r = the required return on investment and the portion of revenue deductions associated with such return (generally
taxes dependent on such return)

or it can be stated as:

$$C = O + F \tag{2.03}$$

where

O = that portion of revenue deductions called operating expenses
F = the required return on investment and that portion of revenue deductions associated with such investment (generally allowances for depreciation, insurance premiums,

property taxes and other taxes dependent on the return). This item is frequently called the "carrying (or fixed) charge component of the cost"

While the foregoing classification of costs provides an adequate definition of the broad economic *nature* of the two major portions of the total costs, it is insufficient to convey a good understanding of the incidence of costs or cost causation or the manner in which costs are incurred on an electric utility system in the supply of service under the wide variety of customers' load requirements.

Parametric Cost Components. To meet this requirement, the total cost-to-serve must be resolved into components which conceptually reflect the major parameters which our judgment, experience or intuition tell us, from technical and economic considerations, to be responsive or related to the incidence of the costs, or to their causation or to the manner in which they are incurred in the supply of service. In the original establishment of such parameters we, like many others in science and technology who want to understand the workings of complex phenomena, postulate relationships which, at the then existing level of our observation, appear to offer possibilities for such understanding; and if, from experience, it is found that through their use we can foretell satisfactorily the behavior of the phenomena, their parameters become accepted as workable tools.

From studies of, and lengthy experience on, cost of rendering service on electric utilities, I have established, and will use here, the following general equation to describe the incidence of the costs, their causation, or the manner in which they are incurred, in the supply of unrestricted electric service:

$$C = C_C + C_D + C_P + C_E \qquad (2.04)$$

where the four parametric components are:

C_C = the "Customer" component, comprising costs which are caused by the presence of customers on the system, irrespective as to their demand and energy requirements

C_D = the "Customer Demand" component comprising costs which are caused by the individual customers' maximum kilowatt demands, irrespective as to their load diversity and kilowatthour energy requirements

C_P = the "Class Peak or Diversified Demand" component,

comprising costs which are caused by the kilowatt peak
load of a class, a system or its functional subdivisions,
or by customers' diversified maximum kilowatt demands

C_E = the "Energy" component, comprising costs which are
caused by customers' kilowatthour energy requirements,
irrespective as to their demands and load diversity

In accordance with the General Unified Theory of cost-to-
serve described herein, the form of this general equation remains fixed throughout its entire range of application, but each
of the classes of service into which an electric utility's business is homogenized through subdivision will possess its own
unit cost for each of the four parametric components. Thus the
cost to serve (C_T) a customer of a given class will be expressed
by the following equation:

$$C_T = c_c + c_d D_c + c_p P_c + c_e E_u \qquad (2.05)$$

where the component unit costs and the corresponding parameters are:

c_c = the unit cost of the "Customer" component expressed
per customer

c_d = the unit cost of the "Customer Demand" component expressed per kilowatt of customer's maximum demand as
at the customer's meter

c_p = the unit cost of the "Class Peak or Diversified Demand"
component expressed per kilowatt of class peak as at
the meters, or per kilowatt of customer's diversified
maximum demand as at his meter

c_e = the unit cost of the "Energy" component expressed per
kilowatthour of customer's use as at the customer's
meter

D_c = the customer's maximum kilowatt demand

P_c = the customer's diversified maximum kilowatt demand
with respect to the class peak

E_u = the customer's kilowatthour energy use

It will be observed from equation (2.05) that the total cost-to-
serve a customer of a given class depends upon the magnitudes
of the four parametric unit costs and upon the customer's three
load characteristics. Since the interrelationships of the two
demand characteristics with the third—the volume of service

rendered—are not necessarily linear in nature over the entire range of customers' service requirements (shown in Chapter 4), the total cost-to-serve is likely to be nonlinear too (as demonstrated in Chapter 7).

Throughout our discussion of equations (2.04) and (2.05) we have employed the word *cost*, as applied to the total as well as to the parametric components. Each of such components comprises the cost features reflected by equations (2.01) to (2.03), inclusive. Therefore, each of these components integrates the two cost classifications indicated by these equations, and thus can be subdivided into them if required. Unless otherwise specifically stated, my general concept of such costs, as they apply to the cost-to-serve function of operational economics throughout this book, will comprehend the fully-analyzed, assigned, or allocated amounts of all elements entering these components.

Consideration of equation (2.05) provides a definite indication that the subject of the cost-to-serve resolves itself into three major parts: *one deals with the determination of costs by the four parametric components; the second, with the determination of the service load characteristics; and the third, with the combining of the results of the first two, to obtain the cost-to-serve.* All three parts of this endeavor are coordinated through a General Unified Theory of behavior of the models underlying the parts. Such models should not be too complex, but at the same time must be sufficiently refined to provide consistency throughout the largest possible range of their application. They should be enduringly stable over a long period of time; be harmonious with the basic principles underlying the American juridical principles of propriety, equity, and fairness; reflect the physical manner of service supply; and provide meaningful averages of a stratified mass of individual elements.

Cost Periods. The fundamental period for the cost determination in the operational economics is a year comprised of twelve consecutive calendar months. It is usually called an annual period and basically stems from the periodicity of the time cycle covered by the planet Earth around the sun. This period integrates within itself the twelve calendar months, the two solstices, and the four seasons—spring, summer, fall, and winter. It is the only generally accepted time period which reflects all of the seasonal variations in the use of electric service by customers of a utility, and thus integrates the significance of these variations in the operational economics of service supply.   Under existing conditions of cost accounting, it usually comprises a calendar year; but sometimes could cover any other twelve-month period, or even any period of fifty-two consecutive weeks.   In these latter cases its description should specifically indicate the twelve months ending what month or the fifty-two weeks ending what week.

The pricing in rate schedules, generally prevailing throughout the United States for the service rendered by electric utilities is usually expressed for convenience on a monthly basis, sometimes for calendar months, and sometimes for thirty-day months. However, the revenues derived from such rate schedules can be readily obtained for an annual basis to integrate seasonal variations and to permit direct comparisons with the annual cost-to-serve.

Of course, cost-to-serve data developed on an annual basis, reflecting annual component unit costs and the corresponding annual parameters in equations (2.04) or (2.05), can be readily converted to average monthly conditions.   Similarly, revenue data on an annual basis, reflecting the sum of the twelve-months' values can be readily converted to an average monthly basis.   But, under the functional behavior of capacity costs of electric service, which are inherently created by the annual maximum demand requirements, the reverse procedure, that is, employing average monthly demands for this parameter for determining cost-to-serve, should be avoided as improper in any meaningful studies of the operational economics of electric utility services.

3. COST MODEL OF AN ELECTRIC UTILITY SUPPLY SYSTEM

The supply system of a modern electric utility is a complex conglomerate of numerous facilities, equipment, and activities. Such a system integrates within itself the functions of electricity production, its bulk transmission, its distribution, and in some cases also its utilization, together with the associated business functions of work performed on consumers' premises, of customers' billing, of sales promotion, and of general administration. As of a given time, such a system reflects the evolutionary inheritance of the past, the historical spread of piecemeal coverage of the territory served, the plans for the future and the heterogeneity of equipment employed in rendering a large variety of service requirements.

The production of electricity on a modern utility is accomplished in either thermal or hydro generating stations. These stations are usually interconnected among themselves and with those of neighboring utilities through a grid of high-voltage transmission lines to allow at all times of day and night, and throughout all seasons of the year, an economical loading of all such production facilities of the interconnected system, and to provide a high reliability of service from the production system throughout the territory. Electricity thus produced and transmitted is then distributed in bulk at other high voltages either directly to large-size users or to other load centers, where it is stepped down to intermediate, called "primary," voltages and either delivered in bulk directly to medium-size users or to local distribution points for conversion to low, called "sec-

ondary," voltages suitable for delivery to and direct utilization
in premises of residential or other groups of small-size users,
or for conversion to constant current for street lighting application.   In addition to these functions, generally present on all
modern utility supply systems in the United States, a number of
utilities possess special purpose facilities reflecting individualized functions such as frequency changers for use in electrified railroads, direct current conversion equipment for lo-
calized distribution inherited from the past or for use by electrified street railways, and other facilities functionally devoted
for individualized applications.

The business functions of a utility comprise customers' billing with its required metering and often service-control facilities; sales promotion of the available services with the related
aspects of appliance repairs, merchandising, and public rela-
tions; and general administration comprised of activities of
management, keeping property records and general accounts,
purchasing all supplies, and performing other duties such as
required for stores, payrolls, personnel, treasurer, legal, rates,
and other corporate requirements.

The supply system and the business functions in reality con-
sist of many individual entities: the plant is made up of land,
structures, buildings, boilers, dams, turbines, generators, transformers, switchgear, towers, poles, wires, cable, meters,
switches, fuses, office buildings, storerooms, cars, trucks, tools,
office equipment, and the like; and the personnel comprises:
operators, maintenance crews, linemen, patrolmen, meter-read-
ers, billing clerks, salesmen, servicemen, bookkeepers, accountants, engineers, chemists, lawyers, secretaries, stenog-
raphers, managers, and others.   In reality each of these
entities performs its own assigned task in its own peculiar
manner within its own prescribed scope. Many of these entities
in their physical existence are comingled with each other and
cannot be segregated, or separated, in a physical sense into
functional subdivisions, which can only be accomplished in a
statistical manner through the creation of a conceptual model
in such a manner as to make each of its functional parts act in
its entirety as a single entity reflecting a single conceptual
behavior of the part.

Cost Model.   The cost model of an average electric utility
supply system is composed of the following major functional parts:

1. Production System
2. Bulk Transmission System
3. Distribution System
   a. High Tension Voltage Distribution
   b. Primary Voltage Distribution
   c. Secondary Voltage Distribution
   d. Constant Current Distribution
   e. Service Conductors
4. Metering and Control System
5. Special Purpose System (including the transfer of constant current distribution from 3d.)

And the cost model of such a utility's business system is composed of the following major functional parts:

6. Work on Consumers' Premises and related activities
7. Customers' Billing and related matters
8. Sales Promotion and related activities
9. General Administration activities, including appropriations for pensions and employees' welfare expenses

TABLE 1. COST MODEL OF AN ILLUSTRATIVE ELECTRIC UTILITY

Functional Subdivisions	Annual Cost		
	Percent of Each Total		Each Total in Percent of Sum Total
	Operating Expenses	Carrying Charges*	
Production System	56	44	54
Bulk Transmission System	15	85	6
Distribution System:			
High tension voltage distribution	13	87	7
Primary voltage distribution	19	81	9
Secondary voltage distribution	20	80	5
Service conductors	28	72	1
Metering and Control System	37	63	3
Special Purpose (incl. Constant Current Distribution)	30	70	2
Work on Customers' Premises	88	12	1
Customers' Billing	95	5	3
Sales Promotion	100	—	3
General Administration	73	27	6
Sum Total			100

*On plant and working capital; comprising return, depreciation, taxes dependent on such return and insurance.

Table 1. provides an illustration of the economic significance of each of the functional parts in relation to the total for an illustrative electric utility of a relatively large metropolitan-suburban type, operating in the northeastern section of the United States.

Having established this cost model of the supply system, let us now analyze each of its functional parts with the object of establishing qualitatively the significance of each with respect to their contributions to the parametric components of equation (2.05).

THE PRODUCTION SYSTEM

The production system is the most significant single functional element of a modern electric utility and represents over one-half of the over-all total cost-to-serve.   Under modern practices, it functions as an entity, the operations of its individual elements of capacity blocks being subordinated to the over-all economic significance of the system.

The simultaneous interactions of the requirements for and the production of electricity have been always a unique economic feature of the electric utility business.   As a result, the peak loads over short intervals of time, measured in minutes, with an adequate allowance for reserve needs throughout the year, have always determined its capacity needs.   The generally used measure of this capacity is expressed in kilowatts, under specified conditions; but two other measures, peculiar to the alternating current electricity now commonly produced by utilities, form additional determinants.   They are the capability of the production system to meet the reactive requirements of the load, which is expressed as reactive kilovolt-amperes, and the total current-carrying capability of the electric portion of the production system, expressed in kilovolt-amperes, which in accordance with the fundamental principles of electricity, is in effect the square root of the sum of the squares of the other two determinants.   Thus,

where
$$Kva = \sqrt{(Kw)^2 + (Kvar)^2} \qquad (3.01)$$

Kva = the total current carrying capability
Kw = the active power carrying capability
$Kvar$ = the reactive power carrying capability

The ratio of kw to kva is called the power factor.

While the measures for kilowatts and kilovolt-amperes, in a mathematical sense, are always positive, that for kvar can be either positive or negative depending upon whether the reactive requirements in an electrical sense are of a lagging or of a leading nature. This feature of *kvar* provides a convenient means for recognizing cost-to-serve credits or debits due on account of difference in the nature of reactive requirements of the load, which cannot be reflected mathematically by either the kilowatt or the kilovolt-ampere measures.

By and large, the production system is provided and operated for the economic benefit of the entire business of the utility considered as a whole without regard to any of its individual production components. (There may be exceptions to this generalization, and where present such exceptions will require special and individualized considerations.) Conceptually, such a production system "feels," at any given time only the coincident and the total load requirement of the enterprise, and thus all of its costs are jointly incurred by all of the load components.

As of any given time the production system reflects the evolutionary developments of the past and the modern developments of the present. It can be composed of hydro and thermal generating plants; high efficiency and lower efficiency capacity blocks; large-size and smaller-size units; facilities operating on different types of fuel (such as coal, oil or gas or even nuclear) under different operating practices (attended and unattended); and is comprised of relatively large central stations and small decentralized installations. Notwithstanding the heterogeneity of this conglomerate, its costs can be resolved into such functional elements as we choose to establish to meet the requirements of our cost-to-serve concept. The number of such elements and their scope of coverage are matters of individual judgment. Herein we shall set forth a methodology which has provided good and consistent indications on the economic aspects of the cost to serve.

Under this method the original cost, or as it is frequently called investment (or the fair value where this basis is used), of each electric generating station, after the elimination of "special purpose" facilities, is resolved into three elements, comprising equipment and related land and structures. One element is related to the kilowatt aspects of the capacity and comprises the facilities of the thermal cycle (or hydraulic cycle as

the case may be) of a generating station from the coal pile (or
water pond) to and including the prime-movers and the electric
generators, less the estimated value of the reactive capability
built into the electric generators which forms the second element related to the *kvar* aspects of the capacity. The third element is related to the kilovolt-ampere aspects of the capacity
and comprises the remainder of the electrical facilities of the
station.

To provide the reader with a general indication of the relative
magnitudes of these elements, studies of the illustrative utility
system show that of the total investment in facilities of a thermal production system about 90 percent would be applicable
to the kilowatt element, 2 percent to the *kvar* element, and
8 percent to the *kva* element.

Thermal Stations. Under the established method of analysis,
the operating expenses of each thermal electric generating station, after elimination of those applicable to "special purpose"
facilities, are resolved into four elements each comprising
labor, maintenance materials, and supplies, and the first, third,
and fourth, in addition—the fuel. They can be expressed by
the following general equation:

$$C_g = C_1 + c_2 K + c_3 P_{pf} + c_4 E_g \qquad (3.02)$$

where

C_g = the total annual operating expense of a generating station

C_1 = a "Constant" element comprising expenses which are
constant in nature and independent of either the installed
capacity, or the peak-prepared-for, or the amount of
energy generated

c_2 = a "Capacity" element comprising expenses which are
caused by the total installed capacity in a plant, and its
unit value is expressed per kilowatt of such capacity K

c_3 = a "Peak-Prepared-For" element comprising expenses
which are caused by requirements to be ready to carry
load, without producing an energy output to the system, and its unit value is expressed per kilowatt of
average peak-prepared-for requirements P_{pf}

c_4 = "Energy" element comprising incremental expenses,
primarily in the use of fuel and maintenance, which

are caused by the generation of energy output E_g to the system and its unit value is expressed by the kilowatthour of net generation

The last two elements of the above equation ordinarily comprise a number of individual capacity blocks of a plant whenever they differ materially within themselves in their thermal efficiencies.

It is beyond the scope of this presentation to describe the details of the procedures involved in establishing the constants of this equation. The pioneering work by the distinguished engineer N. E. Funk,[1] followed by the expert analyses of experienced students of this problem H. Estrada,[2] and F. Light,[3] have been outlined by them in their papers on this subject. Other operators and engineers of the Philadelphia Electric Company and of other electric utilities have used this or similar techniques successfully in the preparation of budgets and forecasts, and in studying various economic problems of electric power production. The economic significance of the last two elements of equation (3.02) have had wide applications in day-to-day transactions of energy and operating capacity interchanges in interconnected operations of electric utility systems and power pools. Suffice it to say, however, for the reader's appreciation of the relative significance of these elements, studies of a specific utility system show that of the total production expense of thermal generating stations, about 20 percent is attributable to the constant and the capacity elements, 10 percent, to the peak-prepared-for element, and 70 percent, to the energy element. The unit cost per kilowatthour of the latter element is frequently referred to as the incremental cost of energy production. It is this element that basically determines the scheduled loading of specific thermal capacity blocks of a well-integrated electric production system, and provides the distinguishing features for classifying such capacity into base, semi-base,

[1] N. E. Funk, "Allocation of Load on Generating Stations," United Gas Improvement Annual Conference (May, 1928, unpublished).
[2] H. Estrada, "Preparation of Power Station Increment Coal Rate Curves," System Operators Meeting (Pennsylvania Electric Association, December, 1930, unpublished).
[3] F. H. Light, "Application of Digital Computer Technique for Development of Incremental Maintenance Cost," *AIEE Transactions*, Vol. LXXII, Part 3 (1958), p. 1562.

semi-peak, and peaking types. The base type has relatively low incremental costs of energy production, and the peaking type, the highest, with the other types falling between these limits.

Hydraulic Stations. The investment costs of facilities of a hydraulic station, and its operating expenses, can be resolved also into elements. When this is done, it will be found that, of the total annual costs, a very small portion will appear in the "energy" element, by far the predominant portion falling into constant and capacity elements. For example, for the illustrative utility system, the energy element of its hydraulic generating station is less than 5 percent of the total of its carrying charges on investment and operating costs. But, since hydraulic generating stations of a modern utility are operated on a fully integrated basis with their thermal ones for over-all economies of production, and where the magnitude of the hydraulic stations' output constitutes a relatively minor portion of the total output of the system (or where it is anticipated that it will become so in the foreseeable future), it has been found desirable, from experience and from practical considerations of cost causation, to realign the actual cost elements of the hydraulic stations to an equivalency of an appropriate subdivision of the thermal system. In this manner, the cost elements of the over-all production system become harmonized to the predominance of its thermal nature, thus introducing a stabilizing influence on the future economic significance of the parametric components of the cost-to-serve.

The method of realignment of the cost of hydraulic generating stations to the equivalency of a thermal one will differ from one utility system to another, because it will depend upon many factors including the differences in the physical natures of hydraulic stations, such as whether they are of the storage, run-of-the-river, or pumped-storage types; the nature of the stream-flows over a period of years, that is, whether they are steady or subject to wide fluctuations; the physical and dollar magnitudes of the installations and their vintage; and the nature of the thermal production plants, the extent of their integration, and the level of their costs of investment and of fuel. Thus, such realignment of costs of hydraulic stations is a matter for individual engineering-economic determination in the light of conditions existing on the production system of the particular utility.

Parametric Components. Under the concept of cost incidence, or cost causation, with respect to the parametric components of the fundamental cost-to-serve equations (2.04) and (2.05) the *kw, kvar,* and *kva* cost elements of investment, and the C_1, $c_2 K$, and $c_3 P_{pf}$ cost elements of expenses of the production system are assigned to the "Class Peak or Diversified Demand" component of the cost-to-serve equation, and the $c_4 E_g$ cost element—to the "Energy" component thereof. However, as will be brought out in Chapter 6, *the individual elements of the demand component will reflect a different weight in different classes of service*, which in turn will result in different numerical values of the unit cost per kilowatt of diversified demands, for each of the classes because of the differences in their power factors, in the nature of their reactive power requirements, and the difference in their conceptual location on the supply system.

THE BULK TRANSMISSION SYSTEM

Bulk transmission comprises facilities of lines and substations operating at high tension voltages and performing the functions of interconnecting the sources of electricity production of the utility and of those of its neighboring utilities, to permit an economic loading of such sources under a unified operation, and to provide a high reliability of the output of the production system throughout the territory of the utility. In effect the bulk transmission system is an extension to bulk load centers of the electric facilities of the generating sources in a form of a network. Under modern practices it, like the production system, functions as an entity, the operations of its individual elements of physical facilities being subordinated to the over-all economic significance of the system. Its economic nature is determined fundamentally by the over-all capacity of the production system which in turn is determined by the over-all peak load requirements of the system. The generally used measure for the current carrying capability of this functional component of the supply system is expressed in kilovolt-amperes.

Under the concept of cost incidence with respect to the components of the fundamental cost-to-serve equations (2.04) and (2.05), the cost of this functional system is assigned to the "Class Peak or Diversified Demand" component of the cost-to-serve. However, being of a kilovolt-ampere nature, its unit cost per kilowatt of diversified demand will be different for different classes of service because of differences in the power factors of the class loads, and the difference in their conceptual location on the supply system.

THE DISTRIBUTION SYSTEM

The distribution system of a modern utility is a most complex conglomerate of physical facilities whose function is to distribute electric service from the production sources and their interrelated bulk transmission system throughout the service area in an economical, highly reliable, and good quality fashion. No two distribution systems can be alike because each must reflect the peculiarities of the individual terrain, the climatological environment, the idiosyncrasies of the people served and of those that serve them, the historic evolutions of the techniques, current developments, future plans, and the load and the customer densities of the territory served. While dealing with a large mass of individual items of physical plant and of individual customers' loads, the operational economics of distribution systems follow the laws of average behavior, but the service rendered must always satisfy the requirements of individual customers.

Although the physical facilities of an electric distribution system may appear to remain intact for long periods of time, their electrical nature undergoes continuous changes. As load requirements grow, new transformation centers are established, existing circuits are cut over, rearranged and subdivided, and new feeders are brought into affected areas.

Starting with humble beginnings of originally serving the more central areas, distribution systems have constantly expanded in area coverage so that today almost all inhabited sections of the continental United States of America are served with electricity from utility systems. In addition, such distribution systems have also grown in load-carrying abilities in order to meet the ever-growing requirements for electric service by existing and new customers, and in mechanical strength to withstand the onslaughts of weather.

Policy Decisions. To fit the economics of a distribution system into the components of the cost-to-serve equations (2.04) and (2.05) requires the establishment of a conceptual cost model on the basis of the fundamental engineering principles used in the design of this system, and the engineering philosophy of its behavior as a dynamic, ever-changing, and always-growing entity.   To do that requires the establishment, for analysis of operational economics, of a number of basic policies along which the utility is to function.   Once established such decisions will exert a powerful influence on the type of cost-to-serve information that can be made available.

The following constitutes a partial listing of some of the more important of such questions of policy and the answers under the author's method of analysis:[4]

Question 1.   For cost-to-serve determinations, shall the service area of the utility be split into two or more subdivisions to reflect natural differences in load and customer densities; or should it be treated in its entirety?

Answer. Where zone rates are in effect or contemplated to be established in the future, the cost-to-serve of distribution must be determined on the basis of a corresponding subdivision of the territory served, and all basic records on the distribution plant and expenses must be kept on that basis.   However, the general method of cost determination for any given subdivision should be substantially the same as for any other.

Question 2.   Shall the cost-to-serve be determined on the basis of types of distribution facilities, that is, aerial *versus* underground, single-phase *versus* polyphase, two-wire *versus* three-wire; or should such cost-to-serve reflect averages for each class of service on the basis of the manner the various types affect each class?

Answer. Where rates for the service rendered are independent of the type of distribution facilities, experience indicates that fully informative cost-to-serve data are obtained when they reflect averages for each class of service on the basis of the conditions applicable to the individual classes.

Question 3.   Shall the cost-to-serve reflect the significance of individualized distances of distribution; or shall it reflect the average conditions?

Answer. From practical considerations, the author's method reflects the principle of determining distribution costs for gen-

[4]In general, however, the answers to these questions are matters of individual utility policies, and will depend upon immediate and long-range objectives.

eral classes of service on the basis of average applicability of
general purpose facilities. Direct assignment of special facilities is confined to special classes of service.

Question 4. Shall the parametric components of cost be determined as nearly as possible on the basis of fundamental engineering principles of distribution system design and behavior;
or shall they be established by ratios reflecting only the judgment of the analyst?

Answer. The author's method for determining the parametric
cost components of the distribution system is based on the
fundamental engineering principles of distribution system design, and the behavior of that system with time. Arbitrary ratios
are avoided in these assignments. This method requires extensive engineering studies such as were made by A. H. Kidder and
W. T. Brown in the Middle Thirties[5] and subsequently reported
by A. H. Kidder and J. H. Neher in their 1955 AIEE paper[6] and
referred to by H. P. Seelye in his book.[7]

Conceptual Model. The conceptual cost model of the distribution system and the treatment of the costs of its various
major functional elements are shown in Figure 1.

It shows that the distribution system is subdivided into the
following functional elements:

High-Tension Distribution: comprises facilities operating at
voltages of 10,000 volts or higher and used directly in the delivery of service to a class of customers at these voltages or to
input centers of the primary voltage distribution system or for
special purpose loads. The portion applicable to high-tension
customers becomes the "Customer Demand" parametric component for that class because the individual loads are so large
in relation to the carrying capacities of the individual facilities
that the probability of any appreciable load diversity on them is
practically nonexistent.

The portion applicable to the primary voltage distribution system becomes the "Class Peak or Diversified Demand" com-

5A. H. Kidder and W. T. Brown, "Distribution System Investment
Allocation," study for Philadelphia Electric Company (September,
1933, unpublished).

[6]A. H. Kidder and J. H. Neher, "Power Distribution System Parameters," *AIEE Transactions*, Vol. LXXIV, Part 3 (1955), p. 125.

[7]Howard P. Seelye, *Electrical Distribution Engineering* (New York,
McGraw-Hill Book Company, 1930).

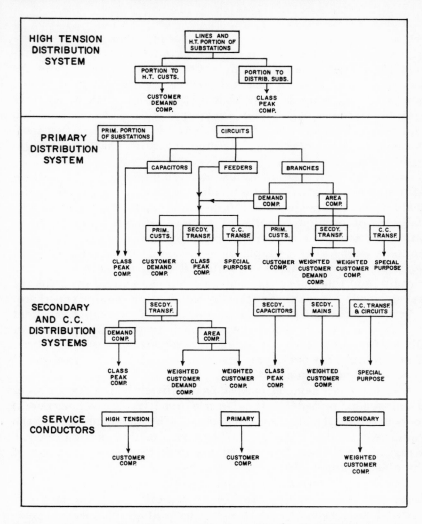

Figure 1. Example of cost model of a utility's distribution system showing functional elements

ponent of the classes to which it applies because the individual loads are small enough in relation to the carrying capacities of the individual facilities to permit a full interaction of load diversity on these facilities. The special purpose facilities of this system are assigned directly to the special purpose loads.

It will be noted that in this model the physical facilities of the high-tension distribution system comprise not only the lines but also their switching facilities at substations which functionally act and operate as part of such lines. In this model the switching facilities of these lines at the production system, however, are retained under that system in order to permit this portion of the costs of this functional system to be included automatically under the "Class Peak or Diversified Demand" component of all classes of service including that of the high-tension class.

Primary Voltage Distribution: comprises facilities operating at voltages from over 1,000 volts to less than 10,000 volts (usually in the range of 2,400 or 4,000 volts) and used in the delivery of service directly to a class of customers at these voltages, to the input centers of the secondary voltage distribution system or to the input of the constant current distribution system. Here too the physical facilities comprise not only the circuits and line capacitors but also the associated facilities at substations, as well as the transformation equipment there.

In this model of this system, the primary voltage component of distribution substations is assigned to the "Class Peak or Diversified Demand" component of the cost-to-serve equation. The circuits, however, are first subdivided into "capacitors," "feeders," and "branches."

The capacitor portion comprises facilities which, in an electrical sense, provide leading *kvar*'s (reactive kilovolt-amperes) to counteract the lagging ones created by the load and by the equipment used to supply it. The costs of this portion become a part of the "Class Peak or Diversified Demand" component of the classes supplied from this system.

The feeder portion comprises the physical facilities of circuits from substations to the first "tap-off" point on each circuit, whether such tap-off is a primary voltage customer, a secondary transformer, a constant current transformer, or a branch of the circuit. The branch portion is the remainder of facilities of the primary voltage circuits. The cost of this remainder is further subdivided into a "Demand" component and an "Area Coverage" component, the former representing the cost of wires in excess of No. 4 wire gauge, the latter becoming the remaining costs of the branches.

The costs of feeders and of the "Demand" component of the

branches are then merged, and the portion applicable to primary voltage customers becomes a part of the "Customer Demand" component of this class, and the remainder becomes a part of the "Class Peak or Diversified Demand" component of other classes supplied from the secondary voltage distribution transformers and from the constant current transformers.

The "Area Coverage" component of branches is subdivided among the three types of tap-offs: primary voltage customers, secondary voltage transformers, and constant current transformers. The portion applicable to primary voltage customers becomes a part of the "Customer" component of this class; the portion applicable to the constant current transformers becomes a part of the "lamp" component of the street lighting class; and the portion applicable to secondary voltage transformers is resolved into two parametric components of "Customer Demand" and "Customer" of the classes supplied from the secondary voltage distribution system. The amount assignable to the "Customer Demand" component is obtained by first dividing the unit cost of a polyphase tap-off by a nominal kilovolt-ampere size of the largest distribution transformer installation likely to be found on the distribution system of the territory served, and then multiplying this unit cost by the sum of the noncoincident secondary customers' maximum demands in excess of 5 kilovolt-amperes. The amount assigned to the "Customer" component becomes then the remainder of the total area coverage component assigned to the secondary voltage transformers.

Secondary-Voltage Distribution: comprises facilities operating at voltages below 1,000 volts (usually 120–240 volts) and used in the delivery of service directly to classes of customers at these voltages. The physical facilities here also comprise not only the mains but also the transformation equipment to secondary voltages.

In this model, the costs of secondary voltage transformers are resolved into two parts: one is assigned to the "Class Peak or Diversified Demand" component of the classes supplied from the secondary voltage distribution system, and the other is treated as an area coverage component and is further subdivided into "Customer Demand" and "Customer" components of the classes supplied from this system in a manner similar to the method used in segregating into these components the area coverage portion of the primary voltage branches assigned to the secondary voltage transformers.

In this model, the costs of capacitors are assigned to the "Class Peak or Diversified Demand" component of the classes supplied from the secondary voltage distribution system, and the costs of the secondary voltage mains are assigned to the "Customer" component of the classes[8] using this functional portion of the distribution system, because under the established general engineering philosophy of distribution system design and its behavior with time, these mains provide an area coverage, any load growth being accommodated through a subdivision of such mains through the introduction of additional transformation or tap-off points on the primary voltage distribution system.

Constant Current Distribution: comprises facilities operating at constant current and used in the delivery of service exclusively to street lamps. (This system is gradually disappearing as more and more street lights are converted to a "multiple" supply from the secondary voltage distribution system.) The physical facilities comprise here not only the circuits but also the constant current transformation equipment and frequently the utilization facilities of street lighting posts, brackets, luminaires, time switches, lighting fixtures and lamps. It is a functional system of a highly individualized nature, and is assignable completely to the street lighting class of service. It has, therefore, been included in the statistical data contained herein as part of the Special Purpose system. In any studies dealing with the cost of different lamp sizes, the cost of this system can be resolved into components similar to those shown in equations (2.04) and (2.05) by substituting the word "lamp" or "lighting" unit for the word "customer."

General. This method of analysis of the electric distribution system is most effective when property records are kept in a way to provide cost data of wires and cables and their appurtenances, together with related statistical material, by the described functional classifications. But with additional work it can be applied under other methods of record keeping. The costs of poles and underground conduits and their accessories,

---

[8]With the advent in street lighting of "multiple" supply from the secondary voltage distribution system a lighting unit is considered equivalent to a "customer."

together with related statistical material, are usually recorded in total and are not susceptible to direct identification by functional groupings. In this method of analysis they are allocated to the functional subdivisions of the distribution system as follows: the distribution poles—on a conductor-foot basis of open wires and aerial cables—and the distribution conduits— on the basis of the average of cable feet and conductor feet of underground wires. There is little doubt as to the reasonableness of the basis for the allocation of poles. The basis of allocations for conduits, I hasten to state, has been tested from detailed analyses of random-selected samples and found to provide confirmation.

Service Conductors: comprise wires and conductors with their appurtenances which extend from the utility's supply facilities in or on the streets to the customers' premises in accordance with specific rules established by the utility with respect to the point of termination of the utility's ownership and the connection to the customer-owned facilities needed for the utilization of the utility's service. Such facilities as are applicable to the supply of service at high tension and primary distribution voltages usually can be specifically isolated from the records, and become the "Customer" parametric components of the respective classes. The remainder is then assigned to the classes supplied at secondary voltages on a weighted customer basis, the weighting reflecting the relative proportion of customers supplied from aerial and underground circuits, the number of single-phase and polyphase customers, and the number of two-wire and three-wire customers. The cost thus derived becomes the "Customer" component of the respective classes.

The types of load and capacity data required for the functional cost analyses of the distribution system of a modern electric utility, along the lines of the model just described, are shown in Item I, and the corresponding statistics in Item II, of the following outline:

I. Capacity of Equipment and Loads:
   1. *Kva* Capacity:
      a) Distribution   substation transformers and capacitors
      b) Line capacitors
      c) Secondary voltage and constant current transformers
   2. *Kva* Peak Loads:
   Sum of distribution substations

3. Sum of Customers' Maximum Kva Demands:
   a) High tension customers
   b) Primary voltage customers
   c) Secondary voltage customers' maximum demands over 5 Kva
4. Class Maximum Kva Demands and Corresponding $RKva$ Demands:
   a) At input to high tension voltage distribution system
   b) At input to primary voltage distribution system
   c) At input to secondary voltage distribution system
   d) As at point of metering

II. Distribution System Statistics:
1. Conductor Feet and Cable Feet Segregated between Aerial and Underground:
   a) High tension special purpose lines
   b) High tension general purpose lines
   c) Primary voltage distribution circuits:
      c-1) Feeders
      c-2) Branches
   d) Secondary voltage distribution mains
   e) Series street lighting mains
   f) Service conductors:
      f-1) High tension voltage
      f-2) Primary voltage
      f-3) Secondary voltage
2. Number of Equivalent Single-Phase Primary Distribution Tap-off Points:
   a) Primary voltage customers
   b) Secondary voltage transformers
   c) Constant current transformers
3. Number of Customers:
   a) High tension voltage
   b) Primary voltage
   c) Secondary voltage:
      c-1) As recorded
      c-2) Weighted as to cost differential of underground and aerial supplies
      c-3) Weighted as to single-phase and polyphase supplies
      c-4) Weighted as to two-wire, three-wire and four-wire supplies

THE METERING AND CONTROL SYSTEM

This system comprises all metering facilities and related equipment, including controls wherever required for a predetermined manner of the customer's use of the utility's service, which are needed for billing customers in accordance with established rates and practices of the utility. The costs of these facilities are resolved, to the extent possible, by major subdivisions such as metering for special purpose customers, for all customers supplied at high tension, for all customers supplied at primary distribution voltages, and for customers supplied at secondary voltages with and without demand registrations, and with or without time-control devices. Once so segregated these costs become the "Customer" parametric component of the particular class, or group of customers.

THE SPECIAL PURPOSE SYSTEM

The Special Purpose system comprises facilities of a special nature which are devoted exclusively for the supply of individualized service to such customers as railroads needing frequency changers or railways needing 600 volt direct-current conversion equipment or special voltage transformation equipment for industrial customers. These facilities can exist either at generating sites, at utility's substations, or on customers' premises. The aggregate of all such facilities constitutes in this model a special purpose system, is segregated from the other functional subdivisions, and is assigned directly to the classes of customers which require their use on an individualized basis. As previously indicated (see Constant Current Distribution), the statistical data contained herein include under this subdivision the constant current distribution system, which is of a highly individualized nature being applicable exclusively to the street lighting class of service.

WORK ON CONSUMERS' PREMISES

This activity, assumed by the utility, can comprise many functions ranging from free replacement of burned out fuses of residential customers, or the free servicing on major appliances, to maintaining industrial substations. Its costs on a modern utility system can be analyzed readily by classes of service, and once obtained generally become the "Customer" parametric component of the class to which they are assigned.

CUSTOMERS' BILLING

This functional activity covers all expenditures of the utility in connection with the preparation of bills and their collection. It includes such functions as meter reading, bill computation, bill delivery, cash receiving, bill collection, answering customers' inquiries, administration of contracts, etc. The cost of these activities per customer of various classes can differ widely depending on many elements generally stemming from the rate structure and the cyclical periodicity of rendering statements and collecting the moneys due. These costs can range from a few dollars per year per customer for the residential class to several hundreds of dollars per year per customer for some of the large users which require special demand determinations, adjustments of rates for changes in fuel costs, billing deviations from specified power factor standards, contract minimums, guaranteed load factors, and the like. However, through careful studies of this functional activity, accurate cost information can be secured for each class of service. Data thus obtained become the "Customer" parametric component of the cost-to-serve for the individual classes of service.

SALES PROMOTION

This activity generally includes two functions: customers' contacts and sales of new or increased use of the utility's service. It covers many diverse functions of contacts between the utility and its customers or customers' representatives such as contractors, architects, builders, appliance salesmen, distributors, dealers, and the like. It usually includes cost of local and national advertising, demonstrations of utility's availability of service, sales engineering studies, and others. Here a close study of cost records by functional activities will provide an adequate segregation to classes of service. Once determined for classes of the mass market type, these costs become the "Customer" component; for other classes they are split in an equitable manner from special studies between the "Customer" and the "Customer Demand" components.

GENERAL ADMINISTRATION

This functional grouping covers the costs of all activities of a general administrative nature, including general management, general accounting, property records, payrolls, corporate administration, legal, rates, statistical, employees welfare, pensions, and a multitude of similar and related matters.[9] Fundamentally, these costs are of an "overhead" nature, and in the author's method of cost analysis are related to the payroll expenses of the functional operations of the utility and, therefore, are spread on that basis over all of the parametric components of the cost-to-serve for all classes of service.

[9]This functional part should not be confused with the Administrative and General Expense group of the Uniform System of Accounts for Electric Utilities. Expenses now included in that group which are clearly applicable to any functional part other than General Administration should be included under such appropriate functional part.

4. MODEL OF AN ELECTRIC UTILITY'S LOAD STRUCTURE

The study of electric-service loads may be divided into two major parts: one dealing with the gradual ebb and flow of loads which are integrated over specified intervals of time measured in terms of minutes, and the second dealing with momentary surges of load which last for short intervals of time measured in terms of seconds. The load characteristics of each of these parts in turn may be subdivided into four distinct components: one taken as at the terminals of the individual appliances and applications, the second one as at the service entrance of individual consumers of electric service, the third one for the diversified conditions of groups of consumers or groups of specified appliances and applications, and the fourth for all classes of consumers or for all classes of appliances and applications, which results in what may be called the "system" conditions. In this book the discussion will be confined to the interrelation of some of the factors of the first part of the subject.

It is a well-known fact, but often forgotten in the day-to-day operations of an electric utility that its basic "raison d'être" in the operational economic sense is the diversity which exists in the load requirements of its customers. It can be said that a utility trades on that diversity, and thus provides service to the individual customers at less cost than would be the case if each had to provide the facilities required by its own load for the same reliability of service supply. The natural and statistical laws governing the behavior of such diversity are quite complex. They will be described more fully later in this chapter. But it should be noted that the establishment of a conceptual model of the load structure carries with it the operational economic implications regarding the applicability of load diversity.

Diversity factor, which is a measure of the degree of diversity present between maximum loads of individual parts of a system, is defined by the American Institute of Electrical Engineers (AIEE) as "the ratio of the sum of the maximum power demands of the system or part of the system to the maximum demand of the whole system or part of the system under consideration measured at the point of supply." Here, however, it will be easier to visualize and deal with the reciprocal of this relation, that is, with the coincidence of power demands. Its measure is expressed as a "coincidence factor" and has been defined by the Load Research Committee of the Association of Edison Illuminating Companies (AEIC) as the "ratio of the maximum demand of a group, class or system as a whole to the sum of the maximum demands of the several components of the group, class or system."

While the diversity factor can never be lower than unity, the coincidence factor can never be greater than unity, and, therefore, in dealing with the coincidence factor, we deal in values between zero and unity, while in the case of diversity factor we deal in values between unity and infinity. Since a large part of the facilities required to render electric service depends upon the coincident or diversified maximum demands of groups of consumers, it is evident from the foregoing definition that the higher the coincidence factor, the larger becomes the amount of facilities required per kilowatt of the noncoincident maximum demands of individual consumers, and the lower the coincidence factor, the smaller it becomes.

MAJOR FACTORS AFFECTING THE COINCIDENCE IN THE USE OF SERVICE

The manner in which electric service is used by individual consumers or groups of consumers, and thus the degree of coincidence in this use, is determined by many factors. Among the more important ones may be mentioned population habits, community and business practices, weather and other climatic conditions, design of utilization equipment, and methods employed in the control of use of the service rendered. The significance of these factors may become clearer from the following discussion.

Population Habits and Community's Business Practices. Population habits and community's business practices exert a powerful influence upon the degree of coincidence in the consumers' use of electric service. The difference in the time when people get up; when they go to bed; how, when, and what they eat; where they live; the holidays they observe; where, when, and at what they work; the amount of leisure they have; and, generally speaking, how they live, work and play on different days of the week and in different seasons of the year; all of this is reflected in the degree of coincidence of consumers' use of electric service. These conditions are not subject to precise mathematical formulations, and their resultant effect will be different for different communities and different climatic, social, and political conditions. But for any given community, operating under a given set of social and political conditions, the resultant effects of population habits and community and business practices upon the manner of use of electric service usually fall into some general pattern and thus result in some determinable values of the degree of coincidence of individual consumer's use of service. These forces are generally too strong to be subject to control by individuals, although major policies of service-supply may have some minor influences upon them. They are, however, very susceptible to social and political controls, as, for example, by the general behavior of the community during a war as contrasted to its behavior in peacetime; by the artificial changes in the setting of clocks from the normal setting on sun-time; by social and political revolutions and by the lack or the presence of regimentation of the people's lives.

Weather and Other Climatic Conditions. Weather and other climatic conditions also exert a powerful influence upon the degree of coincidence in the consumers' use of electric service. For example, the advent of severe darkness because of an oncoming storm during otherwise daylight hours may create a coincidence of the power and lighting loads, wiping out the normal diversity between their individual maximum demands. A severe cold spell causing the almost continuous operation of individual heating plants increases the extent of coincidence in the use of electric service in connection with such plants. A severe hot spell, causing an almost continuous operation of individual air conditioning plants and other forms of cooling and ventilating equipment, increases the extent of coincidence in the use of electric service in connection with these appliances. These forces are beyond the control of individuals. They are not subject to exact mathematical determinations. But they are susceptible, in general, to appraisals from available weather records for maximum, minimum, and average conditions.

Design of Utilization Equipment. The design of utilization equipment has a considerable influence upon the degree of coincidence of consumers' use of electric service. For example, generally speaking, to perform a given task through expenditure of a given amount of energy, devices which are "overcapacitied" may have lower coincidence factors than devices which are "undercapacitied," although the coincident maximum demand of the former may be higher than the coincident maximum demand of the latter. Devices designed for full automatic operation under intermittent cycles may have lower coincidence factors than those designed to accomplish the same purpose under manual operation. These design features are well within the control of design engineers, although it should be realized that the effects of different designs cannot be ascertained from laboratory tests, but must be obtained from extensive research and tests of sample applications in actual use.

Methods of Control. Methods for artificial control in the use of service also have important influences upon the degree of coincidence of consumers' demands. Generally speaking, a group of identical devices operating without any restrictive control will experience a smaller coincidence in their individual maximum demands than the same group of devices operating under a predetermined control cycle, even though the group of uncontrolled devices may possess features which are undesirable from other considerations affecting the system while the controlled devices may not have such undesirable features.

LOAD STRUCTURE

An adequate knowledge of the load structure of a modern electric utility system is essential to enable one to foresee or to predict the effects of changing conditions on the physical features and operational economics of electric service supply. The details of this structure and the forces acting on it are numerous and complex. To understand their nature, their behavior, and their workings, the mind must simplify and, as in science, reduce things to basic elements through the establishment of a conceptual model. Obviously, all such simplifications are relative, and as pointed out in Chapter 1, reflect the scale of observation of which we are capable at the time. But without such simplifications, we estop ourselves from proceeding.

In this chapter we shall set forth a general theory on the composition of the load structure of a modern electric utility system, which I originally set forth in a paper presented before the Sixteenth Annual Meeting of the American Power Conference,[1] and will demonstrate its practical significance by describing the general features of the model which has been in use for over a quarter century on a large electric utility system operating in the eastern part of the United States. Load structures of other utilities will undoubtedly differ in details from those which are described herein. But the general principles underlying the establishment of such a model are believed to be of fundamental nature in the broader aspects of their significance for the operational economics of electric service supply.

General Theory. In the quest for an understanding of the behavior of the load structure of an electric utility system, we are confronted at the outset with a mass made up of a large number of individual elements, such as the hundreds of thousands of the utility's customers and the millions of electric appliances and applications such customers employ in the use of electric service. The response in the supply of that service is immediate and simultaneous with the demand for it.

To study the behavior of each and every one such individual elements is obviously impractical, economically infeasible, and of little, if any, practical significance. As stated in Chapter 1, the general method now employed in science in studying the behavior of a mass is a statistical method, which is based upon the behavior of the average of a great number of active elements. Such method presupposes that, on the average, each element obeys the laws of chance. Any method of load analysis, also must provide means for studying the behavior of the

[1]Constantine W. Bary, "Load Structure of a Modern Electric Utility System," *Proceedings* (Chicago, American Power Conference, 1954), Vol. XVI. Paper reprinted in *Electric Light and Power*, XXXII (May, 1954), 85.

average of the elements comprising the mass of the total load.

Experience has shown that for a modern electric utility system the simple combination into one total of all individual elements of the entire load for averaging does not provide the necessary means to predict reliably the physical or economic impacts on the system of the behavior of loads over a wide range of service requirements. The reason for that is found in the heterogeneity of the uses of electricity and in the mathematical significance of coincidence factors, which become meaningless as averages when combining loads that widely differ in the sizes of their demands.

A highly refined subdivision of the load structure for averaging, unrelated to the operational economics of electric service supply, is also undesirable, because it may not reflect the proper significance of load diversity and in this way hinder a proper understanding of behavior of the load. Thus, under present-day conditions, a conceptual model of the load structure should be not too complex, but at the same time should be subdivided into sufficient parts to provide consistency throughout the largest possible range of its application, should be enduringly stable over a long period of time, should reflect adequately the physical manner of service supply, and should provide meaningful averages of a stratified mass of individual elements.

In such a model, the total load of the electric system, in a statistical sense, forms the "universe." This total is conceived to be made up of half-a-dozen, or so, comparatively large blocks which we shall call "classes" each being its own "subuniverse." Each of the classes is made up of a number of smaller blocks which we shall call "strata." Each of the strata is further made up of still smaller blocks which we shall call "elements." In this model, the element is the smallest subdivision which we care to establish within a class. It represents either the loads of individual customers, or of a particular electric appliance, or an electric service application.

Within each class, groups are the composite of a number of elements which are classified in accordance with some common controlling characteristic of the load, and strata are the composite of a number of individual groups which distinguish themselves from other groups of the class in respect to some outstanding feature, preferably of load characteristics. A class is the composite of all strata comprising it, all its groups, and all its elements. It may be defined in the broadest sense as the result of collective grouping of individual customers of electric service possessing essential properties or characteristics in common, the nature of which forms the distinguishing attribute of the group.

In the author's model of the conceptual load structure, load-diversity benefits within a group of customers belong to the customers of that group; those existing between groups belong first to the groups and then to the customers comprising them; and those existing between classes belong first to the classes, then to the groups forming them, and then to the individual customers forming the groups. This principle is far different from the one which proclaims that the benefits of the entire load diversity on a utility system belong to all customers, irrespective of size, classification, or grouping of their individual load characteristics. In other words, load diversity within a group is captured and retained by that group, just as the load diversity within a class is captured and retained by that class.

Such a structure of the model reflects the basic features of load diversity in utility's service supply and provides adequately and effectively under a general unified theory of diversity applicability, the fundamental means to explain, to foresee, and to predict the impacts of the behavior of loads over a wide range of service requirements upon the operational economics of service supply.

Model of Load Structure. There are many features to the load of a modern electric utility system, its classes of service, and the groups and elements comprising them. They do not remain fixed either from year to year, or season to season, or from day to day, or hour to hour; but are subject to continuous fluctuations depending on the ebb and flow of the requirements for electricity by the community served. Strictly speaking, therefore, there is no such thing as one set of load characteristics. For the purpose of establishing a conceptual model of a utility's load structure for operational economics, however, the more important features will be defined adequately by the following:

System Load Characteristics:
1. Kilowatthour energy output and kilowatt peak loads for selected periods of the year

2. Average weekday load curves for the selected periods of the year

3. Power factors at time of peak loads

4. Period load factors

5. Load-occurrence and load-duration curves

Class of Service Characteristics:

1. Kilowatthour energy sales; kilowatt diversified maximum demands, kilowatt noncoincident maximum demands

2. Average weekday load curves for selected periods

3. Power factors

4. Load factors, based on diversified and noncoincident maximum demands

Empirical Relationship establishing the probable behavior of certain basic load characteristics of groups of customers within a class, with such groups arranged, for averaging, in accordance with the significant controlling characteristic under which the particular class has been chosen to be administered in the operational economics of the utility.

Figures 2 through 4 depict the essential load characteristics of all Class I utility systems in the United States of America and of an illustrative utility system. These data show that the load patterns of this system closely resemble those for the combined of all Class I systems.

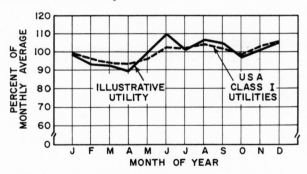

Figure 2. Example of monthly patterns of peak loads

It is a system whose summer peak is somewhat higher than the following winter peak, while the reverse is true of the Class I systems.

It is of interest to note from Figure 3 that the monthly energy outputs in the summer months of July and August are of magnitudes substantially equal to those of the winter months of the preceding January and the succeeding December.

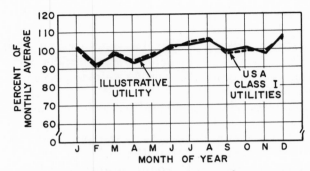

Figure 3. Example of monthly patterns of energy outputs

Its annual load factor, see Figure 4, is close to 63 percent, and its generated power factor at time of peak is in the order

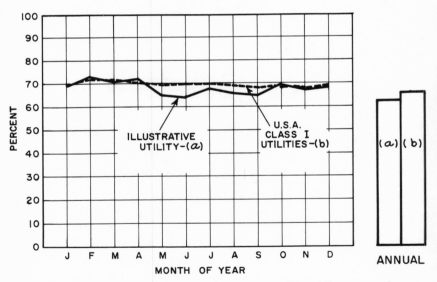

Figure 4. Example of monthly patterns of load factors and their annual values

of 90 percent. The seasonal patterns of the average weekday load curves of the illustrative utility are shown in Figure 5.

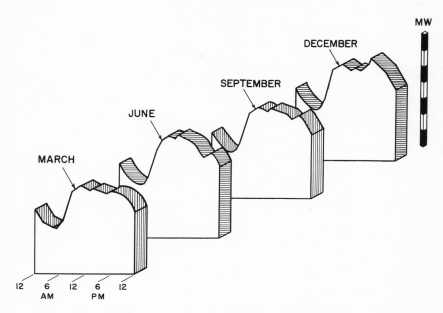

Figure 5. Example of seasonal average weekday load curves

The load occurrence curve of the illustrative utility shown in Figure 6 indicates that the upper 10 percent of its annual kilowatt peak load provides less than 1 percent of the annual kilowatthour output, and its duration curve shown in Figure 7 indicates that the upper 10 percent of its load lasts for less than 3 percent of the total hours in the year.

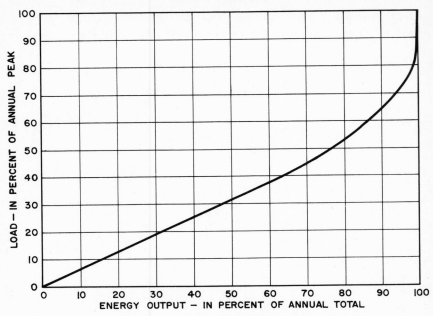

Figure 6. Illustrative annual load occurrence curve

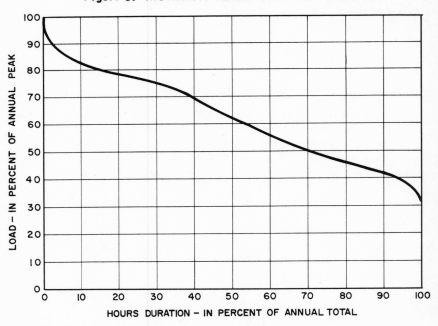

Figure 7. Illustrative annual load duration curve

The model of the load structure of this system is illustrated in Figures 8 through 10 inclusive, showing its physical and operational economic nature. Figure 8 shows a complete

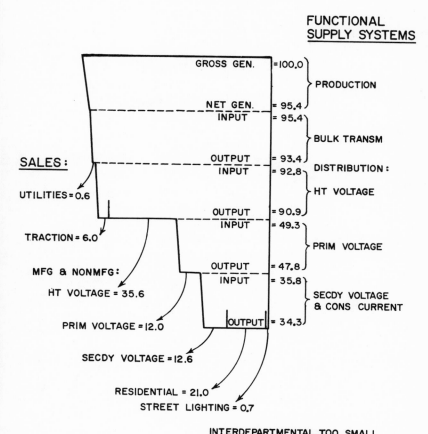

**FUNCTIONAL
SUPPLY SYSTEMS**

**Figure 8. Illustrative functional structure of energy
in percent of annual production**

energy balance by the functional elements of the supply system. Figures 9 and 10 show the average weekday load curves for the six of the eight classes of service used as major building blocks of this system's load structure. The two classes of service comprising "Sales to Other Electric Utilities" and "Interdepartmental Use" are too small to be shown on these charts.

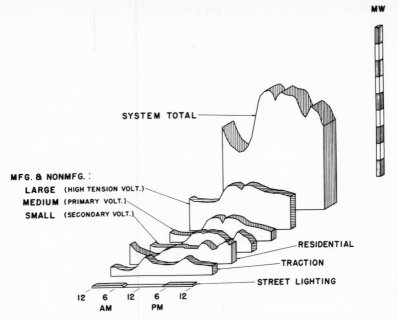

Figure 9. Example of a June average weekday load structure by classes of service

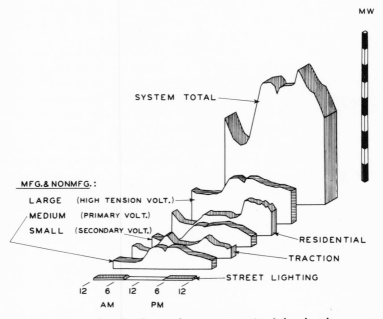

Figure 10. Example of a December average weekday load structure by classes of service

The classification of the major load blocks of this load structure follows that generally in use on electric utility systems in the United States, although the terminology used is more descriptive of the functional nature of the classes and amplifies it by introducing the distinction as to the magnitude of customers' loads within the manufacturing and nonmanufacturing category which is also made synonymous with the differentiation in the voltage level of service supply corresponding to the functional elements of the supply system described in Chapter 3. Thus, the concepts underlying this model of the load structure are harmonious with those reflected in the model of the supply system. Under such unified approach the load model reflects adequately the physical manner of service supply. It also provides an inherent and relative homogeneity to the sizes of loads within classes, thus providing for the derivation of mathematically significant factors on load diversity within each of such classes, which in turn permits the establishment of significant and meaningful relationships on the cost-to-serve over a full range of customers' load requirements within each of the classes, under a unified theory of load behavior.

Classes of Service. The author's General Unified Theory of an electric utility's load structure has been established some thirty years ago. The model of this load structure reflects basically the principle of the physical manner of supplying service, and establishes the following classes:

Residential covers the supply of single phase service at secondary voltages (generally at 120–240 volts) to individual dwellings for the personal convenience of the household.

Secondary Voltage Manufacturing and Nonmanufacturing covers the supply of single phase or polyphase service at 120–240 volts generally to small size customers, other than residential, ranging basically up to 25 kilowatts but including some as high as 100 kilowatts, and averaging around 5 kilowatts.

Primary Voltage Manufacturing and Nonmanufacturing covers the supply of polyphase service at 2,400 and 4,000 volts, generally to medium size customers, ranging from 25 kilowatts to 500 kilowatts, and averaging around 200 kilowatts.

High Tension Manufacturing and Nonmanufacturing covers the supply of polyphase service at 13,200, 33,000, 66,000, and 132,000 volts, generally to large size customers, in excess of

500 kilowatts but including a few as low as 100 kilowatts, and averaging around 2,500 kilowatts.

Traction covers the individualized supplies of 60 cycle polyphase and 25 cycle single or polyphase services at high tension voltages to electrified railways and railroad systems.

Street Lighting covers the individualized supply of service for street illumination of a series or multiple type, where the utility either owns or does not own the utilization facilities.

Sales to Other Electric Utilities covers individualized firm service supplies from the bulk transmission system to neighboring utilities for resale.

Interdepartmental Use covers the supply of service to other departments of the utility.

The basic determinants of classification in this model of the load structure are (a) the physical character, that is, voltage level, of service supply and (b) the general nature for which the service is used. Accounting and rate classifications are made to fit the structure of this model, rather than the other way around.

EMPIRICAL RELATIONS

The quest for knowledge and understanding of the behavior of the load structure cannot stop with the class loads. To understand the behavior of the class, it is necessary to understand what goes on within it. To obtain that knowledge, means must be found for establishing for each general class the probable trends that are going on in the load behavior of its individual elements, arranged in groups according to the significant controlling characteristic under which the particular class is administered in the utility's operations.

There are two such controlling characteristics of significance on a modern electric utility system: the individual customers' energy use; and, the individual customers' monthly load factors by billing demand intervals. The former applies in our model primarily to customers of the residential class, the latter, to the manufacturing and nonmanufacturing classes.

Energy versus Diversified Demands. Figure 11 depicts relationships between customers' annual energy use and their diversified maximum demands for average weekdays around the peak period of the residential class (more fully defined at the end of this chapter). The quantitative significance of these

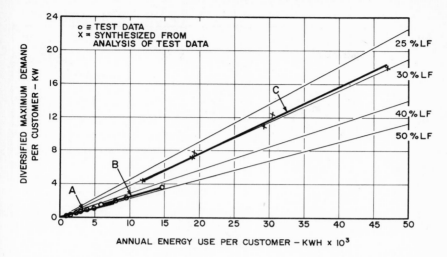

Figure 11. Illustrative relationship of energy uses *versus* average weekday diversified maximum demands of residential customers

A. "Base use" comprising lighting and miscellaneous appliances

B. "Base use" plus electric cooking and water heating (uncontrolled)

C. "All-electric home" (reflecting B plus electric cooling and heating)

relationships is constantly undergoing changes, and undoubtedly will continue to do so in the future. It, thus, behooves us to be alert to any significant changes in these relationships. One such change looms over the horizon: studies indicate that by projecting data into the conditions of an all-electric home, which would include electric space heating and air conditioning (under uncontrolled methods of operation), the energy *versus* group demand relationship, shown in Figure 11, will not only move into a much higher energy and diversified maximum demand region, but at the same time, into a band of much lower annual load factors than is obtained now with the load of a full-use home, before the introduction of electricity for the performance of the heating and cooling jobs.

Coincidence Factors versus Load Factors. Figure 12 depicts an empirical relationship between group coincidence

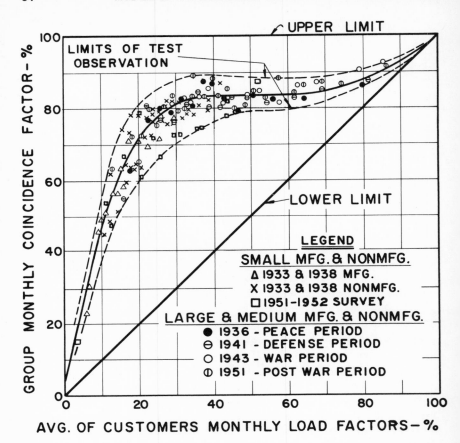

Figure 12. Empirical relationship between coincidence factors and
load factors—based on integrated 30-minute demands
in December for groups of 30 customers

factors for customers of the manufacturing and nonmanufacturing
classes and individual customers' monthly load factors. This
relationship and its underlying theory have been described in
detail by me in 1945[2] and were first outlined in my 1937
presentation to the Association of Edison Illuminating Com-

[2]Constantine W. Bary, "Coincidence-Factor Relationships of Electric Service Load Characteristics," *AIEE Transactions*, LXIV (1945),
623.

panies (AEIC).[3] It has been studied in a thorough manner and verified first in 1939 by a subcommittee, F. M. Terry chairman, of the Special Committee on Load Studies of AEIC,[4] and then again in 1952 by a subcommittee, B. P. Dahlstrom chairman, of the Load Research Committee of AEIC.[5] H. E. Eisenmenger rationalized and verified the shape of the empirical curve in a classical manner, from mathematical considerations, in his 1939 paper before the 55th Annual Meeting of AEIC.[6] It has become known as the Second Law of Load Diversity,[7] or the "Bary" curve. It provides conveniently the means for obtaining the probable diversified maximum demands per customer for a given set of customers' monthly energy uses and their noncoincident maximum demands, which are the necessary ingredients for computing customers' load factors.

It will be noted from the actual test data shown, that over nearly two decades of observations, covering pre-war, defense, war, and post-war conditions, the probable average relationship of test observations remain unaltered.

(Recently completed studies of 1961 data on load patterns of customers of the manufacturing and nonmanufacturing class, which resulted in 118 test-observations spread over a wide range of monthly load factors, again substantiate the qualitative and quantitative nature of the relationship between monthly coincidence factors and load factors established for the month

[3]Constantine W. Bary, "Economic Significance of Load Characteristics as Applied to Modern Electric Service," Minutes, 53d Annual Meeting (New York, Association of Edison Illuminating Companies, 1937, unpublished).

[4]"Report of Subcommittee on Coincidence Factors of the Special Committee on Load Studies of the AEIC," Minutes, 55th and 56th Annual Meetings (New York, Association of Edison Illuminating Companies, 1939 and 1940, unpublished).

[5]"Report of General Subcommittee on Nonmanufacturing and Manufacturing Customers of Load Research Committee of the AEIC," Minutes, 69th Annual Meeting (New York, Association of Edison Illuminating Companies, 1953, unpublished).

[6]H. E. Eisenmenger, "Study of the Theoretical Relationship between Load Factor and Diversity Factor," Minutes, 55th Annual Meeting (New York, Association of Edison Illuminating Companies, 1939, unpublished).

[7]The first law of load diversity is the relationship which exists between group coincidence factors and the number of customers in the group, described in my 1945 AIEE paper (see footnote 2).

of December.   From a recent compilation of equally comprehensive data for customers of this class for the 1961 summer period, a similar relationship has been established for the warmest month which reflects heavy use of air conditioning equipment.   The qualitative nature and the quantitative magnitudes of this relationship are virtually the same as for the month of December, and the new test-observations follow the patterns of dispersion outlined by the limits of observation shown in Figure 12.)

This relationship can be considered, therefore, as of a fundamental nature in the general behavior of electric loads.   But being of an empirical nature the following qualifications must be kept in mind:

1. It is an empirical relationship and is based on the conditions and experience of one utility system supplying a given community.   Other communities with different population habits, different definition as to what constitutes a class of service, different weather and other climatic conditions, may differ in the actual magnitudes of the coincidence factors shown throughout the entire load-factor range.

2. The relationship is confined to consumers of substantially the same size, taking the same class of service, operating at the same load factors, and always taken in sufficient numbers for each type, size, and load factor to produce representative results on a coincidence factor of the group.   It is obvious that, unless these qualifications are observed fully, different coincidence factors may be obtained.

3. The coincidence factors obtained from Figure 12 are those for individual consumers within a group applied to monthly conditions.   There will be additional coincidence factors between different groups of any one class of service, for longer periods than a month, and between different classes of service of a system.

INTERGROUP AND INTERCLASS COINCIDENCE FACTORS

Experience with the two probable relationships just described has shown that no matter which of the controlling characteristics is used for arranging individual load elements by groups, the major effects of load diversity within a general class are captured and retained in the load characteristics of the groups, whether they be expressed in terms of diversified maximum demands or group coincidence factors.   But it is known that additional effects of load diversity exist between groups of a given class and between classes. Their measures are called "intergroup," and "interclass" coincidence factors, respectively. Table 2 provides an indication of the general magnitudes of the intergroup, and interclass coincidence factors obtained on the illustrative utility system.

TABLE 2. ILLUSTRATIVE INTERGROUP AND INTERCLASS COINCIDENCE FACTORS

Intergroup

Between all groups of present-day residential customers (without ranges and water heaters)	0.98
Between all groups of present-day residential customers (with ranges)	0.99
Between all groups of present-day residential customers	0.96

Interclass

Between two classes at secondary voltage level	0.99
Between four classes at primary voltage level	0.92
Between all eight classes at production system level	0.87

The establishment of probable trend relationships between certain parameters of load characteristics at the group level of the load model is susceptible to actual determination through the statistical method of averages, because of the large mass of individual elements which can react to the laws of chance. But at other levels of the model, say that of the classes, there are so few individual things to be dealt with that, from mathematical considerations, they cannot produce trend relationships, but only individualized spot values.

Distribution of Load Diversity Benefits.   Obviously, the establishment of any classification carries with it the implications regarding the applicability of load diversity benefits which exist on a modern electric utility. Much has been written on this subject in terms of the allocation of demand-related costs of an electric utility enterprise. An excellent critical résumé by P. Schiller of the better-known methods is contained in the 1943 Technical Report K/T 106 of the British Electrical and Allied Industries Research Association,[8] and an "Im-

---

[8] P. Schiller, "Methods of Allocating to Classes of Consumers or Load the Demand-Related Portion of the Standing Costs of Electricity Supply," Technical Report Reference K/T 106 (London, The British Electrical and Allied Industries Research Association, 1943).

proved Method" developed by that group has been published in
its 1945 Technical Report K/T 109.[9] I have been cognizant of
these methods for many years; have studied them and have
found that each, in its own way, has attempted by various in-
genious ways to distribute the benefits of load diversity between the individual components of a combined system load supplied by a single enterprise.   The one which is farthest from
meeting the requirements of the General Unified Theory is the
so-called System Peak Responsibility method, which reflects
the demand-cost assignment to individual components on the
basis of their loads at the *time* of the system peak load. This
method reflects little conceptual perception of the nature and
the mutual benefits of load diversity, nor the complex laws of
probability governing its behavior.   Historically, it has had
favor with the early students of this subject.   But, with an
ever-growing understanding of the significance of the probability
relationships existing in the factors pertaining to load diversity,
coupled with the ever-increasing realization of the instability of
the results obtained through its application in modern operations
of electric utilities and the lack of consistency resulting therefrom, it has been generally superseded by other methods. Most
of them, especially those which are in one way or another
derivatives of the System Peak Responsibility method, fail to
conform to the concepts of the General Unified Theory, as set
forth in this book.   Only the well-known Noncoincident Peak
(NCP) method, as will be shown in this chapter, conforms to
that theory in the practical aspects of its application to the
operations of modern electric utilities, because it is but a
simplification of the method developed to conform to the concepts of the General Unified Theory.   The afore-mentioned
"Improved Method," while not fully conforming to that theory
because of its requirements for the establishment of a "potential peak" period and of an "off-potential peak" period for the
system load comprised of component loads which can be im-
posed without regard to such periods, in its practical signifi-

[9]Committee on Electricity-Supply Technology, Chairman Capt.
J. M. Donaldson, M.C., and Sub-Committee on Cost Research, Chairman Mr. D. J. Bolton, "An Improved Method for Allocating to Classes
of Consumers the Demand-Related Portion of the Standing Cost of Electricity Supply," *Technical Report Reference K/T 109* (London, The
British Electrical and Allied Industries Research Association, 1945).

cance with respect to the distribution of benefits of load diversity among classes of service of a modern electric utility system produces, I have found, results which closely approximate the NCP method.

Considering the complex interrelationship of all elements entering the determination of complete or full cost-to-serve, and to meet the principles of the General Unified Theory, the distribution of benefits of load diversity *among customers of a given class*, in the author's concept, is best accomplished through the application of the probability trends which exist between the manifested diversified load characteristics of groups of customers within a class and some selected controlling feature common to all customers of the class, such as either their energy uses, or their load factors. The same basic principle should hold for the distribution of the benefits of load diversity existing on the system *between different classes* of service. It seems to me that Professor Bonbright, in reviewing the various methods suggested in the past for the allocation of capacity-related costs, arrives at a similar conclusion by expressing it in the following manner: "But when resort must be had to these 'stochastic' or 'probabilistic' methods of capacity cost imputation, no general formula is worthy of much respect. Instead, empirical studies of the relationship between load factors and coincidence factors for different uses of service (air conditioning, water heating, elevator operation, etc.) are required." [10]

With extensive research, for relatively large masses, the existence of general trends within classes can be readily observed and reveal the *most probable behavior* of the diversified characteristics with the change in the selected common controlling characteristics. But no trend can be obtained between classes, such as between their load factors and the interclass coincidence factors, because here one deals with very few individual elements which do not provide the necessary quantity of data for the establishment of such a trend relationship. Available facts provide us only with spot values, at any given time for any given system.

However, we can postulate from the concepts underlying the Second Law of Load Diversity that the behavior of the *interclass* coincidence factors with a change in the average of the

[10] James C. Bonbright, *Principles of Public Utility Rates* (New York, Columbia University Press, 1961), p. 353.

class load factors would be probably quite similar in shape to the curves established for the intercustomers' coincidence factors with changes in their load factors for groups within classes, as shown in Figure 12. The classical, mathematical rationalization of this relationship by Eisenmenger in 1939[11] lends further credence to this postulation.

This conceptual behavior of coincidence factors *between* classes, and the empirical relationship established for groups *within* the classes, can be set forth by the following two similar equations:

Between Classes:

$$P = D\, f(L) \tag{4.01}$$

Within Classes:

$$P_c = D_c\, f(L_c) \tag{4.02}$$

where

> P = the diversified maximum demand of a class with respect to the system peak load
>
> P_c = the diversified maximum demand of a customer with respect to its class peak load
>
> D = the maximum demand of a class
>
> D_c = the maximum demand of a customer in a class
>
> $f(L)$ = the interclass coincidence factors as a function of class load factors,
>
> $f(L_c)$ = the intercustomers' coincidence factors by homogenized groups as a function of customers' load factors

The similarity of the two equations is striking, thus causing us to view our general theory of applicability of load diversity, as of a unified nature at all levels of the load structure, and which I, therefore, have called the General Unified Theory. Under this theory, the benefits of the load diversity existing between classes are distributed in proportion to the diversified maximum demands of the classes. By definition, a diversified maximum demand of a class is the product of the individual

[11]H. E. Eisenmenger, "Study of the Theoretical Relationship between Load Factor and Diversity Factor," Minutes, 55th Annual Meeting (New York, Association of Edison Illuminating Companies, 1939, unpublished).

maximum demand of the class and an appropriate interclass coincidence factor. To obtain this latter factor it is first assumed to correspond to the established basic empirical coincidence-factor *versus* load-factor relationship, curve B_b in Figure 13 reflecting diversity between elements of load. If the

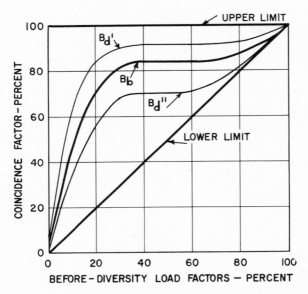

Figure 13. Bary type coincidence factor *versus* load factor curves

B_b = Basic probability relationship reflecting diversity between elements of load

$B_{d'}$ = Derived probability relationship, antecedent to the Basic, reflecting diversity between subelements of load

$B_{d''}$ = Derived probability relationship, succedent to the Basic, reflecting diversity between groups of elemental loads

sum of such diversified maximum demands of the classes on this first try is found to be either higher or lower than the actual peak load of the system, successive approximations are made by using either of the other derived curves: $B_{d'}$, which reflects diversity between subelements of load, or $B_{d''}$, which reflects diversity between groups of elemental loads. These curves are shown in Figure 13, and interpolation between two adjoining curves will provide as close a fit as is desired to obtain equality between the sum of such class diversified maximum demands and the actual peak load of the system. It will be noted that under this procedure, a class with a 100 percent load factor receives no benefit of load diversity, as it should be, because it is a certainty that such a class contributes nothing to the diversity between classes. Other classes receive benefits in varying degrees in accordance with the probability relationship of their conceptual ability to contribute to such diversity in accordance with the Second Law of Load Diversity, or its antecedent or succedent determinants.[12]   For ready reference,

[12]For those who may be curious to know how these determinants are obtained, the following example will illustrate the procedure of deriving the Succedent Curve B_d'' in Figure 13: For a "Before-Diversity" load factor of, say, 10 percent obtain from the Basic Bary Curve B_b a coincidence factor of 48 percent. Thus the After-Diversity load factor of this group becomes 10 percent ÷ 48 percent, or 20.8 percent; and the coincidence factor for this load factor, from the Basic Curve B_b is 72.5 percent. Thus for the original (Before-Diversity) load factor of 10 percent, the Succedent Determinant of coincidence factor becomes 48 percent × 72.5 percent, or 34.8 percent, as shown on the Succedent Bary Curve B_d''. Similar calculations for other values of "Before-Diversity" load factors produce the derived relationship depicted by Curve B_d''.

The establishment of the Antecedent Determinant of the relationship B_d' employs the following procedure: On the basis that all Bary Curves are of a "family type," characterized by a relatively level coincidence factor in the region of Before-Diversity load factors of 35 to 60 percent, it can be postulated that the coincidence factors of the Antecedent Curve in the same load factor region will be also relatively level. Since the values of the coincidence factors corresponding to the Before-Diversity load factors and to the After-Diversity load factors are the same in this limited region, the product of the two similar values of coincidence factors of the Antecedent Curve must be equal to the coincidence factor of the Succedent Basic Bary Curve in this same load factor region. A coincidence factor value of 91.5 percent can thus be established for the Antecedent Curve in the load factor region from about 35 percent to 60 percent. A series of probable curves, similar in trend to the Basic Bary Curve, are then projected downward to zero percent load factor and upward to 100 percent load factor.

By a "cut and try" procedure the most appropriate curve is then obtained, so that the Basic Bary Curve becomes its Succedent. For example, at 10 percent load factor the coincidence factor of the Antecedent Curve B_d' is 63 percent. The After-Diversity load factor of

this method of distributing the benefits of load diversity between classes of service will be called the "Coincidence
Probability" method.

However, in practice and without violating the mathematical
aspects of this theory, the distribution of the benefits of load
diversity between classes can be made in a much simpler manner. For conditions now generally encountered, the magnitudes
of load factors for *classes* of service in the month of their maximum demands generally fall into the region where the conceptual
coincidence-factor *versus* load-factor relationship for the classes
should be flat, that is, where the coincidence factor is substantially constant with a change in load factor. Thus the magnitude of the probable coincidence factor applicable to a class is
the same as that of any other class. This being the case, the
interclass coincidence factor becomes the ratio of the peak load
of the system (i.e., the coincident maximum demand of the
classes) to the sum of the class maximum demands (i.e., noncoincident class peaks with respect to themselves and to the
system peak). Hence for this practical condition the diversified
maximum demand of a class can be expressed by the following
equation:

$$P = D \frac{P_s}{D_n} \qquad (4.03)$$

where

P_s = the peak load of the system, i.e., the coincident
maximum load of all classes

D_n = the summation of the maximum demands of the n
classes of service, i.e., the sum of the noncoincident
class peaks (NCP)

P & D = as defined in equation (4.01)

---

this group becomes 10 percent ÷ 63 percent, or 15.8 percent, and from
this same Curve B_d' the coincidence factor for this load factor is
found to be 77 percent. Thus, for the original (Before-Diversity)
load factor of 10 percent, the Succedent Determinant of coincidence
factor becomes 63 percent × 77 percent, or 48 percent, which agrees
with the value of the coincidence factor at 10 percent load factor on
the Basic Bary Curve B_b. Similar calculations for other values of
"Before-Diversity" load factors establish the suitability of the selected "cut and try" Antecedent Curve.

It will be observed that the ratio term of equation (4.03) is in effect the average interclass coincidence factor, which in the practical case encountered in the actual operations of modern electric utilities, is also conceptually the most probable value for each of the classes in their ability to contribute to the load diversity.

From equations (4.01), (4.02), and (4.03), it becomes evident that the NCP method of determining demand-related class of service costs is but a practical simplification of the author's fundamental concept of applicability of the benefits of load diversity under the General Unified Theory. [13]

In the author's model of the utility's load structure, the half dozen, or so, classes of service constitute, in a statistical sense, sub-universes, each having its own peaks and its own valleys. The significance of any load on the operational economics of the cost-to-serve becomes dependent on the class of which it is a part and not on that of the entire system, except as such load may affect the interclass coincidence factor. Similarly, the significance on operational economics of introducing restrictions in the time availability of utility's supply of service for an "off-peak" load becomes primarily dependent on the load characteristics of the class of which it is a part, and not on the system; and secondarily on the effects (if any) such load produces on the interclass coincidence factor. This will be further explained in Chapter 10.

AVERAGE WEEKDAY LOADS

In the practical application of this model of an electric utility's load structure the class peaks and the class load curves are conceived as being those for an average weekday around the peak period of the class, or of the system. While not a fundamental prerequisite of the General Unified Theory, it is an important feature of it, because over the many years of experience in studying the operational economics of cost-to-serve I have found that the use of such an average weekday (comprising the average day of one or more weeks of Mondays through Fridays, inclusive, without holidays) provides consistent results and sound indications on numerous phases of rendering utility service. It provides high reliability in such information, depicting

---

[13]The foregoing description of the author's theory can be illustrated also through the following examples:

firmly the outstanding characteristic inherently peculiar to each of the classes. Being of an *average* nature it stabilizes the sig-

A. General Case. Let us assume a hypothetical electric utility with five classes of service having the load characteristics shown in lines 2 and 3 of Table 3. Let us further assume two values of system peak: no. 1 providing an average interclass coincidence factor of 0.80, and no. 2 providing an average interclass coincidence factor of 0.90. In other words, one system condition is with a lower, and another with a higher, coincidence factor than the level value of the Basic Bary Curve:

TABLE 3. HYPOTHETICAL ELECTRIC UTILITY SYSTEM

	A	B	C	D	E	Total
1. Class of service	A	B	C	D	E	Total
2. Maximum demands—Mw	600	500	800	700	400	3,000
3. Load factors in month of maximum demands—%	20	40	60	80	100	
4. Coincidence factors—Basic Bary Curve	.70	.83	.83	.84	1.0	
5. First-try of diversified maximum demands	420	415	664	588	400	2,487
Peak No. 1 Conditions = 2,400 Mw						
6. Coincidence factors—Succedent Bary Curve	.58	.70	.70	.81	1.0	.80
7. Second-try of diversified maximum demands—Mw	348	350	560	567	400	2,225
8. Interpolated probable diversified maximum demands—Mw	402	398	637	563	400	2,400
9. Distributed load diversities—Mw	198	102	163	137	0	600
10. Distributed load diversities—% of maximum demands	33.0	20.4	20.4	19.6	0	20.0
Peak No. 2 Conditions = 2,700 Mw						
11. Coincidence factors—Antecedent Bary Curve	.83	.91	.91	.92	1.0	.90
12. Second-try of diversified maximum demands—Mw	498	455	728	644	400	2,725
13. Interpolated probable diversified maximum demands—Mw	492	450	720	638	400	2,700
14. Distributed load diversities—Mw	108	50	80	62	0	300
15. Distributed load diversities—% of maximum demands	18.0	10.0	10.0	8.9	0	10.0

In accordance with the procedure outlined in the text, we obtain from the Bary Curve B_b, for each of the classes, the coincidence factor which corresponds to the class load factor. These values are shown in line 4 of Table 3. We now make the first approximation toward obtaining the probable diversified maximum demand for each

nificance of such characteristics from year to year, and eliminates the spurious fluctuations inherent in a single day, espe-

---

of the classes. By definition, it is the product of the maximum demand of the classes and the corresponding coincidence factors. The
values of the first-try are shown in line 5 of Table 3.

To obtain the desired balance for the conditions of peak no. 1, we
make the second approximation, by employing the Succedent Bary
Curve B_d'', which reflects lower coincidence factor values, and peak
no. 1 is lower than the sum of values of the first-try. The results of
this second-try are shown in lines 6 and 7 of Table 3. But the sum of
these values is lower than peak no. 1. We, therefore, interpolate between the values of lines 5 and 7, so as to produce a sum equal to
peak no. 1. The results of this interpolation are shown in line 8, and
become the probable diversified maximum demands of the classes
corresponding to peak no. 1.

To obtain the desired balance for conditions of peak no. 2, we
proceed as outlined in the preceding paragraph, except we use the
Antecedent Bary Curve B_d', because it reflects higher coincidence
factor values, and peak no. 2 is higher than the sum of values of the
first-try. The results are shown in line 13 of Table 3.

From these results we can obtain now the distribution of the system's load diversity between the classes, as shown in lines 9 and 10
for conditions of peak no. 1, and in lines 14 and 15 for conditions of
peak no. 2. It is quite evident from an analysis of these results that
the 100 percent load factor class E receives no distribution of load
diversity since in fact it contributes nothing to it. Class A, with a
low load factor in the descending region of the Bary Curve, where the
probability of coincidence is conceptually lower than in the higher
load factor region, receives a proportionately larger amount of the
available load diversity than the classes with higher load factors.
Classes B and C, both having load factors in the region of the Bary
Curve where the probability of coincidence is constant, receive
proportionately the same amount of the available load diversity. Class
D, with a high load factor in the ascending region of the Bary Curve
where the probability of coincidence is conceptually higher than in
the lower load factor region and approaches the limiting value, receives a proportionately lower amount of the available load diversity
than the classes with lower load factors, but never lower than established by the lower limit of the coincidence factor *versus* load factor
relationship.

B. The Special Case Prevalent in Practice. In practice, all class
load factors generally fall in the level region of coincidence factors
of the Bary Curve. It can be demonstrated that, where such load
factors are between 35 and 60 percent, the preceding arithmetic computations, of the "cut and try" nature, can be simplified by the employment of equation (4.03).

For example, let us assume for this purpose the basic data of line
2 of Table 3, the class load factor as shown in line 3 of Table 4, and

cially when such a single day reflects abnormal conditions which are not inherently present in day-to-day behavior of the class loads.

---

the system peaks for the two conditions as shown in lines 8 and 13 of Table 3. The P_s/D_n quotients of equation (4.03) for these conditions become 0.80 for peak no. 1 and 0.90 for peak no. 2. The most probable diversified maximum demands of the classes thus become as shown in lines 8a and 13a of Table 4, which check the interpolated values shown in lines 8 and 13, respectively, of that table:

TABLE 4. ILLUSTRATIVE UTILITY SYSTEM

		A′	B′	C′	D′	E′	Total
1.	Classes of service						
2.	Maximum demands—Mw	600	500	800	700	400	3,000
3.	Load factors in month of maximum demands—%	35	40	45	50	60	
4.	Coincidence factors—Basic Bary Curve	.83	.83	.83	.83	.83	
5.	First-try of diversified maximum demands—Mw	498	415	664	581	332	2,490
Peak No. 1 Conditions = 2,400 Mw							
6.	Coincidence factors—Succedent Bary Curve	.70	.70	.70	.70	.70	
7.	Second-try of diversified maximum demands—Mw	420	350	560	490	280	2,140
8.	Interpolated probable diversified maximum demands—Mw	480	400	640	560	320	2,400
8a.	Calculated probable diversified maximum demands from equation (4.03)	480	400	640	560	320	2,400
9.	Distributed load diversities—Mw	120	100	160	140	80	600
10.	Distributed load diversities in % of maximum demand	20	20	20	20	20	20
Peak No. 2 Conditions = 2,700 Mw							
11.	Coincidence factors—Antecedent Bary Curve	.91	.91	.91	.91	.91	
12.	Second-try of diversified maximum demands—Mw	546	455	728	637	364	2,730
13.	Interpolated probable diversified maximum demands—Mw	540	450	720	630	360	2,700
13a.	Calculated probable diversified maximum demands from equation (4.03)	540	450	720	630	360	2,700
14.	Distributed load diversities—Mw	60	50	80	70	40	300
15.	Distributed load diversities—% of maximum demands	10	10	10	10	10	10

While the average weekday conditions are conducive to all loads which are not directly affected by climatological conditions of the area, this concept has been extended to cover loads affected by climatological temperature conditions. For loads affected by winter temperatures I have established the "average weekday of a normal coldest spell." The coldest spell of a heating season is defined as the period of the lowest average daily mean temperatures comprised of consecutive days with daily mean temperatures of some value (such as 23 ° F. or less for Philadelphia conditions), which, on the basis of weather records for the territory, is certain to occur there every year. Similarly, for the load affected by summer temperatures, I have established the "average weekday of a normal warmest spell" of the cooling season which is based on the effective degree-hour records over a ten-year period developed from weather data for hourly dry bulb and wet bulb temperatures. For Philadelphia conditions, an effective degree-hour is taken as one-third of the sum of the dry bulb hourly temperature in excess of 75 ° F. and twice the corresponding wet bulb hourly temperature in excess of 65 ° F. [14]

Since, in this case, the most probable value of the interclass coincidence factor applicable to each class is in effect the *average* of all classes, the load diversity of the system is distributed uniformly over all classes, that is, for the peak no. 1 conditions it becomes 20 percent of the maximum demand of each of the classes, and for the peak no. 2 conditions it is 10 percent of these demands.

Thus the preceding examples demonstrated with numbers the procedure outlined in the text on the "Coincidence Probability" method of distributing load diversity among classes of service, and illustrated that the well-known NCP method is but a simplification of the author's basic theory.

[14]For a more detailed explanation, see, Constantine W. Bary, "Dollars and Sense of Electric House Heating," Minutes, 75th Annual Meeting (New York, Association of Edison Illuminating Companies, 1959, unpublished), Appendix I.

5. CLASS LOADS AND LOAD-CARRYING CAPABILITIES OF THE SUPPLY SYSTEM

Determination of class of service loads is not a simple task. The information sought on diversified maximum demands, in kilowatts and kilovolt-amperes, at various levels of the supply system is not available in the general record-keeping routines of the present-day utility systems. To secure the necessary information requires a systematic activity known as load research. It embraces a whole gamut of engineering, statistical, and mathematical methods and procedures, ranging from a simple application of judgment to available data, to refined mathematical probes into significance of sampling techniques. In this chapter, I shall describe a general method which has been found practical on the illustrative system. However, there may be other methods, more or less refined, more or less reliable, more or less costly, more or less time-consuming which could provide the required information under specified conditions and for specified objectives.[1]

In securing the required information an endeavor is made to obtain as much of it as possible from a compilation of data from available records, and the remainder, from an expansion of the results of load surveys conducted periodically by sampling customers of various classes of service. Under this approach the breakdown of the system load into its components by classes of

[1]For a detailed description of a number of methods, see, AEIC Load Research Committee, "Manual of Procedure for Load Surveys" (New York, Association of Edison Illuminating Companies, 1961, unpublished).

service and by functional subdivisions of service supply should be made annually for an average weekday of one or more peak periods. The total load for the entire system used for the "universe" of this analysis is the arithmetic average of the hourly loadings of five to ten weekdays, Monday through Friday (exclusive of holidays), around the peak periods. When the system definitely peaks in December, year in and year out, such analysis can be confined to the average weekday of that month. With a change in system load patterns in recent years to dual peaking levels in summer as well as in winter, the analysis should be made for the average weekday of a summer month and for the December month. For simplicity, these periods will be referred to as "average weekdays." For the purpose of this analysis, the system load and the loading of all of its component parts reflect 30-minute clock-hour intervals ending on the hour and certain selected half-hours around the time of the morning and evening system peaks.

A question can be raised as to why the 30-minute demand interval is used for such load analysis work. There are several reasons. First, for systems where the demands of practically all demand-billed customers are measured on a 30-minute demand interval basis, it seems consistent to use it throughout all load analysis work. Second, the Load Research Committee of AEIC has established the 30-minute interval as a preferred standard for its studies, which thus affords a convenient basis of comparison. And, third, the 30-minute basis appears to me as a reasonable compromise between the 60-minute interval employed for record-keeping of the total load of the system at the production level, which can be converted, however, to the 30-minute basis from data provided by instantaneous load recorders used in load dispatching, and the shorter intervals of 15 minutes and even lower needed by the requirements of high-grade service at various distribution levels of the supply system.

It must be realized, too, that consistency in demand intervals, at noncoincident and diversified levels, is essential for a proper interpretation of empirical relationships between load factors and coincidence factors and between energy use and diversified maximum demands. Those depicted in various charts of this book have been standardized to reflect 30-minute demand intervals.

Class Load Curves from Billing Records. The service load

curves of individual classes are determined in general either by
an analysis of registrations of the billing demand instruments of
all, or nearly all, individual customers in a class, or by an
analysis of the loading characteristics of sample customers obtained from periodic load surveys, and their ultimate expansion
to include all of the customers comprising such classes. Average weekday load curves determined from registrations of billing
demand meters are usually those for the high tension manufacturing and nonmanufacturing, for the traction, and for other
utilities classes of service when these customers are equipped
with standard-recording instruments. Such load curves of the
street-lighting class are determined from the billing records of
the connected load of lighting units and their specified hours of
operation. The average weekday load curves of the primary
voltage manufacturing and nonmanufacturing class of service are
determined by the expansion of the summated load curve shapes
of customers with recording demand meters so as to include the
energy use of all customers of this class of service.

Class Load Curves from Surveys. The average weekday load
curves for the residential and secondary voltage manufacturing
and nonmanufacturing classes of service are developed from
load curve shapes of sample groups of these classes, obtained
from periodic field load surveys and expanded to include the
entire energy use of these classes. Field tests should be made
periodically to determine the load patterns of sample customers
of these two classes of service. Such tests could alternate from
year to year between the two classes, so that at no time are the
basic data more than one year old. Test groups of sample customers are best prepared in accordance with the requirements of
the stratified method of sampling—the sample customers being
chosen at random from a large number comprising each stratum
which has been homogenized to include customers of specified
energy use characteristics. Winter period tests are made usually for several weeks spanning the period of the system peak
load and each sample customer is tested for a period of one or
two weeks, although the entire winter test of all sample customers is spread over a four- to six-week period. Summer period
tests, on a reduced scale, should be made for several months
spanning the period of the probable system peak load. Such
peak load occurs as a result of high ambient temperatures which
in many parts of this country can occur from June to September,

inclusive. This procedure is dictated largely by economic considerations of conducting such tests and by the availability of manpower and test-metering equipment. It can be said, however, that the results derived therefrom have been found to provide reliable indications on the fundamental load characteristics of the classes.

System Losses. The foregoing description dealt with the methods of developing classes of service average weekday load curves as at the level of customers' meters. To the hourly demand values of these load curves are then added the hour-to-hour losses inherent in the supply of electricity from the point of generation through the functional supply facilities to the points of metering. The main analysis of system losses is made on an annual basis. The total system energy losses from the point of net generation to the customers' meters are obtainable from billing and operating records. The subdivision of this volume of energy loss into functional components of the supply system basically uses a method which involves the compilation of available kilowatthour meter registrations at the level of primary voltage distribution substations, which form an intermediate check point between the registrations of energy output at the level of the production system and at the level of sales; and estimates of the losses in various parts of the supply system which are obtained from a knowledge of line and circuit loadings, their physical characteristics of length and wire sizes, and the efficiency characteristics of transformers, voltage regulators, meters and other distribution facilities.

The annual losses of the various functional subdivisions of the supply system developed from such studies form the basis for the determination of the corresponding hour-to-hour losses for the average weekday load curves. For the bulk transmission system, they reflect detailed calculations based on metered or test-derived values. For the functional components of the distribution system, they are derived from established load-loss relationships reflecting a segregation of the losses into components which do not vary with the load, such as the meter and transformer iron and dielectric losses; those that vary directly with the load, primarily in substation transformers which are switched "on" and "off" with changes in load; and those that vary with the square of the load, such as the copper losses in lines, mains and circuits, and in transformers permanently connected to the supply system irrespective as to the ebb and flow of the load.

Table 5 shows a numerical set of delivery efficiency data for the four functional subdivisions of the illustrative supply system. It will be noted that, by and large, the annual efficiencies are not materially different from those at time of peak loads.

TABLE 5. ILLUSTRATIVE PHYSICAL DELIVERY EFFICIENCY OF FUNCTIONAL SUBDIVISIONS OF SUPPLY SYSTEM

	Percent Efficiencies	
	For Energy Supply	For Peak Load Supply
Bulk Transmission System	97.9	98.5
Distribution System:		
High Tension Voltage Distribution	98.0	97.6
Primary Voltage Distribution	96.0	96.3
Secondary Voltage and C.C. Distribution	95.8	95.4

Load Balance. With the use of the developed class of service, average weekday load curves, as at the level of sales, and the calculated loss factors, it is possible to convert each of the load curves of individual classes of service to the levels of each of the functional subdivisions of the supply system and then, by summing them up as at the level of the production system, compare the sum with the average weekday load curve of the system as derived from load-dispatching log records. This comparison provides an over-all check on the accuracy of the analytical work. With a good correlation between the sum of the derived and the actual curves, a high degree of confidence is obtained in the practical significance of the analytical work. When the correlation is not too good, an investigation of the reasons for the deviations will frequently reveal either arithmetic errors in the analytical work, the necessity for changes in sampling techniques, or the malfunctioning in the field of some control devices from predetermined settings. However, in my over-thirty-years' experience, I find that under a careful analytical work, backed by sound sampling data, the sum of the derived class load curves for average weekdays should correspond well with the system actuals. Figure 14 provides demonstration of such a comparison for the illustrative system for the average weekdays of a summer and of a winter period.

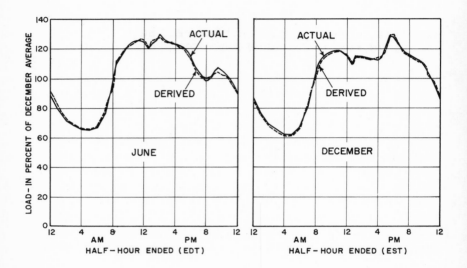

Figure 14. Derived *versus* actual load curves for average weekdays in June and December

Annual Class Peaks. While the detailed analyses of load segregation by classes of service are made for the average weekdays of a summer and of a winter (December) period, the diversified maximum demands of the classes for the year in question are obtained through the application of "pk" factors developed from a study of the seasonal variations of energy sales, billing demands, or from considerations of climatological data reflecting conditions of the average weekday of the normal warmest spell and of the normal coldest spell for the temperature sensitive loads.

These adjustments are desirable from theoretical considerations, and from practical objectives for an adequate reflection of the manner facilities are provided to meet load requirements of classes of service.

Reactive Peak Loads. Upon completion of this analysis, the peak loads of the classes, expressed in kilowatts, are supplemented by an analysis of their reactive kilovolt-amperes at each level of the functional subdivisions of the supply system, starting with their values, based on known power factors of the classes at the time of their peaks, at the sales level, and progressing through the functional subdivisions of the supply system by adding the lagging or leading vars inherent in its physical facilities. Here too a rough check can be had: the sum of the class of service vars at the level of the production system should be consistent with the vars of the system load at the time of its peak, which is usually available from a detailed engineering analysis of the system's peak load.

Customers' Maximum Demands. In addition to the maximum demands (or peak loads) of classes, the fundamental cost-to-serve equation requires the knowledge of the noncoincident maximum demands of customers within each of the classes. Such demands are readily obtainable from billing records for all classes whose customers are billed on a demand basis; and for the other class they are obtained through the expansion to class proportions of sample data secured from periodic load surveys.

FUNCTIONAL SYSTEMS' CAPABILITIES

Interrelated with the class load data is the information on the capabilities of the various functional subdivisions of the supply system. This information is ordinarily available in the engineering, operating, or statistical records of the utility and comprises the following:

For the Production System: The total *kw*, *kvar* and *kva* capabilities of the entire production system, including firm purchases

For the Bulk Transmission and the High Tension Voltage Distribution Systems: The total reactive kilovolt-ampere capability of synchronous condensers

For the Primary Voltage Distribution System: The total capability of primary distribution transformers, the sum of their noncoincident *kva* peaks, and the total reactive kilovolt-ampere capacity of condensers

> *For the Secondary Voltage Distribution System and Constant Current Street Lighting System:* The total capacity and number of secondary distribution and constant current transformers, and the total reactive capacity of condensers
>
> *For the Special Purpose System:* The total (usually leading) reactive kilovolt-amperes of special purpose facilities, as frequency changers, rotary converters, and the like

Development of class loads in all of their essential aspects, and of capacities of functional subdivisions of the supply system, permits the derivation of a set of important factors for use in establishing meaningful and consistent parametric component unit costs pertaining to the load parameters of the fundamental cost-to-serve equation. The comprehensive information on class loads described herein provides at various levels of the supply system data on interclass coincidence factors, power factors, reactive factors, and loss factors; and the comprehensive information on capacities provides means for establishing the basic unit costs for some of the functional subdivisions under their normal loadings.

6. STANDARD COMPONENT UNIT COSTS

In the concept of component unit costs used herein, the word "component" refers to the four parametric entities of the basic equation (2.05) for the cost-to-serve. The word *costs* means the sum of the fully analyzed, assigned, or prorated expenses, allowances for depreciation, taxes, and a specified return on net plant and working capital. Such costs are derived from actual data of the immediate past, or, preferably, from pro forma estimates of the immediate future. Although it is true that knowledge of the past is needed to provide a basis of foreseeing the future, and, as the saying goes, "what is past is prologue," pro forma estimates of the future are even more important from practical considerations of rate making. The unit cost values of these components should reflect *standard* conditions of system capacity loading and of the more important factors dependent on the established models of the supply system and of the load structure. Under these standard unit costs, means are provided for establishing uniform and meaningful criteria to gauge, in an absolute or relative sense, the significance of operational economics of the loads of classes or of the loads within the classes.

It should be noted that the *method* of cost evaluation described herein is independent of the basis employed in establishing the dollar amounts of a utility's plant in service. It matters not whether it reflects the "original cost" concept of the Uniform System of Accounts prescribed for electric utilities or the "reproduction cost" or the "fair value" concepts employed in some regulatory jurisdictions in compliance with established laws.

The important thing is that the annual carrying charge rate, used to convert them to annual costs, is compatible with the basis reflected by the dollar amounts of the plant. As stated in Chapter 2, different purposes may require the use of different bases, even though the method of evaluation is the same. However, for the purposes of operational economics, standard component unit costs, employing the original cost basis coupled with a compatible carrying charge rate, should be quite adequate under the economic conditions in the United States existing now and foreseeable in the immediate future.

The following description provides illustrations of some of the types of cost assignments employed in the author's scheme of developing various parts of parametric standard component unit costs. They are confined to the stated functional elements of the supply system in order to bring out in a concise fashion the various salient features which are likely to be encountered; but by this approach it is not intended to minimize the significance of cost assignments of other functional elements; most of them resemble the features of one or the other of the types described in the examples. Numerical data used reflect practical conditions; but they do not necessarily represent typical or average values; they are simply illustrative of the methods, which would be well nigh impossible of explaining without numbers.

Cost Assignment No. 1, peculiar to the production system's plant and its carrying charges, reflects the combining of three cost elements of this functional system into a single parametric component unit cost, under specified standard conditions of the system and of each of the classes of service. Its detailed steps are shown in the upper portion of Table 6.

Let us assume that the investment cost of the production plant is 160 cost units per kilowatt of production system capability. From detailed studies, as more fully described in Chapter 3, it is found that 90 percent of this cost is related to the kilowatt capability of the plant, 8 percent to its kilovolt-ampere rating, and 2 percent to its *kvar* rating. Let us further assume that for each kilowatt of plant capability there is built in 0.57 *kvar* of reactive capacity and thus 1.15 kilovolt-ampere of current carrying capability. The unit costs of these three elements of the production system are therefore as follows:

1) Kw element = $0.90 \times 160 \div 1$ $= 144$ per Kw of plant capability
2) Kva element = $0.08 \times 160 \div 1.15 =$ 11 per Kva of plant capability
3) $Kvar$ element = $0.02 \times 160 \div 0.57 =$ 6 per $Kvar$ of plant capability

Under these basic unit cost elements of the production plant we are now in position to develop their contribution to the "Class Peak or Diversified Demand" parametric component of unit costs of the four general classes of service, as shown in Table 6.

Lines 2, 10, and 19 reflect normal loading factors of the respective capacity elements of the production system; that is, they represent the measure of the amount of normal capacity provided on the system, in the respective elements, to assure a high degree of reliability of the supply from the production system. The lower these factors the higher the reserve, and therefore the higher the unit cost per kilowatt of the allowable peak loads which can be carried on such a system for the specified reserve standard. These loading factors need not be the same for the three cost elements, because the trigonometric relationships of the built-in reactive capability of the system need not be the same as that of the kilowatt peak load. As a matter of fact in practice they are seldom alike.

Lines 3, 11, and 20 reflect the factors which define the normal relationship between the system average weekday peak load and the absolute single-day peak on the production system, thus enabling the conversion of the unit cost of the elements to conditions of the average weekday, established as a prerequisite of the conceptual model of the class load structure.

Lines 4, 12, and 21 are the interclass coincidence factors for each of the three capacity elements of the production system. Their uniform application to all classes of service is in accord with the conceptual behavior of the load structure and the underlying applicability of the benefits of load diversity under the Coincidence Probability method, explained in Chapter 4.

It will be noted from a careful study of the factors thus described that all of them relate to *system* conditions of each of the elements and are therefore uniformly applied to all classes of service. Of course, under the General Unified Theory as more fully set forth in Chapter 4, the interclass coincidence factors could differ for different classes of service. Similarly, the loading factors could differ too. But in practice these differences

TABLE 6. PRODUCTION SYSTEM

Plant		Mfg. & Nonmfg. Classes			Resid. Class
		HT	PD	Sec.	Sec.
KW Element					
1. Cost per KW of production system net capability		144	144	144	144
Conversion factors:					
2. System loading factor	a	0.87	0.87	0.87	0.87
3. Ratio of system avg. weekday pk to single-day pk	b	0.97	0.97	0.97	0.97
4. Interclass KW coincidence factor	c	0.87	0.87	0.87	0.87
5. Combined joint-use factor $\quad c \div (a \times b)$		1.03	1.03	1.03	1.03
6. Class-KW efficiency of supply	d	0.97	0.92	0.86	0.86
7. Total Multiplier $\quad (5) \div d$		1.06	1.12	1.20	1.20
8. Cost per KW of class peaks as at meters $\quad (1) \times (7)$		153	161	173	173
KVA Element					
9. Cost per KVA of production system net capability		11	11	11	11
Conversion factors:					
10. System loading factor	a_1	0.85	0.85	0.85	0.85
11. Ratio of system avg. weekday pk to single-day pk	b_1	0.97	0.97	0.97	0.97
12. Interclass KVA coincidence factor	c_1	0.87	0.87	0.87	0.87
13. Combined joint-use factor $\quad c_1 \div (a_1 \times b_1)$		1.06	1.06	1.06	1.06
14. Class KVA efficiency of supply	d_1	0.96	0.89	0.82	0.82
15. Class power factor as at meters	e_1	0.95	0.91	0.92	0.97
16. Total Multiplier $\quad (13) \div (d_1 \times e_1)$		1.16	1.31	1.41	1.33
17. Cost per KW of class peaks as at meters $\quad (9) \times (16)$		13	14	16	15
KVAR Element					
18. Cost per KVAR of production system net capability		6	6	6	6

	Description	Formula				
	Conversion factors:					
19.	System loading factor	a_2	0.79	0.79	0.79	0.79
20.	Ratio of system avg. weekday pk to single-day pk	b_2	0.97	0.97	0.97	0.97
21.	Interclass $KVAR$ coincidence factor	c_2	0.89	0.89	0.89	0.89
22.	Combined joint-use factor	$c_2 \div (a_2 \times b_2)$	1.16	1.16	1.16	1.16
23.	Class $KVAR$ efficiency of supply	d_2	0.88	0.84	0.70	0.55
24.	Class tangent corresponding to pf as at meters	e_2	0.33	0.46	0.43	0.25
25.	Total Multiplier	$(22)\, e_2 \div d_2$	0.44	0.64	0.71	0.53
26.	Cost per KW of class peak as at meters	$(18) \times (25)$	3	4	4	3
	Total					
27.	Total cost per KW of class peaks as at meters	$(8) + (17) + (26)$	169	179	193	191
28.	Total annual carrying charges per KW of class peaks as at meters	$(27) \times 0.12$	20.3	21.5	23.2	22.9
	Expense: Annual					
	KWH Energy Element					
30.	Cost per KWH of production system net output $\times 10^{-3}$		3.31	3.31	3.31	3.31
	Conversion factors:					
31.	Class KWH efficiency of supply		0.96	0.92	0.88	0.88
32.	Total Multiplier	$1 \div (31)$	1.04	1.09	1.14	1.14
33.	Cost per KWH of class sales $\times 10^{-3}$	$(30) \times (32)$	3.44	3.61	3.77	3.77

Notes: In Tables 6 to 11 inclusive, the column designations:

HT stand for supplied at High Tension voltage
PD stand for supplied at Primary Distribution voltage
Sec. stand for supplied at Secondary Distribution voltage

The same numerical value of carrying charge rate was used in all of the tables of this chapter. This was done for simplicity of presentation and not necessarily as an indication that in actual practice the carrying charge rates of different functional parts of the supply system are the same. Further details of this subject are described in Chapter 14.

could not be material; in the case of the coincidence factors, because of the fundamental shape of the Bary type coincidence factor curves; and in the case of the loading factors, because of the functional composition of the reserve requirements of present-day production systems of electric utilities. The major portion of such requirements is comprised of an allowance for spinning reserve and of a provision for probable departures of estimated loads from actual. Both of them, however, should be of uniform proportion for all regular and unrestricted components of the system load. However, other factors which are of an individual nature in relation to each class introduce the needed differences in the conversion of the basic unit costs of the capacity elements to the unit costs per kilowatt of each of the class peaks as at the level of their metering points on the supply system. Thus in fact, the parametric component unit cost of a class, while reflecting the same basic unit costs of the three capacity elements, is different from any other classes only by differences inherent in some features of the class loads, and by the differences in the locations of the classes on the established model of the supply system.

Cost Assignment No. 2, peculiar to the energy element of the production system expenses, is a simple conversion of a basic unit cost per kilowatthour of net system output to the "Energy" parametric component unit cost per kilowatthour of a class' energy sales. Its details are shown at the bottom of Table 6, previously referred to in discussion of Cost Assignment No. 1.

Cost Assignment No. 3, typified by the bulk transmission system, reflects a simple conversion of a single cost element into a single parametric component unit cost for each of the classes, as shown in Table 7, and needs no further explanation since it is identical in treatment to the kilovolt-ampere element of the production system.

Cost Assignment No. 4, typified by the high tension distribution system, reflects a dual parametric assignment of a basic unit cost of a functional supply system. In this case the parametric component unit cost of the high tension (HT) class is of the "Customer Demand" nature, while those of the other classes are of a "Class Peak or Diversified Demand" nature, the reasons for which were provided in Chapter 3. To carry out this principle, the basic unit cost of the functional system

TABLE 7. BULK TRANSMISSION SYSTEM PLANT

		Mfg. & Nonmfg. Classes			Resia. Class
		HT	PD	Sec.	Sec.
1. Cost per KVA of production system net capability		30	30	30	30
Conversion factors:					
2. System loading factor	a_1	0.85	0.85	0.85	0.85
3. Ratio of system avg weekday pk to single-day pk	b_1	0.97	0.97	0.97	0.97
4. Interclass KVA coincidence factor	c_1	0.87	0.87	0.87	0.87
5. Combined joint-use factor	$c_1 \div (a_1 \times b_1)$	1.06	1.06	1.06	1.06
6. Class KVA efficiency of supply	d_1	0.96	0.89	0.82	0.82
7. Class power factor as at meters	e_1	0.95	0.91	0.92	0.97
8. Total Multiplier	$(5) \div (d_1 \times e_1)$	1.16	1.31	1.41	1.33
9. Cost per KW of class peaks as at meters	$(1) \times (8)$	35	39	42	40
10. Annual carrying charges per KW of class peak as at meters	$(9) \times 0.12$	4.2	4.7	5.0	4.8

is expressed per kilovolt-ampere of the sum of HT customers' maximum demands and of the average of substations' sum of noncoincident peaks and their capacities. This basic unit cost is then modified by the appropriate factors, which translate it to the parametric component unit costs of the classes, as shown in Table 8.

Cost Assignment No. 5, typified by the branch element of the primary voltage distribution system, reflects another type of unit cost for the basic value, that is, per weighted equivalent single-phase tap-off, and the final unit cost for the parametric value, that is, per customer. Its details are shown in Table 9. The weights used account for differences in costs of aerial and underground construction and of the number of conductors utilized by single-phase and polyphase supplies which are relatively utilized by the classes.

TABLE 8. HIGH TENSION DISTRIBUTION SYSTEM PLANT

		Mfg. & Nonmfg. Classes			Resid. Class
		HT	PD	Sec.	Sec.
1. Cost per KVA of sum of HT cust max demands and avg of prim subst capacities and pks		35	35	35	35
Conversion factors:					
2. Ratio of class peaks on prim distr system to avg of prim subst capacities and pks	a_3	—	1.14	1.14	1.14
3. Class-KVA effic. of supply	b_3	—	0.89	0.83	0.83
4. Class pf as at meters	c_3	0.95	0.91	0.92	0.97
5. Total multiplier	$a_3 \div (b_3 \times c_3)$	1.05*	1.41	1.49	1.42
6. Cost per KW of cust max demands at meters	$(1) \times (5)$	37			
7. Cost per KW of class peaks as at meters	$(1) \times (5)$		49	52	50
8. Annual carrying charge per KW of customers' max demands at meters	$(6) \times 0.12$	4.4			
9. Annual carrying charge per KW of class peaks at meters	$(7) \times 0.12$		5.9	6.2	6.0

*Equals $1/c_3$

TABLE 9. PRIMARY VOLTAGE DISTRIBUTION SYSTEM BRANCH PLANT

		Mfg. & Nonmfg. Classes		Resid. Class
		PD	Sec.	Sec.
1. Cost per weighted no. of equiv single-phase tap-offs		300	300	300
Conversion factor:				
2. Ratio of weighted no. of equiv single-phase tap-offs to number of customers	a_4	3.93	.08	.07
3. Total Multiplier	a_4	3.93	.08	.07
4. Cost per customer	$(1) \times a_4$	1,179	24	21
5. Annual carrying charge per customer	$(4) \times 0.12$	141.5	2.9	2.5

Cost Assignment No. 6, typified by the circuit element of the secondary voltage distribution system, reflects a simple basic unit cost expressed per *average* of all customers on that system and its translation to a per-customer value of each class for the "Customer" parametric component of unit cost. The details of it are shown in Table 10. The weights used account for differences in costs of aerial and underground construction, of the number of conductors utilized for single-phase and polyphase supplies and for two-wire and three-wire requirements, which are relatively utilized by the two classes.

TABLE 10. SECONDARY VOLTAGE DISTRIBUTION SYSTEM MAINS PLANT

		Mfg. & Nonmfg. Class	Resid. Class
		Sec.	Sec.
1. Cost per average customer		45	45
Conversion factor:			
2. Customer weighting factor	a_5	1.66	0.88
3. Total Multiplier	a_5	1.66	0.88
4. Cost per customer of the class	$(1) \times a_5$	75	40
5. Annual carrying charge per cust. of the class	$(4) \times 0.12$	9.0	4.8

Cost Assignment No. 7, peculiar to the functional costs of the general administrative activities, which in the author's concept of a utility's cost structure are of an operational "overhead" nature, and therefore relatable to all parametric components of the cost-to-serve, is shown at the bottom of Table 11 which serves also as a general summary of the manner of building up the four parametric component unit costs for the four general classes of service used for illustration. Crosses indicate the applicability of a functional cost item for a class in the parametric components of the cost-to-serve; dashes indicate the opposite, that is, their nonapplicability. The lines with arrows at each end indicate the extent overhead items are distributed to the parametric components of the classes, using the indicated bases of allocation.

Significance of Parametric Components of Cost. In concluding this chapter, an analysis is provided of the relative economic significance of the parametric components of cost-to-serve on the illustrative electric utility system. Specific values will

TABLE 11. ILLUSTRATIVE SUMMARY OF ASSIGNMENT OF FUNCTIONAL COST ELEMENTS TO PARAMETRIC COMPONENTS OF COST-TO-SERVE OF FOUR GENERAL CLASSES OF SERVICE

	"Customer" Component				"Customer Demand" Component				"Class Peak or Diversified Demand" Component				"Energy" Component			
	Mfg. & Nonmfg.			Res.	Mfg. & Nonmfg.			Res.	Mfg. & Nonmfg.			Res.	Mfg. & Nonmfg.			Res.
	HT	PD	Sec.	Sec.	HT	PD	Sec.	Sec.	HT	PD	Sec.	Sec.	HT	PD	Sec.	Sec.
Production system	–	–	–	–	–	–	–	–	X	X	X	X	X	X	X	X
Bulk transmission system	–	–	–	–	–	–	–	–	X	X	X	X	–	–	–	–
Distribution system																
High Tension distribution (Substations & lines)	–	–	–	–	X	–	–	–	–	X	X	X	–	–	–	–
Primary voltage distribution																
Substations	–	–	–	–	–	–	–	–	–	X	X	X	–	–	–	–
Capacitors	–	–	–	–	–	–	–	–	–	X	X	X	–	–	–	–
Feeders	–	–	X	–	–	X	–	–	–	X	X	X	–	–	–	–
Branches	X	X	X	X	–	–	–	X	–	–	–	–	–	–	–	–

Secondary voltage distribution												
Transformers	—	—	X	X	X	X	X	X	X	X	—	—
Capacitors	—	—	—	X	X	X	X	X	—	—	—	—
Mains	—	—	X	X	X	—	—	—	—	—	—	—
Service conductors	X	X	X	X	—	—	—	—	—	—	—	—
Metering and control system	X	X	X	—	—	—	—	—	—	—	—	—
Work on consumers' premises	X	X	X	—	—	—	—	—	—	—	—	—
Customers' accounting	X	X	X	—	—	—	—	—	—	—	—	—
Sales promotion	X	X	X	—	—	—	—	—	—	—	—	—
General administrative:												
General plant (carrying charges)	←——————— (at fixed rate per dollar of foregoing plant) ———————→											
General & administrative expenses	←——— at fixed rate per dollar of direct expenses (excluding fuel, energy purchases, and fixed charges) ———→											
Total cost-to-serve per unit of the parameter as at meters	X	X	X	X	X	X	X	X	X	X	X	X

Note: Functional costs include expenses and carrying charges on investment in plant and working capital.

differ for individual utilities now and with the passage of time. Those shown in Tables 12, 13, and 14 are provided only as illustrations to form a general idea of the relative order of magnitude of these components of cost under existing conditions of the load structure of that utility.

TABLE 12. ILLUSTRATIVE HORIZONTAL COMPOSITION OF PARAMETRIC COMPONENTS OF COST BY FUNCTIONAL SUBDIVISIONS—PERCENT

Functional Subdivisions	Total	Parametric Components			
		Customer	Customer demand	Class Peak	Energy
Production system	100	–	–	59	41
Bulk Transmission system	100	–	–	100	–
Distribution system:					
High Tension voltage distribution	100	–	38	62	–
Primary voltage distribution	100	23	11	66	–
Secondary voltage distribution	100	77	4	19	–
Service conductors	100	100	–	–	–
Metering & Control system	100	100	–	–	–
Work on customers' premises	100	100	–	–	–
Customers' billing	100	100	–	–	–
Sales promotion	100	92	8	–	–
General administrative	100	35	5	52	5
Total*	100	18	4	53	22

*Percentages shown do not add up necessarily to 100, because the remainder is applicable to the special purpose system, not shown.

Table 12 reveals that of the total cost-to-serve, the parametric component which is related to "Class Peak or Diversified Demand" occupies the most prominent position. Over fifty percentage points of the total are lodged in this component. This provides a convincing reason why *adequate knowledge of class peaks and customers' diversified maximum demands must be had before any reliable information can be obtained on the cost-to-serve*. It can be surmised also that with the ever-growing load requirements of individual customers, the significance of this parametric component should increase with time, and will be significantly affected by the diversified demand requirements of new loads. The component of costs related to the "Energy" is second in significance; that related to "Customers" is third, and that related to "Customer Demands" is fourth.

From Table 13 it will be observed that costs of the production system form the largest contributions to the two major parametric components of the cost-to-serve, that is, the "Class Peak or Diversified Demand" and the "Energy"; and again points up the overwhelming economic significance of this functional part of the supply system.

TABLE 13. ILLUSTRATIVE VERTICAL COMPOSITION OF PARAMETRIC COMPONENTS OF COST BY FUNCTIONAL SUBDIVISIONS—PERCENT

Functional Subdivisions	Parametric Components			
	Customer	Customer demand	Class Peak	Energy
Production system	–	–	60	99
Bulk transmission system	–	–	12	–
Distribution system:				
High Tension voltage distribution	–	61	9	–
Primary voltage distribution	12	23	11	–
Secondary voltage distribution	23	5	2	–
Service Conductors	7	–	–	–
Metering & control system	14	–	–	–
Work on customers' premises	3	–	–	–
Customers' billing	16	–	–	–
Sales promotion	13	4	–	–
General administrative	12	7	6	1
Total	100	100	100	100

Relative Magnitudes of Parametric Component Unit Costs. The relative magnitudes of the component unit costs differ among the four general classes of service in relation to the averages of the system, as shown in Table 14.

For example, the component unit costs related to the "Class Peak or Diversified Demand" for the classes supplied from the secondary voltage distribution system are in the order of 1-1/4 to 1-1/3 of the system average, while for the class supplied from the high tension voltage distribution system it is 3/4 of such average, and for the class supplied from the primary voltage distribution system it is 1-1/10 of such average. The reverse is true for the "Customer" parametric component unit

TABLE 14. ILLUSTRATIVE COMPARISON OF PARAMETRIC COMPONENT UNIT COSTS OF FOUR GENERAL CLASSES OF SERVICE IN RELATION TO SYSTEM AVERAGES

	Parametric Component Unit Costs (Annual)			
	"Customer" per customer	"Cust dem" per KW of cust max dem	"Class peak" per KW of div max dem	"Energy" per KWH
System average: relative range of cost units	35–40	3.5–4.0	45–50	0.0038–0.0040
Class of service (as ratios to system avg.):				
Residential-secondary voltage supply	0.87	0.80*	1.26	1.05
Manufacturing & nonmanufacturing:				
Secondary voltage supply	1.46	1.20*	1.30	1.05
Primary voltage supply	17.0	0.75	1.08	1.00
High Tension voltage supply	19.0	1.60	0.74	0.95

*Applies to customers' maximum demands in excess of 5 KW.

costs. Here such unit costs are from 15 to 20 times the system average for the classes supplied from the primary voltage distribution and from the high tension voltage systems respectively, while they are from 7/8 to 1-1/2 of such system average for classes supplied from the secondary voltage distribution system.

The component unit costs related to "Energy" are more nearly uniform for all classes of service in relation to the system average, the variation ranging from 5 percent under, for the class supplied from the high tension voltage distribution, to 5 percent over, for the classes supplied from the secondary voltage distribution system.

The parametric component unit costs related to "Customer Demand" vary from 1-2/3 of the average for the class supplied from the high tension voltage distribution system, to 3/4 of the average for the class supplied from the primary voltage distribution system.

The foregoing description provided basic information on the significance of the parametric component unit costs of the four general classes of service in relation to the system averages. The following Chapter 7 will expand this information in relation to the individual customers' loads within some of these classes, over a wide range of requirements.

7. COST-TO-SERVE RELATIONSHIPS

In Chapter 4, we have learned that on a modern utility system there are two of the better known controlling characteristics which can serve to establish for each general class of service the probable trends that are going on in the load behavior of its individual elements. One of such controlling characteristics is the individual customers' energy use, and the other, their monthly load factors. In our model of a utility's load structure, the former applies primarily to customers of the residential class, the latter, to the manufacturing and nonmanufacturing classes.

It has been shown also in that chapter that, from comprehensive load research studies, empirical relationships can be established between customers' energy use and their diversified maximum demands for the residential class, as shown in Figure 11; and between customers' monthly load factors and their group coincidence factors for the other general classes, as shown in Figure 12.

Energy Use is the Controlling Characteristic. With the availability of such relationship for the residential class of service and with energy-use as the controlling characteristic the fundamental cost-to-serve equation (2.05) can be rewritten in the foling terms:

$$C_T = c_e + c_d D + c_p \, g \, f(E_u) + c_e \, E_u \qquad (7.01)$$

where

$f(E_u) =$ the kw of diversified maximum demand as a function of customer's energy use, such as established in Figure 11

g = an intraclass coincidence factor between individual groups which, when applied to a weighted summation of the individual diversified maximum demands of the groups, establishes the peak load of the class. Experience indicates that on the basis of average weekday loads, used in our concept of a utility's load structure, this factor is in the order of 0.95

From practical considerations, the "Customer Demand" parametric component of this equation does not apply until the customer's noncoincident maximum demand exceeds 5 kw, and then only to the excess over this amount, so that it is relatively small until such demands exceed 10 kw. Therefore, it can be considered to be nil up to such values of demands which in effect eliminates its use for all present-day customers with annual requirements of less than 8,000 to 10,000 $kwhr$. It becomes significant only for customers in all-electric homes.

The "Customer" component is basically constant over a wide range of customers' requirements, except as it may be altered to reflect increases when special facilities are provided for controlling the availability to the customer of the service for some specific applications, such as "off-peak" water heating, "off-peak" heat storage, or the like.

Figure 15 illustrates a cost-to-serve relationship of customers of the residential class for a wide range of their unrestricted and uncontrolled energy requirements. In developing it, use was made of equation (7.01), the load relationships A, B and C depicted in Figure 11 and the parametric component unit costs for the residential class, illustrated in Table 14.

This cost-to-serve relationship which employs the *energy-use as the controlling characteristics* illustrates, among other things, two of the most important features of operational economics of the residential class of service: first, that the cost-to-serve increases at a substantial rate with increased energy use; and, second, that the "Customer" parametric component forms the major portion of the total cost-to-serve in the very low-use region, while the "Class Peak or Diversified Demand" component predominates in the high-use region.

Load Factor is the Controlling Characteristic. With the avail-

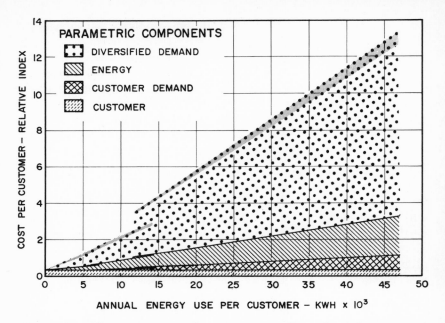

Figure 15. Illustrative annual cost-to-serve of residential customers by parametric components

ability of a coincidence-factor *versus* load-factor relationship for the manufacturing and nonmanufacturing classes of service for some month, as shown in Figure 12 for the month of December, and under a postulation that such relationship also applies to an average month, for which there is theoretical support from Eisenmenger's mathematical rationalization of this relationship[1] and from indications of available test information—the fundamental cost-to-serve equation (2.05) can be restated in the following form:

$$C_T = c_c + c_d\, D_c + c_p D_c f(M) + c_e 730\, D_c\, L_m \qquad (7.02)$$

where all values are expressed on the basis of an average month, L_m being the customers' load factors as a fraction, and $f(M)$, a composite of several factors as a function of L_m. The predomi-

[1]H. E. Eisenmenger, "Study of the Theoretical Relationship between Load Factor and Diversity Factor," Minutes, 55th Annual Meeting (New York, Association of Edison Illuminating Companies, 1939, unpublished).

nant portion of this function is the coincidence-factor versus load-factor relationship shown in Figure 12, the other factors being: the intraclass coincidence factor, the maximum month to the December month demand factor, the December month to the average month demand factor, and a conversion factor from a single day to an average weekday of the load conditions. From experience it has been found that these other factors, some of which are also functions of customers' load factors and some of which are larger than unity and others smaller, when applied as multipliers result in an $f(M)$ relationship which numerically does not differ materially from the fundamental values of the Bary Curve of the selected month, such as shown in Figure 12 over its entire load factor range, except in the very high load factor region where it becomes higher than the fundamental values of the Bary Curve.

In other words, the application of these factors results in an $f(M)$ relationship similar in shape and numerical values up to the ultra high load factor region of around 85 percent with a steepening of the slope thereafter resulting in an $f(M)$ value somewhat higher than unity at the extreme values of load factor.

For convenience of use, equation (7.02) can be divided through by D_c to obtain a cost-to-serve expression per kw of customers' monthly maximum demand as follows:

$$\frac{C_T}{D_c} = \frac{c_c}{D_c} + c_d + c_p f(M) + c_e\, 730\, L_m \qquad (7.03)$$

However, since $730\, L_m$ is also equivalent to the hours' use H_m of the maximum demand, equation (7.03) can be further rewritten as:

$$\frac{C_T}{D_c} = \frac{c_c}{D_c} + c_d + c_p f(M') + c_e\, H_m \qquad (7.04)$$

With the use of this equation, of the $f(M')$ function, and of the parametric component unit costs for the manufacturing and non-manufacturing classes of service, shown in Table 14, it is possible to construct cost-to-serve relationships for a wide range of such customers' sizes and over the full range of their monthly load factors. Such cost-to-serve relationships are illustrated in Figure 16 for three maximum demand values of the class supplied from the primary voltage distribution system.

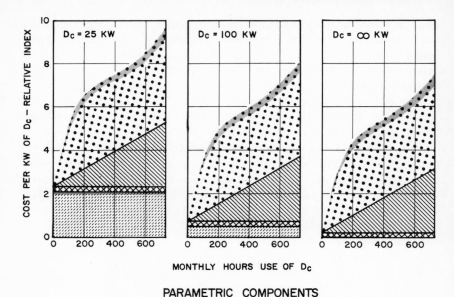

MONTHLY HOURS USE OF D_C

PARAMETRIC COMPONENTS

DIVERSIFIED DEMAND   CUSTOMER DEMAND

ENERGY   CUSTOMER

Figure 16. Illustrative monthly cost per KW of maximum demands of customers of the manufacturing and nonmanufacturing class by parametric components

The infinite value of D_c is provided only to illustrate the mathematical limit of size upon the cost-to-serve relationship. Although purely theoretical, it is nevertheless of importance in the considerations of the effects of customers' sizes upon the asymptotic convergence of unit costs per kilowatt of customers' maximum demands.

These cost relationships illustrate, among other things, three most important features of operational economics of the manufacturing and nonmanufacturing classes of service when employing *customers' load factors, or the hours' use of maximum demand, as the controlling characteristic.* First, the cost-to-serve per kilowatt of customers' maximum demand increases with an increase in their hours' use of the maximum demand similarly in character to the behavior of the Second Law of Load Diversity. Second, for relatively small demand-size customers, the "Customer'' component forms the major portion of the total cost-to-serve in the small hours' use region, while in the large hours' use region the ''Class Peak or Diversified Demand'' component predominates.   Third, unit costs per kilowatt of customers' maximum demands decrease with an increase in customers' sizes through a diminution of the ''Customer'' component, which disappears for ultra high demand values. In other words the asymptote of the cost-to-serve per kilowatt of customers' maximum demands for any given load factor is comprised of the sum of the last three components of the cost-to-serve equation.

8. COST ASSIGNMENT AND COST ALLOCATION

The foregoing chapters outlined the general procedure employed in determining the most probable cost-to-serve over as wide a range of customers' load requirements as the probability relationship of load characteristics provide, and in accordance with the selected controlling characteristics used in administering the operational economics of a class. In addition, if information is also available either on the distribution of customers by selected intervals of the controlling characteristic and its related parameter, or on the over-all numerical values of the four parameters of a class, computations can be made to provide information on the cost to serve such a class under standard conditions reflected by the component unit costs.

The first set of data provides information to guide in designing rate schedules, for each of the classes of service for which such information is available, to conform to the established most probable cost-to-serve relationships. The second set provides us with the ability to determine the over-all economic requirements of such classes under the specified magnitudes of their parameters which are descriptive of the over-all business produced by the class. Both offer also an opportunity to compare existing revenue yields with the most probable cost-to-serve, and, being based on component unit costs, provide sensitive indicators on the significance of the cost data.

There is another method of cost analysis, which differs from the former in that it is directed toward determining the rates of return provided by the classes on the rate bases apportioned to them. This method involves the assignment, allocation, or apportionment of the revenues and revenue deductions; cost, or value, of plant and working capital, with the concomitant accruals for depreciation and of other elements of the rate base. When this procedure is applied to all service classifications, it is usually done in such a way as to obtain a perfect accounting balance between the sum of the apportioned parts and the total being allocated. It is an excellent method for determining the earning ability of a service subdivision, for a given annual test period under either existing or prospective rates; but, in the latter case, it requires special computations of the prospective taxes which depend on the new revenue and on the new income produced by the prospective rates.

There are two mathematical approaches to the effectuation of this method of cost analysis, both of which should result in identical answers. They stem from the basic mathematical features of the apportionment formulas, as can be seen from the following:

Let

C = the cost element to be apportioned among n parts (such as classes of service)

b_T = the base of apportionment, reflecting the total of the values $b_1 + b_2 + b_3 \ldots b_n$ for all of the parts over which the apportionment is to be made

The amounts a_1, a_2, $a_3 \ldots a_n$ apportioned to each of the parts thus become:

$$a_1 = C \times \frac{b_1}{b_T} \tag{8.01}$$

$$a_2 = C \times \frac{b_2}{b_T} \tag{8.02}$$

$$a_3 = C \times \frac{b_3}{b_T} \tag{8.03}$$

$$a_n = C \times \frac{b_n}{b_T} \tag{8.04}$$

Obviously, the terms $\dfrac{b_1}{b_T}$; $\dfrac{b_2}{b_T}$; $\dfrac{b_3}{b_T}$; and $\dfrac{b_n}{b_T}$ are fractions of the total base, and are known as "allocation ratios." When properly computed, their sum will be equal to unity. The use of this "ratio"-approach represents the classical procedure for the apportionment or allocation of joint costs; and the sum of apportioned parts will always equal the whole being allocated provided the sum of the ratios is equal to unity. While this "ratio" approach ordinarily is convenient of application, it does not lend itself, without additional work, to an analytical appraisal of the significance of the resulting values per unit of the allocation base. Although generally this is not too much of a handicap, care should be exercised in the accuracy with which the ratios are established, especially for those which represent a small part of the total.

To overcome the shortcoming of this "ratio" approach, the preceding formulas can be restated, in the following manner without affecting the significance of the results:

$$a_1 = \frac{C}{b_T} \times b_1 \tag{8.05}$$

$$a_2 = \frac{C}{b_T} \times b_2 \tag{8.06}$$

$$a_3 = \frac{C}{b_T} \times b_3 \tag{8.07}$$

$$a_n = \frac{C}{b_T} \times b_n \tag{8.08}$$

Under this approach, the fraction $\dfrac{C}{b_T}$, appearing in each of the allocation formulas, represents, in effect, the cost element being prorated per unit of the allocation base. Let us call it the "unit cost" approach. But immediately I caution the reader not to confuse it with the parametric component unit costs described in the preceding chapters which can be derived, however, from this approach through the expenditure of additional work. This approach, possessing the advantage over the former of providing a sensitive indication on the significance of the cost data in relation to the base of allocation, is generally more difficult of ap-

plication, especially when a meticulous balance is desired between the sum of the apportionments and the total being allocated.   However, this approach is well suited for ascertaining
the amount of a cost element which is to be apportioned to one
or two parts of the whole, whenever such individualized information is desired to be confined to the data of the parts in
question.

Under the General Unified Theory of cost determination, the
bases for these allocations or apportionments are fully consistent with, and responsive to, the concepts and principles reflected
in the established cost model described in Chapter 3, in the
model of the load structure described in Chapter 4, and in the
methods of cost determination described in Chapter 6. The only
bases of allocations not covered in these chapters are those
which apply to taxes that are dependent on revenues and income,
and on the accrued depreciation in the rate base.

Following the well-established principle that distribution of
costs to classes of service should be based upon factors which
reflect the nature of the costs to be distributed, the manner in
which, or the purpose for which, they are incurred, the basis for
the allocation of taxes depending on revenue is the revenue of
the classes subject to the tax; and the basis for the distribution
of taxes depending on taxable income, is the approximation of
the taxable income of the classes.   Such income is susceptible
of determination from available data on class revenues, the distributed revenue deductions (other than income taxes) and the
distributed interest on debt capital, which itself is distributable
on the basis of net plant costs. Following the aforementioned
general principle of cost distribution, the basis of apportionment
of the accrued depreciation, is the depreciable plant subdivided
by its functional elements whenever such accrued depreciation
is itemized by such functional elements, otherwise the allocation basis becomes the entire depreciable plant as it is distributed to the classes.

Such cost allocation studies conducted continuously and on
consistent, well-established, and sound bases of cost determination are valuable guides not only in following the trends of
earnings of the various classes of service in terms of the rates
of return on their apportioned rate bases, but also as indicators
of the relative earning rates of the classes in relation to that of
the entire utility enterprise. They provide valuable information

as a check on the reasonableness of existing rates in relation to existing volumes of business, and offer opportunities, not otherwise available, through additional studies of foreseeing or predicting the future earning abilities of the classes under varying alternatives of load growth, changing load characteristics, and the like, which can serve as valuable aids in managerial decisions for future plans, or actions, and in regulatory judgment on the future effects of its decisions.

9. GENERAL SERVICE RATES

Electric service is sold by utilities to customers at established prices which are known in the United States as "rates," or "rate schedules." Such rate schedules, together with rules, regulations, practices, conditions, or contracts involving any rate or rates, constitute an electric utility's tariff, which is required to be filed with the regulatory commission having jurisdiction. The tariff is usually employed as the vehicle for publishing the utility's conditions of and for service supply.

Well-rounded rates integrate within themselves the essential policies and practices of the utility with respect to:

Engineering of the supply system (such as design, voltage standards, capacity rating of equipment, minimum reserve requirements, etc.)

Operation of the supply system (such as maintenance standards, equipment loading, operating reserves, extent of servicing customers' equipment, etc.)

Accounting (such as periodicity of customers' billing, type of accounting for supplies, size of property units, depreciation standards, methods of establishing tax liabilities, etc.)

Finance (such as ratios of capital structure, dividend payouts, types of financing, etc.)

Sales (such as direction of promotional efforts, competition with other energy sources, administration of contracts, etc.)

Legal (such as franchise requirements, state laws for utilities, Federal utility acts, commissions' rules and regulations, court pronouncements on utility matters, and the established juridical-economic concepts.)

It is beyond the scope of this book to go into the details of the art of rate making, or into the philosophical-economic aspects which have been well covered in such excellent treatises as those by L. R. Nash,[1] James C. Bonbright,[2] and by R. E. Caywood.[3]   Suffice it to say that, while the promulgation of rates is not devoid of emotional considerations, it cannot be arbitrary, capricious, or can it be unreasonably preferential or prejudicial.

While giving consideration toward reflecting value of service to the consumer, rates, in my opinion, must be related also, and perhaps even primarily, to the cost of service incurred by the utility under specified conditions of service availability, that is, whether uncontrolled as to the time of use (reflecting prime degree of service), or whether confined to specified periods of time (reflecting second degree service).   However, because of practical requirements of simplicity, ease of understanding, and convenience of administration, no rate form that has been brought to the author's attention can meet exactly the empirical cost relationships which fundamentally are of nonlinear nature.   Thus, costing techniques resulting in cost curves, as in Figures 15 and 16, Chapter 7, can only serve as guides in the promulgation of a linear price structure which would reflect the general significance of the economics of electric service supply.   Rates also should provide as much as possible self-acting economic inducements to consumers for the use of service at improved load characteristics upon the utility's supply system, and should create desirable psychological attitudes as to their durability and stability.

There are two basic types of electric rates in use in the United States for general classes of service; one employs energy use as the sole parameter for pricing of the service rendered; the other employs energy use and maximum demands as dual parameters

---

[1]Luther R. Nash, *Economics of Public Utilities* (New York, McGraw-Hill Book Company, Inc., 1925); *Public Utility Rate Structure* (New York, McGraw-Hill Book Company, 1933).

[2]James C. Bonbright, *Principles of Public Utility Rates* (New York, Columbia University Press, 1961).

[3]Russell E. Caywood, *Electric Utility Rate Economics* (New York, McGraw-Hill Book Company, Inc., 1956).

of the service rendered.   There are other types, but they are either confined to special applications, or are in process of elimination.   The controlling characteristic of the first type is the energy used by customers, and of the second type, the customers' load factors and their concomitant demands.

Rates which employ the energy as the controlling characteristic in effect reflect the averaging of the operational economics of service supply to individual customers of a class along energy intervals over a wide range of customers' uses.   Rates which employ load factors as the controlling characteristic in effect reflect such averaging by demands along load-factor intervals over the complete range of customers' requirements.

Since the parametric component of cost-to-serve related to the "Class Peak or Diversified Demand" is by far the largest item in the cost-to-serve relationships, as depicted in Chapter 7, it should be noted that energy-type rates basically reflect the operational economics of a fixed load factor, that is, they can be made to satisfy the cost-to-serve for a given diversified load factor, but they will become inadequate for lower load factors, and more than adequate for higher ones.   This is probably one of the major reasons why in classes of service having this type of rate, prospective major load additions which produce high diversified load factors are prized by utilities, while those with low diversified load factors should be approached with caution and often require simultaneous acquisition of other supplementary loads which could provide satisfactory diversified load factors for the combined loads to preserve the operational economics of the established rate schedule.   With energy-demand type rates, properly designed to reflect the significance of the Second Law of Load Diversity, depicted in Figure 12, the operational economics of variable load factors are automatically recognized over the entire range of customers' service requirements.

ENERGY-TYPE RATE

The most common form of the electric energy-type rate in use in the United States is the "block" rate such as is illustrated in the following rate table using relative indices.   The possible annual bills generated by this rate are depicted in Figure 17.

The first two blocks of the rate carry relatively high prices per kilowatthour which are needed to recover as quickly as

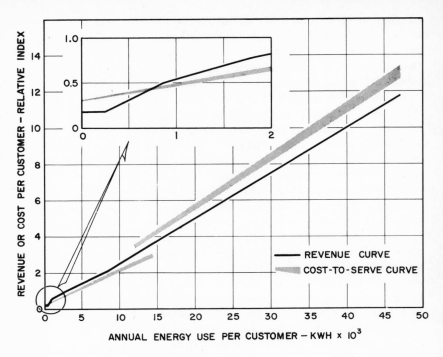

Figure 17. Illustrative block energy type rate for residential customers

Monthly Rate Table*

First	20 Kwh	1.50		
Next	50 Kwh	0.05	per Kwh	
Next	80 Kwh	0.03	per Kwh	
Over	150 Kwh	0.02	per Kwh	
Minimum Earned Rate		0.025	per Kwh	
Minimum Monthly Bill		1.50		

*The numbers used are neither "averages" nor "typical"; they are simply illustrative of the rate forms, which would be well nigh impossible explaining without the use of numbers. Throughout this chapter such numbers, expressed as index numbers, are consistent with the "cost units" used in Chapters 6 and 7.

feasible, within practical limitations, the all-important "Customer" component of the cost-to-serve in this region of energy use. The end blocks are usually priced low enough to induce larger use, but high enough to recover deficits produced by customers with small use and to cover cost-to-serve at a specified diversified load factor for the larger uses. For example, the 0.02 relative index per kilowatthour price of the end block of the illustrated rate would be sufficient to meet the cost-to-serve of all additional loads with annual load factors of better than 40 percent when the parametric component unit cost relative index numbers for "Energy" and for the "Class Peak or Diversified Demand" parametric components are 0.0045 per kilowatthour and 54 per kilowatt respectively.

The minimum earned rate is frequently provided for protection against the possibility of lower diversified load factors in the very high energy use region. For example the 0.025 price of the foregoing illustration becomes effective beyond a monthly use of 680 kilowatthours (8,200 kilowatthours per year) and under the foregoing cost-to-serve values and a substantially uniform monthly distribution of the use throughout the year, would be sufficient to cover them beyond that use, for loads producing diversified annual load factors of as low as 25 percent.

In gauging the significance of the so-called "loss" and "profit" areas of this rate structure in the present-day region of customers' energy use, reference should be had to customers' frequency distribution curves by specified annual kilowatthour-use intervals, such as illustrated in Figures 18 and 19. These curves provide the necessary information which permit deriving

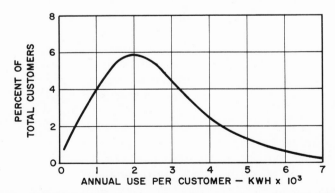

Figure 18. Example of frequency distribution of residential customers in 200 kilowatthour annual use intervals

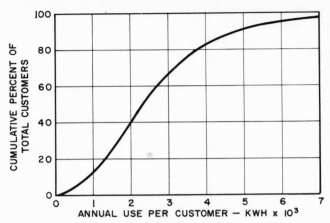

Figure 19. Example of cumulative distribution of residential customers by annual kilowatthour use

the necessary weighting factors to ascertain the relative significance of the loss and of the profit areas with respect to the entire class of service.

DEMAND-ENERGY TYPE RATES

There are three classical forms of demand-energy type rates: the Hopkinson, the Wright, and the Doherty; and a fourth—the Composite one. Their basic features are illustrated in Figures 20 and 21 which provide relationships between the hours' use of customers maximum demands and the customers' bills per kilowatt of their maximum demands. The background curves are the cost-to-serve relationships shown in Figure 16.

All rate statements have been reduced to a minimum in order to show clearly the fundamental differences of the basic rate forms. Any statements as to minimum guarantees, minimum billing demands, or other qualifying features or adjustments which ordinarily are required in practice, especially for seasonal loads widely varying from the average patterns of the class, are omitted in order to keep the comparison down to the fundamentals. To bring out the salient features of these rate forms, each is retained in its simplified and basic form, although for practical applications certain modifications may be introduced either for simplification or to reflect special conditions. Usually all such rates are stated on a monthly basis.

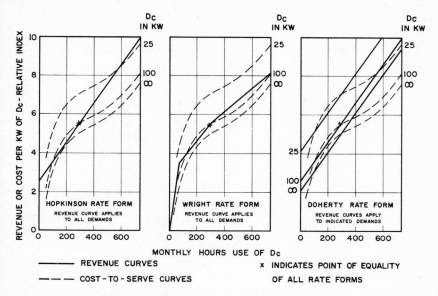

Figure 20. Illustration of the three classical demand-energy type rates applicable to customers of the manufacturing and nonmanufacturing class

The Hopkinson Rate. The basic Hopkinson demand rate is expressed as a Capacity Charge of h_1 per kilowatt of customer's maximum demand, plus an Energy Charge of h_2 per kilowatthour of energy use. In the graphic illustration of Figure 20 the relative index number[4] for h_1 is taken at 2.60 per kilowatt and for h_2 at 0.01 per kilowatthour. It is a rate which, in this comparison, is characterized by an intercept at zero hours' use at the value of the price per kilowatt of the demand charge, and an upward moving straight line whose slope is proportional to the price per kilowatthour of the energy charge. It should be noted that this rate inherently does not, and cannot, follow the general shapes of the probable cost-to-serve relationships nor does its values per kilowatt decline with increasing size of demands.

[4]See note to Monthly Rate Table, p. 106.

The Wright Rate. The basic Wright demand rate is expressed as:

w_1 per *kwh* for the first x_1 hours' use of the maximum demand
w_2 per *kwh* for the next x_2 hours' use of the maximum demand
w_3 per *kwh* for all additional use

In the graphic illustration in Figure 20 the relative index numbers[5] are: w_1 at 0.05 per kilowatthour for the first 150 hours' use; w_2 at 0.009 per kilowatthour for the next 150 hours' use; and w_3 at 0.006 per kilowatthour. It is a rate which, in this comparison, is characterized by a zero intercept at zero hours' use and a series of upward-moving, broken lines, the slopes of each being proportional to the stated prices per kilowatthour of the respective segments. Although this rate follows the general shapes of the probable cost-to-serve relationships, it does not possess an intercept at zero hours' use, as indicated by the cost-to-serve relationships for relatively small loads, nor does its values per kilowatt decline with increasing size of demands.

The Doherty Rate. The basic Doherty demand rate is expressed in three parts: Service Charge of d_1 per customer; Capacity Charge of d_2 per *kw* of maximum demand; and Energy Charge of d_3 per *kwh* of energy used.

In the graphic illustration of Figure 20, the relative index numbers[6] are: d_1 at 50.0 per customer; d_2 at 2.10 per kilowatt, and d_3 at 0.01 per kilowatthour. It is a rate similar in character to the Hopkinson rate, but is characterized, in this comparison, by declining values per kilowatt with increasing size of demands. While this feature is in line with the declining trends in the probable cost-to-serve per kilowatt with increasing size, the other features, being similar to the Hopkinson rate, do not permit this rate to follow the general shape of the cost-to-serve relationship.

Thus neither of the three classical demand rate forms meets the behavior of the probable cost-to-serve when customers' load factors (or the equivalent of hours' use) are employed as the controlling characteristic along which we have chosen to average the operational economics of service supply of such customers. The Hopkinson and the Wright rate forms, in addition, do not reflect the declining costs per kilowatt with increasing demands.

[5] See note to Monthly Rate Table, p. 106.
[6] See note to Monthly Rate Table, p. 106.

However, all these features can be met through the *Composite* rate form which blends within itself the equivalent of the desirable features of the three classical rates.

The Composite Rate. Such a *Composite* rate is expressed in the following form:

Capacity Charge z_1 for the first y_1 kw of maximum demand

z_2 per kw for the next y_2 kw of maximum demand

z_3 per kw over $(y_1 + y_2)$ kw of maximum demand

Energy Charge z_4 per kwh for the first q_1 hrs. use of maximum demand

z_5 per kwh for the next q_2 hrs. use of maximum demand

z_6 per kwh for all additional kwh use

This rate is illustrated in Figure 21 for three values of customers' maximum demands, including a theoretical infinite value to show the convergence of cost and rate to their asymptotic values. The relative index numbers[7] in this rate are: z_1 at 65.0 for the first 20 kilowatts; z_2 at 1.00 per kilowatt for the next 50 kilowatts; z_3 at 0.85 per kilowatt for all additional kilowatts; z_4 at 0.02 per kilowatthour for the first 150 hours' use, but not less than 50 hours' use; z_5 at 0.008 per kilowatthour for the next 150 hours' use; and z_6 at 0.005 per kilowatthour for all additional use.

This rate can be made to follow as faithfully as desired the basic nature of the probable cost-to-serve relationship, such as depicted in Figure 16. It will have an intercept at zero hours' use, it will follow by means of upward-moving broken lines the general contours of the probable cost-to-serve curves which reflect the Second Law of Load Diversity, and it will show declining values per kilowatt of maximum demands for increasing sizes of load, asymptotically approaching a level for very large sizes which will be determined by the end block of the capacity charge. It is undoubtedly these features of rate design that

[7]See note to Monthly Rate Table, p. 106.

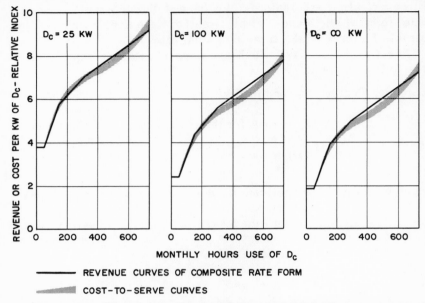

Figure 21. Illustration of a composite demand-energy type rate
applicable to customers of the manufacturing and
nonmanufacturing class

Stuart W. John had in mind in his recent monograph[8] when he referred there to the future impacts of the discovery of the Second
Law of Load Diversity.

GENERAL FEATURES

In this chapter, so far, we dealt with types of rates and rate
forms which would be applicable to the supply of service under
uncontrolled conditions as to the time of its availability. That
is, under such rates, customers could use the utility's service
whenever they require it, in the amounts they want it, subject
only to the limitations in physical facilities connecting them to
the utility's supply system, and the rules and conditions governing such supply.

For classes for which the utility has chosen the energy as the
controlling characteristic, the billing parameter is the kilowatt-

[8]Stuart W. John, "Electric Rates of the Future," *Public Utilities
Fortnightly*, Vol. LXVII, No. 12 (June, 1961), pp. 823–28.

hour meter registering the customer's use irrespective as to its time occurrence. The probable cost-to-serve also employs parameters which are determined from the customers' load characteristics irrespective of their time occurrence, the benefits of the intraclass load diversity being made available to all customers of the class, and those due to interclass load diversity having been made available to all classes of the system.

For the classes for which the utility has chosen the customer's load factors as the controlling characteristic, the billing parameters are the kilowatthour meter registrations and the customers' maximum demands both determined irrespective as to their time occurrence. Here too the probable cost-to-serve also employs parameters which are determined from customers' load characteristics irrespective of their time occurrence, with benefits of intraclass and interclass load diversities handled the same way as explained above.

Thus we have tied together through one single General Unified Theory all the phases of operational economics of service supply under the unconditional availability as to its time of utilization. The application of this theory has had the benefits of a time-test of over quarter of a century, and has yielded consistent results and sound indications on all operational economic phases of electric service supply with which the author has been confronted by managements of utilities and others over this period.

LONG-INTERVAL *VERSUS* SHORT-INTERVAL DEMANDS

The demand-energy type rates described herein ordinarily comprehend the determination of billing demands through the use of integrated values over relatively short intervals of time, such as 15, 30, or 60 minutes. These demand intervals are generally satisfactory measures of demand cost responsibilities where the relationship between customers' short-interval maximum demands and the diversified maximum demands are substantially fixed, as is the case with the large majority of manufacturing and a significant segment of nonmanufacturing customers, especially for those whose group coincidence factors in magnitude approach closely the horizontal portion of the coincidence-factor *versus* load-factor relationship shown in Figure 12. But, where this is not so, as in the case of the large majority of residential customers, the short-interval billing demand becomes less adequate to measure the customer's relative cost responsibility for his capacity requirements, because, as pointed out in Chapter 7, the operational economics of electricity supply for the relatively large energy use customers of this class depend primarily upon their *diversified* maximum demands. I have searched for many years to find a better measure for this cost responsibility pertaining to residential customers, and have finally found it for this class in a long-interval maximum demand measurement for individual customers, such as would be obtained over a 4-consecutive-hour period. We will call it the "4-hour demand."

Figure 22 (right) shows the average relationships, found from tests of a large variety of residential customers, between the customers' maximum demands over longer than one-half-hour periods to their 30-minute maximum demands. The starting times of the longer intervals were spread over the normal working day on a random basis. Although the longer interval demands are always lower than the 30-minute values, different uses reflect different relationships.

Figure 22 (left) shows a rationalization of the phenomena indicated in Figure 22 (right), and demonstrates clearly that residential uses which provide lower coincidence factors also provide low ratios of 4-hour demands to the 30-minute values, and conversely those with high coincidence factors provide higher ratios.

Since, by definition, a customer's diversified maximum demand is the product of the 30-minute maximum demand and the applicable coincidence factor, and since the numerical ratios of the customers' 4-hour maximum demands to their respective 30-minute values approximate closely the numerical values of the respective coincidence factors, it is reasonable to conclude that the magnitude of such 4-hour demand should on the average represent closely the magnitude of the applicable diversified maximum demand. Thus, from theoretical considerations, a 4-hour billing demand finds good support. From practical considerations for residential applications, it has the advantage of minimizing the possibilities of wide fluctuations in billing demands because of extraordinary conditions which may occur on customers' premises that would have a high probability of creating extremely large short-interval maximum demands, but which would have a much lower probability of resulting in higher than normal 4-hour demands.

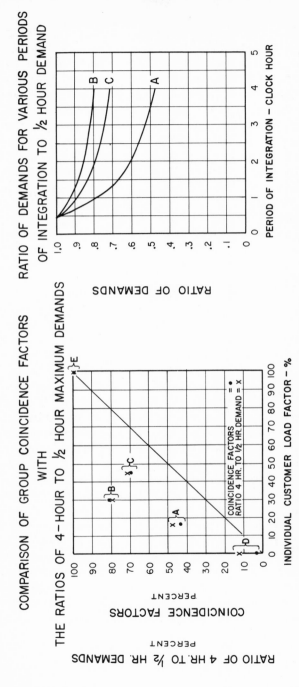

Figure 22. Example of characteristics of long-interval maximum demands of residential customers:

A. Winter (lighting, refrigerators, miscellaneous appliances and range)
B. Summer (lighting, refrigerators, miscellaneous appliances, range and complete cooling)
C. Winter gas house heating (night set-back)
D. Calculated theoretical minimum
E. Theoretical maximum

DEMAND-ENERGY TYPE RATE FOR RESIDENTIAL CUSTOMERS

With the discovery of the theoretical significance of the long-interval billing demands for the residential class of customers that it establishes a good measure of the diversified demand cost responsibilities for the large use customers of this class, I am of the opinion that the operational economics would be served best through the introduction of a demand-energy type rate for the large energy users of this class of customers where the determinations of the billing demands would be based on a 4-hour demand interval. Such a rate could be expressed, for example, in the following manner using relative index numbers:[9]

Monthly Rate Table

Energy Charge Prices:

1.50 for the first 20 *Kwh*
0.05 per *Kwh* for the next 50 *Kwh*
0.03 per *Kwh* for the next 80 *Kwh*
0.02 per *Kwh* for the next 450*Kwh*
0.015 per *Kwh* for the next 300 Hours' use of capacity billed
0.008 per *Kwh* for all additional use

Capacity Charge Price:

3.0 per *kw* for capacity billed.

Determination of Capacity Billed

The use of capacity, to the nearest one-tenth of a kilowatt shall be determined from measurements by a cumulative register recording the maximum rate of use in a month during a consecutive 4-hour period. The capacity billed in a month shall be the positive remainder obtained by subtracting 3.5 from the kilowatts so determined, but shall not be less than 60 percent of the highest remainder so computed in any month of the 11 months immediately preceding the current month.

Based on present-day experience, a cumulative demand register of the long-interval specified in the rate need not be installed until the customers' monthly use exceeds 500 kilowatt-

[9]See note to Monthly Rate Table, p. 106.

hours per month. Thus up to this use the energy is the controlling characteristic; beyond this use, the customer's "load factor" for the additional use becomes the controlling characteristic, but since the billing demand reflects a 4-hour demand interval, and in accordance with the relationship shown in Figure 22 (left), it can be expected with some degree of confidence that on the average this controlling characteristic should be equivalent to the *diversified* load factor of the customer's added use.

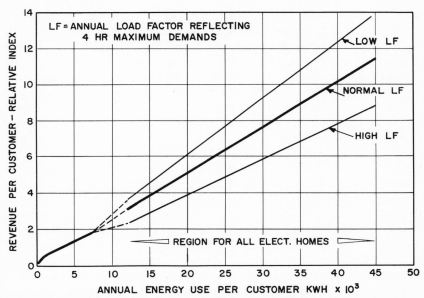

Figure 23. Illustrative residential rate of (a) Block energy type in the low use region; and (b) Demand energy type in the high use region reflecting significance of load factors

Figure 23 depicts this rate, using the energy as the controlling characteristic and indicating the effects of different load factors beyond· 7,000 kilowatthours of annual use. All three of the indicated revenue lines are for conditions of customers' use in the region of all-electric homes, which by definition include the use of electricity for maintaining year-round air comfort in the home. The upper line shown in this use region reflects the home use with electric heating under conventional methods of

operation including a night set-back feature of indoor thermostats; the middle line is for similar conditions but without such
night set-back feature, and the lower one, for reduced size electric heating systems with supplementary controlled heat storage
which perform the same job of heating but with reduced maximum
demands on the supply system of the electric utility, which in
turn results in a reduced cost-to-serve for such loads.

Why is a demand type rate desirable for large use customers
of the residential class? The answer is found in the fact that
such rate tends to encourage such customers to make use of the
utility's service at the highest possible load factor because at
such a rate the customer's bill is lower when his load factor is
higher. Since the large-use region of this class of service is
basically applicable to customers with electric space heating,
the use of electricity to perform this job lends itself very well
to load factor improvement, for example, through the use of supplementary heat storage and a reduced size heating installation.

All of the better known competitive sources of house heating,
such as coal, oil, and gas, possess storage features at various
levels of their supply system which, in an economic sense, enable such businesses to operate at load factors far above the
inherent magnitude of the climatological load factor of house
heating. For example, coal used in house heating reflects
storage of its supply in bins near furnaces at the utilization
level, in silos of dealers at the distribution level, and in piles
at mines at the production level. Similarly, oil and liquified
propane gas reflect storage of their supplies in tanks at all
levels; manufactured gas reflects it in gas holders at the distribution and production levels; and natural gas, in underground
storage fields near marketing areas at the transmission level
and in delivery pipes through line packing.

It is these storage features possessed by all of these heat
sources that permit them to compete economically in satisfying
the requirements of house heating under its inherent low annual
load factor. Electricity, however, does not possess storage features per se at any level of the usual methods of its supply.
But, to perform the function of house heating as economically as
the other heat-energy sources, it too must be provided in some
way with means equivalent to the important storage feature possessed by the competitive sources. At present, we know of no
other way of accomplishing this objective in practice, simply

and economically, except through some form of heat storage at the utilization level of electric house heating.

However, to make heat storage economically attractive to users of electric house heating, economic inducements must be provided in the pricing of the residential service for this purpose. Conventional, simple kilowatthour rates contribute nothing toward the needed incentives. It should be realized that, just as in economics, according to Gresham's law "bad money drives out good," so under conventional simple kilowatthour rates, electric heating systems with bad load characteristics drive out those with good. The quicker the utility industry adopts some form of demand-energy type of rates, such as the one suggested in the foregoing paragraphs, or its equivalent through some other means, reflecting substantial inducements for customers to improve their load characteristics on the utility's supply system, the sooner will efforts be directed from many sources of the country's competitive economy toward accomplishing this aim. To succeed, this idea must have wide support from utilities, broad acceptance by regulatory commissions, and much educational effort upon the public. The facts depicted in Figure 23 show that such a rate could provide substantial inducements. For example, in the probable range of use the annual bill for high load factor is some 35 percent lower than for low load factor and about 20 percent lower than for normal load factor.

10. "OFF-PEAK" SERVICES

The preceding chapters dealt with the operational economics of electric service made available by a utility to its customers on noninterruptible, that is, firm basis, and reflecting seasonal patterns of substantially uniform nature for most of the group intervals of customers of the general classes. Services of this type constitute by far the largest portion of the business of a present-day utility. However, to optimize the operational economics, many utilities in the United States provide other electric services priced at lower than firm-service rates to reflect conditions of an "off-peak" nature.

"Off-peak" services may be defined as types of electric service which, being of a valley-filling nature, do not incur for the utility the major portion of the "Class Peak or Diversified Demand" parametric component of the cost-to-serve, and thus permit the establishment of lower rates to induce their acquisition. However, to be of value to the utility and to its other customers, who in fact have created the load valleys, such services must be priced to cover all *incremental* costs of the four parametric components of the cost-to-serve equation and in *addition* provide something more toward the remainder of the average cost-to-serve, and to the "Class Peak or Diversified Demand" parametric component.

There are several types of off-peak service. Some are specifically limited by the utility to the time of day or the season of the year, when it makes them available to customers desiring them, usually in conjunction with some form of "firm" service;

others are supplied by the utility with an announced understanding that they can be interrupted by it in full or in part at any time of day, at specified periods, or on specified notice to customers. There are other types, usually of a seasonal nature which are inherently valley-filling with respect to the utility's existing load pattern of a class or of the system, but which do not carry an announced label of being off-peak or interruptible. No matter what type, all such loads possess one common feature: they remain valley-filling only so long as there is a valley to be filled. During such period, they are acquired at a low or no demand cost responsibility. Once the valley becomes filled, however, all additional load of this type starts incurring full demand cost responsibilities.

Determinants of "Off-Peak" Service. Under the concept of the utility's load structure described herein, and as stated in Chapter 4, the primary determinant of an off-peak period is the character of the load of the *class* of which it is a part; and the secondary determinant is the effect that a load acquired in such "off-peak" periods may have upon operational economics of the over-all system load at any one of the conceptual levels of the utility's supply system. It is only under this concept that the fundamental economic impact of an off-peak load is properly revealed in regard to the class of service of which it is a part. Similar evaluations along the same consistent lines are then possible for other off-peak loads as they would apply to other classes of service which could use them for their own valley filling, but under their own particular requirements. Of course, if an off-peak period established for a class can at the same time be also off-peak with respect to the system, the significance of its operational economics is placed on a very conservative basis, because under such conditions the acquisition of such a load, within the limits of such off-peak valleys, cannot affect the interclass coincidence factor, since neither the numerator (the system peak) nor the denominator (the sum of noncoincident class peaks) of equation (4.03) will be affected. However, when an off-peak period of a class does not coincide with the off-peak conditions of the system at one or more of its conceptual levels of supply, the significance of its operational economics is not as favorable, because under such conditions the acquisition of such load within the limits of the off-peak valley of the class can affect the interclass coincidence factors at one or more of the conceptual levels of supply, since the numerator of equation (4.03) could now increase, while its denominator will remain unchanged.   Fortunately, however, in practice such changes are likely to be small and are frequently offset by the effects of the year-to-year changes through the ebb and flow normally occurring in the system peak load and in the peak loads of the individual classes of service at the affected conceptual supply levels.   It is here where we have to rely to some extent upon the laws of chance that the interclass coincidence factor will not change. If it does, under the established theory of cost determination its change will affect uniformly the particular elements of the "Class Peak or Diversified Demand" parametric component unit cost of all affected classes, thus retaining the relative relationship between them.

Establishment of "Off-Peak" Periods.   It is much more important to establish a proper off-peak period with respect to a class than with respect to the system.   Such off-peak period should have sufficient depth to its valley to permit the acquisition of a substantial quantity of the off-peak load before the valley is filled up, and the class peak shifts to a new time.   As soon as this happens all additional load of this type will no longer be of an "off-peak" nature, but will establish a new peak period. Thus, great care must be exercised in establishing rates for off-peak services.   If the rates are too low, they may encourage such an avalanche of acquisition of such load as to jeopardize quickly its significance as a valley-filling load. While, after reaching a peak-creating condition, it could be re-priced to a higher rate level, such action would undoubtedly create undesirable repercussions and, from purely economic considerations, could result in a loss of such a load, especially if its original lower pricing corresponded to the full limit of the value of this service to the customers using it.

One of the most effective means of handling off-peak loads is to acquire simultaneously some on-peak loads in a balanced manner.   For example, such balanced acquisition is possible in the residential class through a $1\frac{1}{4}$-to-1 ratio of electric ranges to water heaters the latter time-controlled for off-peak operation. Although balanced load building on electric utility systems is not new in the United States, and has been tried on a number of utilities, it requires well-developed sales techniques, and even then could falter, because fundamentally under established laws, a utility must render service to all those who are lawfully entitled to the service, that is, the customer actually dominates the condition of his wants.

In summary, off-peak service sold by a utility, at prices which cover incremental cost-to-serve plus something more toward the average cost-to-serve, is desirable to the utility from short-range operational economic considerations. The longer such short-range, the safer the economic impacts of that service. The significance of any off-peak service must be viewed primarily from the viewpoint of the class of service of which it is a part, and only secondarily from the viewpoint of the system as a whole or at any of its supply levels. The former determines its operational economics, the latter introduces minor modifications to such determinations.

Illustrations of "Off-Peak" Principles. The following figures illustrate some of the general principles of the foregoing dis-

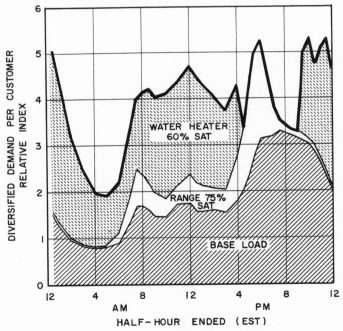

Figure 24. Superposition of loads of electric ranges and "Off-Peak" water heaters on the base load of residential class of service

cussion. Figure 24 shows the highest average weekday load curve of a residential class comprising uses other than those of electric ranges and water heaters. Superimposed on it is a com-

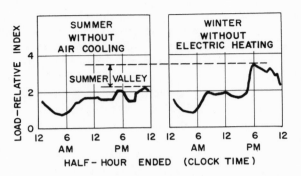

Figure 25. Residential class load a decade ago

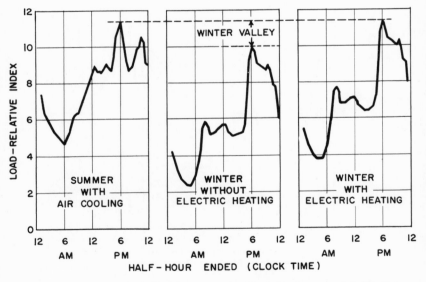

Figure 26. Residential class load a decade from now (showing winter valley without electric heating; and balanced summer-winter peaks when winter valley is filled with 2.2 percent saturation of electric heating)

posite load curve of electric ranges and time-controlled[1] water heaters acquired in the ratio of 1¼ ranges to one of such water heater. Under this control cycle the load of the controlled water heaters can reach a very high saturation without causing the creation of its own class peak. In the illustration, as high as a 60 percent saturation of water heaters has not created a new peak as a result of an accompanying almost 75 percent saturation of electric ranges.

Figures 25 and 26 illustrate two other conditions:[2] the first shows a summer valley in the load of a residential class of a decade ago, which with time becomes filled up with the summer cooling load, shifting the peak to the summer period as shown in the first graph of the second figure which shows an anticipated condition a decade from now, where a valley is created between the summer and winter loads which obviously can be filled up with an electric space heating load. However, since the magnitude of the electric space heating load per customer for climatological conditions similar to those of the illustrative system is many times bigger than that of cooling, the winter valley created by the cooling load, equivalent to about a 20 percent saturation, can be filled with only a 2.2 percent saturation of electric heating installations. In other words, for the equivalent of about 20 percent of homes with electric cooling, we can have only a 2.2 percent saturation of homes with electric space heating without having the heating load establish a new peak.

This simply means that while there is a reasonable assurance for the water heater load to be off-peak over wide limits of saturation, provided its acquisition is accompanied with the load of electric ranges, such assurance cannot be had with the electric house heating load accompanied by the load of summer cooling. In one case a relatively low price for electric service to controlled water heaters possesses a low risk element of becoming inadequate; in the other case a low rate for electric service to

[1] The control cycle of water heaters is as follows: one half the total number of water heaters is "Off" from 4:00 P.M. until 10:30 P.M. and "On" for the remaining hours of the day; the other half is "Off" from 4:00 P.M. until 9:00 P.M.; "On" from 9:00 P.M. until 10:30 P.M.; "Off" from 10:30 P.M. until midnight, and "On" thereafter for the remaining hours of the day.

[2] Summer curves are for the average weekday of a normal warmest spell, and winter curves are for the average weekday of normal coldest spell, as more fully set forth in Chapter 4.

house heating is fraught with a substantial risk of becoming inadequate beyond a relatively small saturation. However, in regions of strong competition for the house heating load a reasonably high price for electric service for house heating together with other desirable actions on the part of the utilities and manufacturers concerning this load, as has been stated in my paper, "Dollars and Sense of Electric House Heating,"[3] should act as economic controls on the acquisition of this load, thus reducing the risks by deferring the peak-creating conditions of this load to an indefinite future, in the hopes that in the future the cost-to-serve may be lower as a result of technological development

[3]Constantine W. Bary, "Dollars and Sense of Electric House Heating," Minutes, 75th Annual Meeting (New York, Association of Edison Illuminating Companies, 1959, unpublished). Among other things, the paper suggests that, to make electric house heating in the long run an economically desirable business at prices attractive to potential users, the following actions are required by the electrical industry:

1) Establishment of criteria for high degree of house insulation with electric heating

2) Improvements in heating COP (Coefficient of Performance) of heat pumps into the region of three or better (see, Constantine W. Bary, "Significance of Heat Pump Coefficient of Performance," *AIEE Transactions Applications and Industry*, Vol. LXXVIII, Part 2 [May, 1959], pp. 90-96)

3) Intensive research on and development of economical heat storage means for use in conjunction with electric heating installations (see, Constantine W. Bary and Joseph F. Paquette, Jr., "Some New Aspects of Electric Heating by Means of Heat Pumps with Supplemental Heat Storage," AIEE Conference Paper No. CP-62-40; also summarized as, "How Much Heat Storage Do You Need with Electric Heating?", *Power Engineering*, LXVI [April, 1962], 38; see also, Joint AEIC-EEI Heat Pump Committee, "Report on Heat Storage," *EEI Bulletin*, XXVI [August, 1958], 261; "First Step on Heat Storage Research Program Completed," *EEI Bulletin*, XXVII [June, 1959], 250; "Second Phase Begins on Research Activity for Development of Heat Storage Systems," *EEI Bulletin*, XXIX [September, 1961], 307; "Promising Heat Storage Material Found Through Research," *EEI Bulletin*, XXX [February, 1962], 49; "Third Phase of Heat Storage Research Project Now Under Way," *EEI Bulletin*, XXX (August, 1962), 261.

4) Establishment of kilowatt-kilowatthour rates for residential customers using electric house heating with self-acting incentives to compensate users for the added first cost of better insulation and supplementary heat storage, and for following good practices in sizing house heating systems and operating them (except those with heat storage) under fixed setting of indoor thermostats.

on the utility's supply system, meanwhile permitting the utility
and its other customers to enjoy the economic benefits of such
a valley-filling load.

Similar considerations reside in possible off-peak loads of
other classes, especially of the manufacturing nature, where it
may be advantageous for customers to obtain electric service for
certain of the applications at relatively low rates but at a certainty of interruptions by the utility at times when required by
its load carrying capabilities. However, here too there is an
economic limit in the magnitude of such load as to its desirability to the utility at the low rates it usually requires. This
limit is usually established far below either the spinning or the
installed reserve obligations of the production system of the
utility.

From what has been said, with adequate safeguards off-peak
services supplied by an electric utility to its customers can be
economically beneficial to the utility and to them; but to be so,
the rates charged must cover not only all incremental costs of all
of the four parametric components of the cost-to-serve equation but
in addition must provide margins which should be as high as
practical to contribute toward the full average cost-to-serve,
and act as economic brakes without completely stopping the acquisition of such loads.

11. PEAKING CAPACITY

In the past, capacity-reserve and peak-load requirements of a growing utility system were usually met through an automatic displacement of the older and less efficient generating units from their original position as base-load plants to peaking operations by the installation of new and more efficient generating units. All this proceeded under the well-established concepts and practices of central stations, with resulting economies due to capacity concentration, large unit sizes, higher efficiencies, and continuously improving system annual load factors. These practices should continue for the major portion of systems' expansion requirements, because of inherent economies of central stations, especially for base-load operations. But, since the rate of improvement in efficiencies of new steam plants is much less than in the past, it is becoming evident that there may be no economic advantage in forcing already high efficiency conventional steam units into the peaking region of operation by installing for load growth new ones of only slightly better efficiency or improved operating economy. Similarly there may be no economic advantage of forcing into peak regions nuclear plants whose over-all economies require them to operate on base load to offset high fixed costs.

The base load of a modern utility system is between one-quarter to one-third of its peak load. Under a uniform growth, therefore, ordinarily only this proportion of new capacity is needed by the load additions to the base portion, and the remainder (65 to 75 percent), by the load growth of the other portion. But, since all of the added capacity of a new operating unit is usually more efficient than the existing, it, therefore, pushes the old ones up into the peak region of operation. However, if it were possible to split the new capacity addition into, say, two completely independent parts, without losing the benefits of low unit investment costs, one to function on base load the other in the peak load region, it would be theoretically possible to keep each of such parts in its functional region of operation over most of its life expectancy.

One way of accomplishing this is through the staggered installation of peaking hydro at existing locations, or of pumped-storage hydro, in conjunction with high efficiency base load steam capacity. In either of these cases the economies are marginal unless the unit costs per kilowatt of hydro installations are very low in relation to the steam plants. Furthermore, the capacity blocks required in such installations, to accomplish their low unit costs are usually of sufficiently large magnitudes to create temporary excess capacity on the supply system which has the effect of offsetting in whole or in part the indicated cost-savings on the basis of a simple kilowatt-for-kilowatt economic comparison.

The basic economics of present-day central station steam plants do not offer attractive possibilities for cost savings by substituting less efficient, and only slightly lower investment cost plants for the more efficient ones; and the more efficient plants are generally obtained at relatively higher unit cost of plant investment.

It, therefore, occurred to me a few years ago to investigate whether over-all economies could be obtained on a utility system through the introduction of a new policy in electric power production, by injecting periodically into future capacity additions certain amount of capacity specifically designed for the operational economics of peaking requirements.

The general equation of economic comparison of alternative power plant proposals is:

$$f'I' + C' + c_4'H' - (f''I'' + C'' + c_4''H'') = D. \quad (11.01)$$

where

f' and f'' = the carrying charge rates of alternatives 1 and 2, respectively

I' and $I'' =$ the investment costs per KW of plant capabilities of alternatives 1 and 2, respectively

C' and $C'' =$ the fixed operating costs per KW of plant capabilities of alternatives 1 and 2, respectively

c_4' and $c_4'' =$ the increment or variable production costs of energy per KWH of plant output of alternatives 1 and 2, respectively

H' and $H'' =$ the average annual hours' use of the capacity of alternatives 1 and 2, respectively

$D =$ the algebraic difference between the operational economics of the two alternatives. When such difference is zero, from economic considerations the two alternatives are alike; when it is negative, alternative 1 possesses lower cost than alternative 2, and when it is positive alternative 1 possesses higher cost than alternative 2

This general equation is well suited in the evaluations of the economic significance of two identical size alternatives which are to operate at substantially the same capacity factors. However, where the capacity size of the alternatives or their capacity factors differ materially, this equation will not provide a proper comparison between the alternatives, because the more efficient (low c_4 cost) capacity on a growing utility system will ordinarily provide greater cost savings in the over-all operations of the production system through bigger displacement in energy production of existing less efficient capacity than would be the case of the less efficient (higher c_4 cost) alternative.

To take advantage of the largest possible potential cost savings, peaking capacity has to be sought in the concept of decentralized installations, comprised of package-type, unattended, remote-controlled, low first-cost electric generating units installed close to the load throughout the distribution system. The establishment of such a decentralized peaking policy in effect provides means for transferring a certain portion of capacity expansion from the "tailor-made" construction practices of central station plants to the principles of mass production of factory-assembled units, requiring the minimum of installation effort in the field and decreasing significantly the time lead for planning additions. These units should be capable of frequent start-ups and short runs without elaborate procedures or excessive maintenance.

Obviously, for such new policy to be acceptable, it would have to provide at the outset definite indications of substantial cost savings over the established conventional practices, since there is no sense in substituting a new idea simply to break even with a well-established practice. It must also provide economic margins of sufficient magnitude to cover foreseeable eventualities that could happen if past trends continue in respect to increasing system load factors, increasing levels of fuel prices, and so on, and should offer attractive incentives for taking the risk which is inherent in any new and untried idea. Accordingly, many combinations of the more important economic factors need investigation to show the significant economic effects of possible variations in the more important parameters.

The words *carrying charges* refer to the levelized values of the allowable return on plant net investment costs, the annual depreciation accruals, insurance expense, and taxes, which depend upon such return and on the total of such carrying charges, as set forth in Chapter 14. The words *cost savings* refer to the difference between the total of operating expenses and carrying charges for the system without peaking installations as compared to the same system utilizing a particular degree of peaking installations.

General Principles. The general procedure employed in the conduct of this type of comprehensive study is basically the same as for most similar economic studies involving the annual costs of both carrying charges and operating expenses of dissimilar size units operating at dissimilar capacity factors. The base for comparison is the total annual costs associated with a system expansion program involving no peaking installations. Compared with this base are the total annual costs resulting from an expansion program employing various combinations of decentralized peaking and central station steam plants. The alternative schemes are studied over long enough period of years, not less than 20, into the future to assure statistical stability. To provide significant indications on the possibilities of variations for unforeseeable eventualities, this span of years is treated in 216 separate ways, each treatment representing one combination of several economic factors and their variations, as shown in the following outline.

The major factors affecting the economic significance of injecting peaking capacity:

1. *Load Growth*: slow and fast
2. *Annual Load Factor Trends*: constant; declining; and increasing
3. *Degree of Peaking Capacity*: 10; 15; and 20 percent (the indicated portion of the estimated peak load for which the need to install central station generating capacity is eliminated by the anticipated installation of decentralized peaking capacity)
4. *Investment Cost Differential*: amounts by which the installed first cost of peaking units is less than that of central station steam plants and their associated bulk transmission
5. *Incremental Cost-of-Energy Production on Peaking Capacity*: low; medium; and high rates
6. *Price Levels of Fuel, Labor, Supplies and Construction*: constant and increasing price levels

With no peaking installations and for each degree of peaking installations, 20-year programs of additions of central station steam units and of various amounts of peaking capacity, under each of the load-growth patterns, are established based on the load-capacity relation existing at the beginning of the forecast period. For each year of the forecast period, carrying charges and the fixed component of operating expenses are computed for the new steam-capacity additions, with their associated new bulk transmission facilities, and for the peaking installations at the indicated investment cost differentials. The variable components of operating expenses are computed for the new and for the existing capacity for all three of the load-factor trends and for all three levels of increment cost of energy production on peaking plants. This latter work is accomplished most effectively with the aid of a digital computer. The sum of these annual costs for each year of the 20-year period for each of the programs and for each of the combinations, together with the fixed costs on that part of the system existing at the beginning of the forecast period, comprises the total cost of the system's production and bulk transmission. With this information, annual cost savings for the 20-year period and for the average year of that period are computed for each combination. With additional work, weighted averages reflecting the well-known "present-worth" concept (described in Chapter 14) can be computed.

The study on decentralized peaking capacity additions interspersed with the addition of conventional high-efficiency steam capacity for base load operation, reported in my 1959 ASME paper,[1] indicated the following conclusions:

Reasonable variations in load growth patterns affect little the cost savings per kilowatt of peaking capacity provided.

In comparison with cost savings obtained through the use of peaking capacity under constant system annual load factor, increasing load factors provide smaller cost savings and decreasing load factors provide bigger ones.

Cost savings increase rapidly from zero to about 10 percent of the degree in peaking capacity, reach a maximum and then decline, and at high levels of the degree of peaking capacity turn into losses.

At the optimum level of the degree of peaking capacity, cost savings are not affected too much by reasonable variations in the incremental unit expenses per kilowatthour of peaking capacity; but installed cost per kilowatt differentials between central station capacity and decentralized peaking capacity affect significantly the total cost savings under a peaking policy.

Increasing trend in fuel prices tends to decrease considerably the cost savings with decentralized peaking capacity from levels obtained under constant or declining load factors. But increasing trend in the price level of labor, supplies and of construction costs tends to increase slightly such cost savings.

A large portion of the cost savings is due to reduced average reserve margins possible under the addition of decentralized peaking capacity.

To illustrate the effects on the operational economics of possible variations in the more important parameters discussed hereinbefore, and to permit their rationalization, the results of such a study can be expressed by the general equation (11.02) under the numerical values of the basic parameters shown in Table 15.

---

[1]Constantine W. Bary, "Decentralized Peak-Shaving—Its Economic Significance to Electric Utilities," *Transactions of ASME*, *Journal of Engineering for Power*, Vol. LXXXIII, Series A, No. 1 (January, 1961), pp. 119–29.

General Equation (11.02) of Cost Savings under a Stated Peaking Policy

Anticipated long-range average annual cost savings in production and bulk transmission systems under a particular peak-shaving policy $\uparrow$

= Anticipated long-range average annual cost savings in carrying charges and operation and maintenance expenses $\updownarrow$

− Anticipated long-range average annual cost penalties in fuel expenses $\updownarrow$

$$
\boxed{C_p} \quad = \quad \boxed{\begin{array}{c} K_c(e_c f_c I_c + e_{Mc} M_c) \\ - K_p(e_p f_p I_p + e_{Mp} M_p) \end{array}} \quad - \quad \boxed{\begin{array}{c} e_{Fc} B_c F_c \\ + e_{Fp} B_p F_p \end{array}}
$$

Definition of Quantities

C_p = the anticipated long-range average annual cost savings in production and bulk transmission systems under a particular peaking policy

K_c = the anticipated long-range average central station steam capacity (gross) in kilowatts which is expected to be displaced under a particular peaking policy

K_p = the long-range average peaking capacity (net) which is required to displace the central station steam capacity K_c under a particular peaking policy

e_c; e_p = the factor for central station steam plants and their associated bulk transmission investment, and for peaking investment, respectively, which reflects average price escalation for future plant additions over a long-range period

f_c; f_p = the annual levelized carrying charge rate on central station steam plants and their associated bulk transmission investment, and on peaking investment, respectively

I_c = the estimated unit investment cost per kilowatt of central station steam capacity (gross) and associated bulk transmission, which is anticipated to be displaced under a particular peaking policy

I_p = the estimated unit investment cost per kilowatt of capacity (net) of the required peaking plants under a particular peaking policy

e_{Mc}; e_{Mp} = the factor for central station steam plants and their associated bulk transmission and for peaking facilities, respectively, which reflects average price escalation on future maintenance and operating costs over a long-range period

M_c; M_p = the anticipated annual operation and maintenance expenses per kilowatt of central steam capacity (gross) and associated transmission, and of peaking capacity (net), respectively

e_{Fc}; e_{Fp} = the factor for fuel costs of central station steam plants
and of peaking plants, respectively, which reflects
average price escalation over a long-range period

B_c = the long-range average annual increase in Mega Btu's of
fuel use in central station steam plants due to post-
ponement of installation of higher efficiency capacities
under a particular peaking policy as compared to no
peaking

B_p = the long-range average annual Mega Btu fuel use by
peaking plants

F_c; F_p = the anticipated unit fuel cost per Mega Btu of central
station steam plants and of peaking plants, respectively

TABLE 15. PHYSICAL FACTORS AFFECTING THE ECONOMIC SIGNIFICANCE OF PEAKING CAPACITY

(Reflecting Average of the Years used in Study)

Degree of Peaking Capacity Policy (percent)	Capacity Component $KW \times 10^3$		Fuel-use Component— Mega Btu $\times 10^6$					
			Under Declining Load Factor Trend		Under Fixed Load Factor Trend		Under Increasing Load Factor Trend	
	K_c	K_p	B_c	B_p	B_c	B_p	B_c	B_p
A. Projected Program Conditions								
10 peaking capacity	608	418	6.04	1.63	6.81	2.58	5.85	4.90
15	833	605	7.45	3.40	7.80	5.21	5.25	9.02
20	1,053	783	8.19	5.77	7.25	9.12	3.14	14.45
B. Theoretical Conditions Reflecting Equalization of Average Reserve Margins "With" and "Without" Peaking Capacity								
10 peaking capacity	601	546	4.30	2.72	4.31	4.14	1.52	7.46
15	820	745	5.05	5.06	3.86	7.92	−0.77	13.00
20	1,020	927	5.09	7.76	1.95	12.45	−4.62	19.35

Note: The variations in the fuel-use component with changes in the
degree of peaking and with changes in load factor trends can vary for
different utility systems. They are influenced by such features as:
the basic shapes of the annual load curves underlying each of the
assumed load factors; the adjustment of load occurrence curves for
increased availability of generating units whose periods for overhaul
do not conflict with the periods in which they can be economically
loaded; the portion of central station steam capacity existing at the
beginning of the forecast period which is unloaded by decentralized
peaking capacity; and heat rates of existing and future capacity installations.

An analysis of equation (11.02) and the values of the parameters in Table 15 shows that the net cost savings result from substantial reduction in the system's carrying charges and a smaller increase in fuel expense.

The general economic significance of a peaking policy can be best understood from the summarized information shown in Figure 27 where the average annual cost savings are expressed per kilowatt of the average annual system peak load of about 4,500 Mw, and the unit costs and related factors used are shown in Table 16. All unit costs are related to that of the unit investment cost per kilowatt of decentralized peaking capacity which is assumed at 100 cost units.

TABLE 16. ILLUSTRATIVE COST VALUES USED IN GENERAL EQUATION (11.02)

	Peaking Capacity	Central Station Steam Capacity and Associated Bulk Transmission
Cost units at constant price level		
Investment per KW	$I_p = 100$	$I_c = 230$
Operation and maintenance per KW	$M_p = *$	$M_c = 3.00$
Fuel cost per Mega Btu	$F_p = 80 \times 10^{-2}$	$F_c = 35 \times 10^{-2}$
Carrying charge rate on plant investment	$f_p = 13\%$	$f_c = 12\%$
Average cost escalation factors**		
Applicable to investment	$e_p = 1.1$	$e_c = 1.1$
Applicable to operation-maintenance costs	$e_{Mp} = 1.4$	$e_{Mc} = 1.4$
Applicable to fuel costs	$e_{Fp} = 1.4$	$e_{Fc} = 1.4$

*These unit costs vary with load factor trends as follows:

for declining load factor—2.00
for constant load factor—2.50
for increasing load factor—3.50

**These factors vary slightly with amount of peaking, type of capacity, and load factor trends; but the variations are too small to be considered significant for purposes of this illustration.

It should be evident that potential cost savings of significant magnitudes are possible on electric utility systems through the

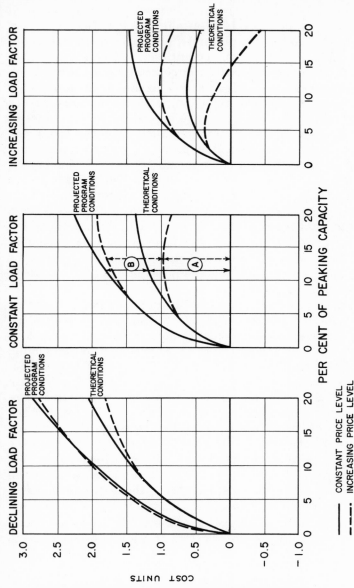

Figure 27. Example of annual cost savings with use of peaking capacity

adoption of a decentralized peaking capacity policy, provided equipment for this purpose is available at low first cost per kilowatt of its capacity, simple and flexible in operation under unattended and remote-control conditions, and low in maintenance cost. To be considered for decentralized locations such equipment must have noise levels and exhaust-gas odors of a tolerable nature. Equipment approaching these requirements is now available in the form of package-type diesel units, gas-jet units, and of simple-cycle gas-turbine units. Of these three, the package-type diesel, at prevailing prices, quality of construction and indicated performance, appears to have a substantial economic edge over the gas-turbine units when the latter are operated on distilate oils and meet peaks under high-ambient temperatures. The gas-jet units appear to run a close economic second to the package-type diesel units, and through more extensive experience which could result in permitting a rise in their unit ratings without a commensurate increase in their first costs, such units could approach and perhaps equal in economic significance the package-type diesel units.

Effect on Operational Economics. The idea of functionalizing the future capacity additions on the production system of an electric utility has important implications upon our concept of the operational economics of service supply. From preceding chapters it will have been observed that the cost of the production system constitutes the largest portion of the "Class Peak or Diversified Demand" and of the "Energy" parametric components of the cost-to-serve equation. The fixed costs of the production system are lodged in the former component and the variable ones in the latter. Thus the introduction of a policy for providing a mixture of peaking and base load capacities with resulting over-all savings will have a tendency to alter the relative proportions of the costs entering these two parametric components, decreasing those of the "Class Peak or Diversified Demand" component and increasing those of the "Energy" component; but the decrease in the former should be very much greater than the increase in the latter.

12. BASE-LOAD CAPACITY, INTERCONNECTIONS AND FUEL CELLS

The preceding chapter discussed the problems of peaking capacity and the solution now available to modern electric utilities of meeting them with cost-savings in their operational economics. However, it was pointed out that over-all economies are obtained only when such peaking capacity is injected periodically into future capacity additions along with the installation of substantial blocks of base-load capacity.

BASE-LOAD CAPACITY

Figure 7, in Chapter 4, shows that about 50 percent of the utility's peak load exists for over 70 percent of a year's total number of hours, or, saying it another way, as in Figure 6, 50 percent of the utility's peak load accounts for over 76 percent of its total annual energy output. The economical means of meeting these requirements rest upon base-load capacities of either hydro plants or, in the great majority of utility systems in the United States, of high efficiency thermal plants. One of the cardinal attributes of such plants is their low incremental cost of energy production (see Chapter 3); and throughout the whole history of electric utilities there was a constant progress toward obtaining higher and ever-higher efficiencies for such plants through increase in steam temperatures and pressures, the employment of reheat cycles, and through an increase in the size of generating units. Today, the highest in the world steam plant thermal efficiency of 8,395 Btu per net kilowatthour or 40.7 percent has been attained by the 360,000 kilowatt Eddystone Unit No. 1 of the Philadelphia Electric Company which operates with steam at a throttle pressure of 5,000 psi, and a temperature of 1,200° F., with double reheat of 1,050° F. and 1,050° F. However, as is well realized by the engineering profession, further improvements in thermal efficiencies of conventional steam plants will be obtained under the law of diminishing returns, with greater difficulties and increased unit cost of installations per kilowatt of capacity, except as they may be offset in whole or in part through ever larger and larger capacity size of units. However, such larger-size units will introduce undoubtedly other economic and operating problems which will require solutions under perhaps new attitudes and new approaches, primarily in the field of top-level managements.

New methods of electric energy production by base-load capacity are around the corner, or looming big on the horizon over the next decade. Nuclear fission plants with incremental cost of energy in the order of two mills per kilowatthour are already offered for construction and operation in the third quarter of this decade by some of the better-known manufacturers of central station equipment, even though the conditions of their steam cycles are those of a quarter-century ago, with thermal efficiency equivalent to that vintage. Notwithstanding that, however, their incremental costs of energy production are estimated to be lower than those of some of the best efficiency modern steam plants when fuel costs are upward of 30 cents per million Btu. But here too to keep down the unit cost of these installations per kilowatt of their capacity, the size of units must be large—upward of one-third million kilowatts.

Another method of power generation, directed primarily toward base-load capacity, which may be available for large-scale installations at the end of this decade, is that which is obtained by using the science of magnetohydrodynamics (MHD), which deals with the phenomena of moving hot fluids or gases through magnetic fields. Gases become electrical conductors when ionized at temperatures of about 5,000° F. Their movement through a magnetic field generates direct-current electricity which can be collected on suitable electrodes. Indications are that large-size generating units of this type would produce electricity at a thermal efficiency in the order of 6,500 Btu per kilowatthour or 52.5 percent, or at incremental cost of production comparable to that of nuclear plants now offered for construction.   However, here too, economies of investment unit costs are obtained only through large-size installations, upward of one-third million kilowatts of capacity.

These are important considerations to keep in mind in a broad gauge analysis of the operational economics of modern electric utilities.   They point to the fact that there are good possibilities that the "Energy" parametric components of the general cost-to-serve equations (2.04) and (2.05) will be kept down through these or similar developments.   But to keep down the "Class Peak or Diversified Demand" parametric components of these cost-to-serve equations will require the utilization of larger and ever-larger unit sizes of this type of capacity, with the concomitant increased centralization of electric generation and the installation of larger bulk transmission facilities for delivery of these large blocks of power to regional load centers.

It is this phenomenon of capital economies residing in large-size units that introduces problems in the operational economics of modern utility enterprises.   Additional production capacity is fundamentally provided to meet load growth.   If the size of the economical unit of the additional capacity is many times the annual load growth increment, the enterprise will experience over a prolonged period of years a substantial capacity surplus over and above the requirements to meet its peak load with normal capacity reserves under a specified standard of supply reliability.   For example, if load growth is at a cumulative rate of, say, 5 percent per year, the maximum reserve requirement at 12 percent, and the additional size unit at 30 percent of the peak load in the year in which it goes into service, the full additional capacity will be assimilated on the system after the fourth year, and the average excess capacity over the period will be in the order of 15 percent.   Improved economies in production, through the introduction of the new base-load capacity, generally will not be sufficient to compensate fully for the carrying charges on the investment in the surplus capacity.   Of course the magnitude of this penalty will vary for different systems depending upon a wide variety of conditions, a discussion of which is far outside of the scope of this book.   However, an indication of its significance can be gleaned from the difference between the upper and lower sets of curves in Figure 27, the latter showing the theoretical cost-saving that is possible if additional base-load capacity for load growth could be provided with unit sizes infinitely variable, as small as required, yet with no sacrifice in unit investment costs, unit operating costs and heat rates over those obtainable from the large-size units. What this really means is that maximum economies are possible with the large-size, base-load units now feasible of manufacture, when their size matches closely the annual load growth of a utility system. There are few, if any, utility systems, that can claim this possibility. But this ideal can be approached through staggered construction of such central station capacity on interconnected systems of two or more of such electric utilities, whose combined load growth requirements approach the kilowatt capability of such a large-size, base-load unit. This involves not only the establishment of interconnections between the bulk power systems of contiguous utilities but coordinated planning for production capacity additions and bulk transmission facilities.

Underlying these requirements is the all-embracing prerogative for individual enterprises comprising the interconnection of subordinating their own whim and wishes in providing such facilities to the dictates of the economic benefits of coordinated planning for the whole interconnection but conforming to the legal intent and economic desirability of individual freedom of action and without creating any implied restraints on trade. That there are many difficulties in the formulation of formal arrangements to accomplish this is realized by most students of this problem, since they involve not only the devising of contractual covenants which would provide equitable compensation for all parties involved over long periods of time under numerous economic conditions encountered in practice, but also conditioning of attitudes at top-management levels away from selfish considerations toward the statesmanship attitude for the welfare of the whole group.

Of course, the end result may be accomplished in two other ways, each of which requires a change of attitude on the part of governing authorities and perhaps even new legislation in Congress. One of these ways is through the merger of contiguous utility enterprises to create large enough systems whose size of annual load growth will be vastly increased over the individual amounts, thus permitting quicker assimilation of large-size production units with concomitant economies not only in production but along other functional organizational lines. The other is through the establishment of holding companies confined to the ownership of contiguous electric utility enterprises, which would provide a consolidation of management policies and practices under established state and federal regulatory authorities.

Of these three alternatives, that involving the concepts of interconnection under individual managements of the interconnected enterprises, but, perhaps, under new principles of ownership of joint capacity projects, deserves most careful study.

INTERCONNECTIONS

The basic principles of interconnection of electric utility systems date back to the early 1920s. The word *interconnection*, in the sense in which it is used today, means the physical tying in together of two or more independently owned and managed electric supply systems at their bulk supply levels. Such interconnections have been made for the purpose of accomplishing economies in the production of electricity of the interconnected systems, in the increase of the reliability of power supply through mutual assistance rendered by one system to another in case of emergency, and for the pooling of benefits of load diversity, operating reserve requirements and energy, and capacity interchange. Throughout the whole length and breadth of the United States there are in effect a number of such interconnections of an area or regional basis.

One of the oldest of such pools, for example, is the Pennsylvania-New Jersey-Maryland (Pa-NJ-Md) Interconnection (formerly Pa-NJ), with a combined peak of about 14 million kilowatts, operating in New Jersey and Delaware, in the major portion of Pennsylvania and of Maryland, in a portion of Virginia and in the District of Columbia. It is a formal pool with coordination of maintenance, operation, and load dispatching, and with informal coordination of construction of production and bulk transmission facilities, except recently on a specific project.

The Canadian-United States Eastern Interconnection with a combined peak of close to 40 million kilowatts made up of several formal and informal pools operates under formal and informal arrangements as a large interconnected group to take advantage of emergency back-up and economic schedules of generation in Maine, New Hampshire, Vermont, Rhode Island, Massachusetts, Connecticut, New York, a portion of Michigan, and the provinces of Ontario and Quebec.

The North Central Area Group with a combined peak of about 20 million kilowatts operates as an informal pool (but includes several formal ones) in Indiana, Ohio, West Virginia, and portions of Maryland, Michigan, Pennsylvania, Virginia, Kentucky, and Tennessee. At times, this entire group has closely coordinated construction, maintenance, and substantial portions of operations.

The Northwest Power Pool with a combined peak of close to 13 million kilowatts operates in portions of Idaho, Montana, Washington, Oregon, Utah, and the province of southwestern British Columbia. It is partly a formal and partly an informal pool with coordination of the use of hydro capacity and energy, load dispatching, and maintenance.

There are other pools and interconnections of a formal and informal nature in the southeastern, southern, southwestern, and western states which operate on bases of coordinated operations, maintenance, and capacity scheduling.

The use of these or similar pools and interconnections in the establishment of formal arrangements and practices for coordinated planning of production capacity additions with concomitant bulk transmission facilities offers the possibilities for almost all utility systems in the United States of obtaining the economic benefits of large-size central station base-load capacity. However, with due regard to the important differences which exist between the significance of coordinated *operations*, involving reversible actions, and of coordinated *construction* of capacity additions, resulting in irreversible commitments, much study of an engineering and operational economic nature will be required to accomplish the objective. Can it be done on this basis? I do not know. Should it be done on one of the other bases mentioned previously? I am not prepared to venture an opinion, because this matter would require much study, far beyond the scope of this book. But that something along these lines will be done is becoming quite evident from considerations of the operational economics of modern electric utilities, although, and without minimizing the other advantages present in interconnections, benefits of any formal actions on coordinated planning of capacity additions by interconnected groups are reduced because of the cost-savings possible by their individual systems through the use of the newly developed technique of package-type decentralized peaking capacity in accordance with the principles and cost differentials described in the preceding chapter; and through the "diversity-of-judgment" approach of individual utilities, especially where incentive pricing is in effect to account for installed capacity deficiencies and surpluses under the split-saving principle of sharing in the benefits.

FUEL CELLS

In the future, there may be another type of capacity available for the production of electric power, which, from present theoretical considerations, could ultimately perhaps supplant our existing economic concepts of base-load and peaking capacities, as well as the central station nature of electricity generation. This type is known as the "fuel cell." [1] It is an electrochemical device which through an interreaction of chemicals called fuels and oxidants, continuously converts chemical energy directly into electrical energy of a direct-current character. In its simplest form it consists of two electrodes and an electrolyte. Gaseous fuel, such as hydrogen, is fed through one of the porous electrodes and a gaseous oxidant, such as oxygen, is fed through the other. The two gases react electrochemically through the electrolyte by producing water and releasing electrons which, with a closed circuit through an electrical load, cause a flow of direct-current electric power. Instead of the hydrogen, which is expensive, the fuel could be such other gases as propane, butane, carbon monoxide, and the like, and in place of pure oxygen stored in tanks, this element might be obtained from the air.

The aim is to develop these devices so that they would possess ultimately the extraordinary features of very low initial unit investment cost, in the order of perhaps one-fourth to one-half of present-day values of base-load central station capacity and of decentralized peaking units, respectively; and, at the

[1] A very interesting treatise on this subject, dealing with the technical and economic analysis of development and opportunities in electrochemical fuel cells, has been prepared recently by nine students at the Graduate School of Business Administration at Harvard. See, Fuel Cell Research Associates, *Fuel Cells. Power for the Future* (Cambridge, Fuel Cell Research Associates, 1960).

same time, also possess a low incremental unit energy cost (in the order of about one-half of that now obtainable in efficient central stations). The latter is feasible in these devices because of their inherently high efficiencies, which are not limited by the thermodynamic laws of the heat cycle, and the hoped-for use of the relatively cheap hydrocarbon products for fuel, such as natural gas, and the availability of air for the oxidant. However, none of this is economically practical at this time. Other advantages of the fuel cells are: they are noiseless; they generate relatively low amounts of waste heat and toxic fumes; and they can operate unattended. They are similar to the well-known electric storage batteries, but should be lighter in weight, need no recharging, and should not wear out in the sense that a storage battery wears out. They are thus well suited for decentralized installations.

Much research effort is being spent by many in this country and abroad on this concept of electricity production, which if successful could revolutionize the supply system of an electric utility. But the problems to be solved in this endeavor are formidable before the objectives can be met. Under existing knowledge, available means require complex apparatuses, which are costly, short-lived, and possess serious problems of safety; and to accomplish the ultimate requires first the discovery and then the development of an inexpensive catalyst which would successfully provide the electrochemical catalysis of hydrocarbon fuels such as propane or natural gas, and the development of inexpensive materials for, and manufacture of, the air electrodes for the oxidants.

How soon these problems will be solved, I am not in position to say. However, that sooner or later they will be solved is, I believe, a reasonable assumption if for no other reason than that the rewards for success are very high. It is, therefore, my opinion, that the electrical industry in all its phases, including regulatory commissions and courts, should be alert to these possibilities because in time they may have a profound effect upon the operational economics of electric utilities and its competitors, especially since they could affect the major cost element of the supply system, which, as shown in Table 1, now represents over 50 percent of the cost of supplying service on a modern electric utility.

13. FUTURE ASPECTS OF BULK TRANSMISSION, DISTRIBUTION, AND BUSINESS FUNCTIONS

The previous two chapters dealt briefly with the significance and future aspects of the production system of electric utilities with respect to its peaking and base-load functions. Now, I shall provide a concise view of the future aspects of the other three major cost systems: bulk transmission, distribution, and business functions.

BULK TRANSMISSION SYSTEM

The total cost of the bulk transmission system of the illustrative electric utility represents about 6 percent of the total. About 85 percent of these costs are in the category of carrying charges on investment, and the remaining 15 percent are of an operating expense nature. Under our model, all of these costs are of the "Class Peak or Diversified Demand" component of the cost-to-serve equations (2.04) and (2.05).

This system is very closely interdependent with that of production. The bigger the concentration of power generation the more extensive becomes the bulk transmission system; conversely, the more intensive is such decentralization the less extensive this system needs to be. Therefore, from considerations of operational economics, its cost significance should always be viewed in conjunction with the production system; and any meaningful economic evaluations of the latter must reflect the effects upon the former.

Under the stimuli of new technologies, some of which are even undertaken for purposes other than the transmission of

electric power, and the constantly increasing needs for economies in the bulk transmission of ever bigger and bigger blocks
of electric power, science and engineering are reaching out toward higher and higher voltages and new, perhaps even radically
different, concepts of performing the job. The reasons for this
drive reside largely in such factors as the resurgence of the
idea of more extensive system interconnections and power pooling, the economies thought to be possible through the installation of large capacity-blocks of power generation, the increasing
costs of rights-of-way, and the special environmental requirements for the location of large nuclear-fission power units away
from heavy concentrations of population where such power has
to be used.

The intensive research work in such fields as extra-high voltage cables, extra-high voltage alternating current and direct-
current aerial transmission, ultra-high-speed switching equipment, and even microwave beam wireless transmission of large
blocks of power over long or short distances, are all directed
toward meeting the needs of the now foreseeable future requirements. What effect these developments will have upon the operational economics of this functional element of electric utilities cannot be stated now with any definite precision. The object of course is to reduce the unit cost per kilowatt of capacity,
which, with all other things equal, should be the case because
the higher voltages permit substantial increases in power-block
potentials of the individual transmission circuits. But other
factors, such as underground in place of aerial construction,
special converter and inverter equipment with direct-current
transmission, increase in the costs of rights-of-way, and of
probable increases in future distances to load centers, may well
offset in whole or in part the economies possible through technological developments. It is safe to say, however, that the
costs of this functional element of the supply system will continue to remain in the "Class Peak or Diversified Demand"
component of the cost-to-serve equations (2.04) and (2.05), that
its proportion is likely to increase in relation to the total, and
that this system's fraction of carrying charges on investment is
likely to be higher than at present.

DISTRIBUTION SYSTEM

The total cost of the distribution system, excluding the metering and control function, of the illustrative electric utility, represents about 20 percent of the total. Over 80 percent of these costs are in the category of carrying charges on investment and the remaining 20 percent are of an operating expense nature. Under our conceptual model, about 35 percent of these costs resides in the "Customer" component of the cost-to-serve equations (2.04) and (2.05), about 15 percent in the "Customer Demand," and 50 percent in the "Class Peak or Diversified Demand" parametric components.

This system is of a highly individualized nature for each and every electric utility enterprise; but it too does not remain static; it is constantly undergoing changes and is not immune to technological developments. On the contrary, although not as spectacular as the production or the bulk transmission systems, it too is experiencing the impacts of research and development under the stimuli of: new technologies, some of which also start for purposes other than electric power distribution; constantly changing service needs through load growths, civic and municipal improvements; community ideas as to aesthetics of its surroundings; and the progress which is being made in the never-ending battle with the elements. For example, lashed and spacer-type cable is finding greater application in place of the former open-wire installations; underground construction of primaries, secondaries, street lighting, and service wires is sought in many residential developments; higher utilization voltages are being studied for such distribution. In other fields of this vast endeavor, discoveries in chemistry and biology are finding applications in the preservation of poles and in the control of harmful vegetation growth. And there are always the possibilities of technological breakthrough in the field of microwave beam wireless distribution of electricity, and, perhaps, even of area illumination through the means of earth-orbiting platforms carrying the necessary power receiving and light-beaming facilities.

Except for these latter and revolutionary possibilities, which may not materialize in the foreseeable decades, the more down-to-earth developments which could affect substantially the general nature of the distribution element of the supply system can influence materially the proportional relationship of the parametric components of the cost-to-serve equations (2.04) and (2.05). For example, heavier aerial construction for mechanical strength, to withstand the onslaught of elements, and a more extensive use of underground construction will tend to increase the unit costs of the "Customer" parametric component of the cost-to-serve equations, and its significance may become greater in the operational economics of supplying electric service. The much bigger loads of individual residential customers, probable in the future as a result of total electric homes, and the concomitant decrease in diversity between such loads will also increase the significance of the "Customer Demand" component of the cost-to-serve equations, even if all other things were to remain the same.

What will be the general level of the unit cost of distribution of electric power in the future is not susceptible to precise answers at this time. Some factors, such as increase in the future density of customers and loads per unit of area served, will tend to reduce them; other factors, such as a decrease in load diversity, heavier aerial construction, more extensive use of underground facilities, will tend to increase them. It thus behooves us to be alert in the continuous task of analyses and evaluations of the costs of the distribution system to the end that we may, at all times, understand its trends and reflect adequately and properly its impacts upon the operational economics of the supply of electric utility service.

BUSINESS FUNCTIONS

The total cost of business functions (including, for sake of simplicity, the metering and control function) of the illustrative electric utility, represents about 15 percent of the total. Over 75 percent of these costs are in the operating expense category, and the remaining 25 percent are in the nature of carrying charges on investment. Under our conceptual model, over 70 percent of these costs resides in the "Customer" component of the cost-to-serve equations (2.04) and (2.05), about 3 percent, in the "Customer Demand," 25 percent, in the "Class Peak or Diversified Demand," and 2 percent, in the "Energy" components.

The large proportion of these functional costs being in the operating expense category, makes them very susceptible to inflationary trends owing to wage increases. But, the large portion of them residing in the "Customer" component of the cost-to-serve equations, causes these costs to increase relatively little with load growth. However, the future trends in these costs are likely to be: in an increasing proportion of carrying charges on investment, as a result of automation of the general office practices and ultimately perhaps even in mechanization of the meter reading function, and in a decreasing proportion of the "Customer" component in relation to the other three components due to load growth. As a matter of fact, with all other things being equal, a double per customer use of service could easily increase the relative significance of these three components by about 50 percent.

Is the nature of these costs subject to change in the future? The answer is undoubtedly "yes," they will change as already mentioned because of the intensification in automation practices in the business activities of the enterprise, in the possibilities of mechanization of meter reading and other practices, and, in the case of combination electric and gas enterprises, in both the level of and the mix within these costs if these two businesses were to be divorced from common ownership and established as independent enterprises. It is far beyond the scope of this book to probe into any details of this matter; nevertheless, it is mentioned here as a consideration which must be kept in mind whenever studying, analyzing, or prognosticating the operational economics of electric utilities.

14. CARRYING CHARGES, PRESENT WORTH, AND "BELOW-THE-LINE" ANALYSES

The words *Carrying Charges* or *Fixed Charges* have been used by engineers and others in and out of the electrical utility industry to describe collectively the charges incurred by utilities in the cost elements of return, depreciation, and taxes, to which are frequently added the cost elements of insurance, operation, and maintenance (exclusive of fuel and exclusive of other production system supplies). It has been customary to express such Carrying Charges as percentages of the so-called "Original Cost" of plant facilities. However, since under the regulatory practices and juridical-economic concepts established in the United States in the economics of utility operations, the return element changes over the life of facilities in percent of their Original Cost as a result of accrued depreciation—even when all other factors remain constant—a necessity arises for the development of techniques which permit the conversion of the annual *variable* charges in percent of Original Cost to the equivalent levelized, or constant, charge in percent of such Original Cost. The concept of equivalency in this technique is reflected through the application of well-known mathematical relationships of discounting future charges to the level of present worth. The levelized Carrying Charges thus obtained then become convenient tools in all kinds of engineering-economic studies or comparisons, and as a basis for the establishment of pricing related to plant facilities. Under this concept, the magnitude of such Carrying Charges becomes synonymous with the concept of levelized revenue requirements to satisfy the over-all magnitude of all elements of the Carrying Charges dependent thereon, all expressed in percent of Original Cost of plant facilities.

GENERAL CONSIDERATIONS OF CARRYING CHARGES

A brief description of the economic aspects of the three elements of Carrying Charges will be helpful in understanding the concepts they represent.

Return. The annual return element is the yearly charge to compensate security holders for the funds that they provide as invested capital for plant facilities. It is equal to the sum of interest on borrowed money, dividends on preferred stock, and the earning requirements on common stock equity. Volumes have been written on what constitutes a reasonable magnitude of this element, on its economic implications, and on the manner of its determination for the natural monopoly conditions of utility system operations under one or several forms of government regulation. Since the magnitudes of the various items which enter into its determination are usually dependent upon each other, it has been the practice to set an over-all rate for it, which is usually defined as a "reasonable" or "fair" or "adequate" rate of return on a rate base which, depending upon the different philosophies of regulation, may be set at "original cost" or at a "fair value" or on some other basis. The product of the rate of return and the rate base, no matter how established, constitutes the total dollars available as compensation to those who provide the invested capital in plant facilities of the enterprise. The return on the invested capital in plant facilities can also be obtained from the financial statement of the utility for any given year, since the interest and dividends actually paid or due, plus earnings transferred to surplus, are reported therein.

The annual return, whether derived from the rate base or from the annual financial statement of the company, may be divided by the invested capital, thus obtaining an annual return rate thereon. The money obtained by the enterprise from all issued securities outstanding, including accumulated earned surplus, is approximately equal to the Original Cost of the plant plus working capital less the reserves for depreciation, any reserves for deferred taxes which might be established in connection with the use of liberalized depreciation in income tax computations, and other similar reserves. The return rate, r, on the invested capital, so defined, can be obtained for several past years and from estimates of future conditions. However, in establishing it for use in the determination of levelized Carrying Charge rates, judgment must be applied by giving consideration to the adequacy of earnings in the period reviewed, as evidenced by the willingness of investors to purchase securities of the enterprise, particularly new issues, to business conditions, and to conditions in the money market in general, particularly as influenced by government fiscal policies. From all such considerations, estimated value can be established for the proper average annual return rate on invested capital to be used in studies of operational economics.

On modern utility systems, generally the Original Cost of a project is financed both by the invested capital and by the reinvested reserve funds in excess of the cost of scattered retirements of plant facilities in the course of time. Hence, the levelized average return to security holders on their invested capital divided by Original Cost, defines the element of the levelized return rate in terms of the Original Cost. It is expressed as a percentage of the Original Cost. The numerical value of this levelized percentage is generally lower than the rate established for the invested capital.

Taxes. The annual tax element of the Carrying Charges is the total of those yearly taxes levied on electrical utilities by local, state, and federal governments, which depend on Original Cost of plant facilities, either directly or indirectly. The tax element of Carrying Charges applicable in whole or in part to the Original Cost of plant comprises such taxes as property taxes, the federal tax on income, state taxes on income, some forms of state capital stock taxes, gross receipts taxes, and other taxes which are dependent directly or indirectly on the elements entering into the computations of Carrying Charges.

The magnitude of annual taxes has become in recent years a very substantial item of total annual Carrying Charges of investor-owned electric utilities. A clear understanding is, therefore, essential to the manner in which such taxes are incurred, so that they may be reflected properly in the over-all magnitude fo the Carrying Charge rates of such enterprises. Under the established concept that Carrying Charges should reflect revenue requirements to meet the Carrying Charge element of the total cost, all taxes based on income are related to the return element of the Carrying Charges.

Other federal, state, and local taxes, usually smaller in magnitude, should also find proper recognition in the annual cost element of taxes. Social security and unemployment insurance taxes, which depend to a large extent upon labor expense can be related to the operation and maintenance expense element whenever that element is included as part of the total Carrying Charge rates. The state gross receipts tax, which is basically levied upon all intrastate revenues derived from customers within the territorial boundry of the utility, is dependent upon the sum of all the components comprising annual charges. Its effective rate for application to the sum of all the components in annual charges is equal to the quotient obtained by dividing its statutory rate by one minus this rate.

Taxes of a local nature to be included in the tax element of annual charges must be determined on bases which approximate most closely or actually correspond to the manner in which these taxes are levied on the utility supplying the service. A careful analysis of their incidence should disclose to what extent such taxes should be included in the annual charges applicable to different functional systems and to the different physical components of each of such functional systems. For example, a local franchise tax levied on the number of poles and miles of overhead wires cannot be considered to apply to the production system, and perhaps not even to the bulk power transmission system. Such tax is obviously related to the secondary, primary, and high-voltage distribution systems, but not to all physical components thereof. Such items, for example, as underground conduits, underground cables, substations, line transformers, and meters should not bear this type of tax in the annual charges applicable to these facilities.

Depreciation. In its broadest sense, this component of annual charges comprises the necessary amount of money required to be set aside annually so that the cumulative annual sums will recover, at the end of the life expectancy, the Original Cost of the facilities used in rendering the service, less net salvage. Here again, volumes have been written on this subject, upon its philosophical-economic implications, methods of accounting, and on its engineering and operating practices.

In problems dealing with individual facilities, care should be exercised to determine depreciation in line with the expected length of life for the item under consideration. However, in problems dealing with projects or physical systems composed of many items, depreciation rates should reflect the weighted composite length of life expectancy of all items of facilities which comprise such a project or physical system.

It has been customary in modern utilities to invest the funds provided by this element of Carrying Charges in new plant facilities, and generally regulatory authorities deduct the reserve created by these funds or its equivalent in establishing a "rate base" to determine the magnitude of allowable earnings.

Summary. The essential elements of Carrying Charge rates are summarized in the following outline, and are arranged into two major categories: (A.) those which are interdependent with each other, such as the elements of return, depreciation and those taxes which depend directly upon such return and upon the treatment accorded depreciation in their computation; and (B.) those which are of individual nature directly expressable in terms of the Original Cost, and other taxes dependent on one or more of the preceding elements.

Elements of Levelized Carrying Charge Rates

A. Interdependent Category

1. Return on invested capital
   a. Basic
   b. Required for interim replacements
2. Straight-line depreciation reflecting average life expectancy
3. Taxes directly dependent on return
   a. Reflecting straight-line method for depreciation
   b. Adjustment for "liberalized" depreciation
4. Tax adjustment a/c of difference in depreciable plant for tax purposes
   a. Reflecting straight-line method for depreciation
   b. Adjustment for "liberalized" depreciation

B. Individual Category

5. Property taxes
6. Insurance
7. Operation and maintenance expense (when specifically stated as having been included in the Carrying Charge rate)
8. Other taxes dependent on one or more of the preceding elements (covering state and federal social security and unemployment, gross receipts, etc.)

MATHEMATICAL ASPECTS OF CARRYING CHARGE RATES

This exposition will be confined to the basic mathematical aspects of Carrying Charge rates as they apply in practical applications to the elements of the interdependent category. A more extensive coverage of this subject is contained in my 1956 AIEE joint paper with W. T. Brown.[1]

A simplified economic behavior with time of a continuous nongrowing plant is depicted in Figure 28 under present-day

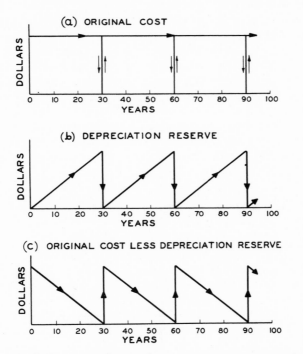

Figure 28. Behavior with time for a continuous nongrowing plant of its (a) original cost (b) depreciation reserve (c) original cost less depreciation reserve

juridical-economic concepts of electric utility operations. It will be seen that, fundamentally, the Original Cost of a plant

[1] Constantine W. Bary and Wilmer T. Brown, "Some New Mathematical Aspects of Fixed Charges," *AIEE Transactions*, Vol. LXXVI, Part 3 (1957), p. 230.

item remains fixed with time; the depreciation reserve grows from zero to the amount of the Original Cost, decreases to zero upon the retirement of the plant, and repeats the cycle upon the replacement of the plant. The net plant, that is, the Original Cost less the accrued depreciation reserve, starts with the amount of the Original Cost of the plant and decreases to zero immediately preceding its retirement, thereupon repeating the cycle with the passage of time.

The fundamentally variable-with-time cost behavior of annual charge rates for the return, taxes, and depreciation is depicted in Figure 29, for a similar elementary case of a nongrowing but continuous plant, with a depreciation reserve accrued on a straight-line basis, with no dispersion in retirements and no net salvage for both income tax calculations and for the recovery of the Original Cost. These *variable* annual charge rates over a period of years can be converted into a single equivalent constant Carrying Charge rate indicated by the horizontal dashed line, labeled $\bar{f}$ in Figure 29, by the well-known mathematical procedure in which a series of future annual payments f_y are discounted to the level of present worth at an appropriate effective earning rate r' which, under the interdependence of income taxes and returns, is equal to the specified return rate on invested capital reduced by the effect of tax ex-

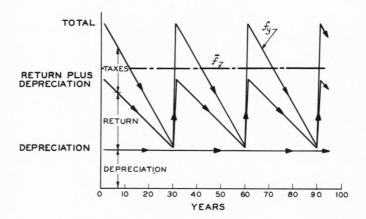

Figure 29. Behavior with time of annual charges in percent of original cost for a continuous nongrowing plant

emption on that portion of such return rate which is represented by the inherent requirements of debt capital, because the conceptually reinvested funds in such present worth evaluation contain no debt capital.[2]

Since the return rate is:

$$r = ib + e\,(1 - b) \qquad\qquad (14.01)$$

where

i = constant average annual interest rate on indebtedness
b = constant average ratio of indebtedness to the total invested capital
e = constant average earning rate on the equity portion of the total invested capital

the effective earning rate becomes:

$$r' = r - Tib \qquad\qquad (14.02)$$

where

T = constant composite effective average annual income tax rate, combining the Federal income tax rate, state income tax rate and any other tax rate dependent on income.

For example, assuming the return rate on invested capital

[2]In most text books, the annual discount rate r' is usually considered synonymous with the return rate r on invested capital. This elementary concept is introduced usually before the introduction of the subject of income taxes; as a matter of fact this elementary concept was created long before income tax laws were even conceived. For enterprises exempt from income taxes, such as those of the government, of states and municipalities, the discount rate for present-worth calculations is equal to the interest rate on their investment; and for enterprises with homogeneous capital structures comprised of equity capital only (without any debt capital) it is equal to their return rates on such capital. But for commercial enterprises with a capital structure nonhomogeneous as to the treatment of its components for determining income tax liability, it is equal to the $r - Tib$ value as shown in equation (14.02). For mathematical demonstrations, see Constantine W. Bary and Wilmer T. Brown, "Some New Mathematical Aspects of Fixed Charges," *AIEE Transactions*, Vol. LXXVI, Part 3 (1957), p. 230; and C. W. Bary, "Economic Evaluation and Choice between Alternative Plans," Minutes, October 1962 Meeting, System Planning Committee (Harrisburg, Pennsylvania Electric Association, unpublished).

$r = 6$ percent; the interest on indebtedness $i = 4.5$ percent; ratio of indebtedness to total invested capital $b = 50$ percent; and a composite rate for federal and state income taxes $T = 55.52$ percent; the effective earning rate r' becomes $= 4.75$ percent.

Retirement Dispersion. In actual practice, the lives of plant items, or units of property as they are called under the Uniform System of Accounts for electric utilities, do not expire all at the same time. Some expire before, others at, and still others after the average life expectancy of the plant. This phenomenon is known as retirement dispersion and is susceptible to actuarial treatment, especially for mass property, such as poles, wires, distribution transformers, meters, and the like. Many studies on such property retirement dispersions have caused students of this problem to establish "Survivor Curves," or "Retirement Dispersion Curves," the better known ones being those of the Iowa type—developed by students of this subject at Iowa State University. As could be expected there are a large variety of such curves. Some are symmetrical about the average life expectancy, peak at that value and are, therefore, known as "S" curves; others are skewed by peaking either to the left or to the right of the average life expectancy and are known as "L" curves and "R" curves, respectively. The numerical subscript carried by each indicates the degree of the sharpness of the curve. Those which are relatively flat carry a low number, those which are relatively sharp, a higher one.

Figure 30 shows three such curves: two curves (L_0 and S_6) provide extreme ranges of effects upon the economic significance of the Carrying Charge rate, and the third curve (curve R_2) represents a more moderate effect on such rate.

The cost of these retirements are in effect reflected as capital requirements through depletion in the accumulated depreciation reserves, and, in accordance with the general theory, create an increase in return requirements and in the concomitant taxes depending thereon, which would not have been present had there been no such interim replacements.

Just as the other variable charge rates over a period of years, those caused by the interim replacements can be converted also into single equivalent constant Carrying Charge rates through the well-known technique of discounting future payments to the level of present worth at the effective earning rate r'. Such calculations have been carried out uniquely by P. H. Jeynes, an earnest student of this subject, and the results presented in a set of tables contained in his 1956 AIEE paper.[3] These tables cover a wide variety of Iowa type dispersion curves, over a wide range of average life expectancies, and for three values of effective earning rates. I have used them to derive for each

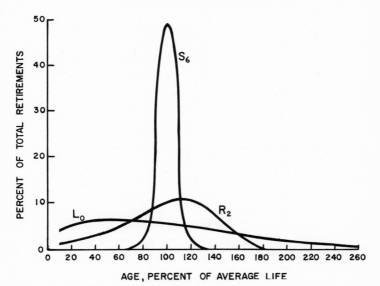

S = SYMMETRICAL DISTRIBUTION
R = RIGHT MODED DISTRIBUTION
L = LEFT MODED DISTRIBUTION

Figure 30. **Examples of Iowa-type frequency curves showing distribution of retirements in 10 percent age intervals**

the numerical values of their increment over the corresponding value of a simple annuity rate. These increment values are shown in Tables 19, 20, and 21 of the Appendix for three effective earning rates, and permit interpolation and extrapolation for other rates which are within those shown or which are not too far outside of their range. Table 18 in the Appendix contains the simple annuity rates at a number of effective earning

[3] P. H. Jeynes, "The Depreciation Annuity," *AIEE Transactions*, Vol. LXXV, Part 3 (1956), pp. 1398–415.

rates in steps of one-quarter of a percentage point ranging from 4 to 6-3/4 percent. [4]

Computation of Carrying Charge Rates. With the aid of these tables and the formulas set forth below, computations can be made of Carrying Charge rates over a wide range of conditions at a high degree of accuracy which would be consistent with large majority of practical problems of electric utilities. [5] The formulas reflecting the theory of ($r - Tib$) possess the unique feature that, for any given method of depreciation for tax purposes, the *total* Carrying Charge rate remains the same no matter what method of depreciation is employed for capital recovery for book purposes, but rearrangement takes place in the magnitudes of its individual elements.

General Formulas. General formulas will be now provided for calculating the elements of levelized Carrying Charge rates:

1. The *levelized return rate* $\overline{r}_r{}'$ over the life expectancy of the plant, expressed in terms of the Original Cost of the plant, is given by the following equation:

$$\overline{r}_r{}' = r + \frac{r}{r'}\left[p\,\overline{q}_r{}' + p\,(\overline{d}_r{}' - \overline{q}_r{}') - \frac{p}{L}\right] \qquad (14.03)$$

where in addition to the symbols already defined,

p = a constant, equal to the ratio of the Original
       Cost less its net salvage at the end of the

---

[4] There is no question that so long as interpolations and extrapolations are required for uneven effective earning rates, the use of these two sets of tables provides a higher accuracy for the sum of the two factors than would be the case by using the single value for them from the Jeynes's tables.

[5] I felt that it was beyond the scope of this book to provide a dissertation of the effects of sustained and rapid growths of plant investment on the level revenue requirement rates in terms of original cost. For a discussion and a mathematical investigation of this aspect of carrying charge rates, see, Constantine W. Bary and Wilmer T. Brown, "Some New Mathematical Aspects of Fixed Charges," *AIEE Transactions*, Vol. LXXVI, Part 3 (1957), p. 230.

We pointed out in that paper that there may be other aspects of the subject of levelized carrying charge rates that could warrant further exploration, and additional studies in the future may show the need for a modification of existing concepts.

useful life of the project to the Original Cost. Net salvage is equal to the salvage of the plant less the cost of removal.

L = average life expectancy of the plant in years

$\overline{q}_r{}'$ = normal annuity rate corresponding to the average life expectancy L under an effective earning rate r', interpolated from Table 18

$\overline{u}_r{}' = (\overline{d}_r{}' - \overline{q}_r{}')$ = an additional amount representing levelized adjustment for retirement dispersion for one of the Iowa type curves corresponding to the average life expectancy and under an effective earning rate r', interpolated, or extrapolated from Tables 19, or 20, or 21

For example, under the foregoing numerical assumptions, and with $p = 1$, $L = 40$, and with an R_2 retirement dispersion curve, $\overline{q}_r{}'$ is interpolated from Table 18 at 0.88 percent; $(\overline{d}_r - \overline{q}_r)$ is extrapolated from Table 21 at 0.305 percent; and the levelized return rate is calculated as 4.33 percent.

2. The *levelized depreciation rate* $\overline{D}_r{}'$ expressed in terms of Original Cost, being on a straight-line basis, is:

$$\overline{D}_r{}' = \frac{p}{L} \qquad (14.04)$$

Under the above numerical assumptions it becomes 2.50 percent.

3a. The *levelized tax rate* $\overline{t}_r{}'$ dependent on income and calculated under the straight-line method of depreciation is:

$$\overline{t}_r{}' = \frac{T}{(1 - T)}\, \overline{r}_r{}' \left(1 - \frac{ib}{r}\right) \qquad (14.05)$$

Under the above numerical assumption it becomes 3.37 percent.

3b. The *incremental change* in the levelized tax rate due to liberalized depreciation for tax computation is:

$$\Delta \overline{t}_r{}' = \frac{T}{(1 - T)}\, p\left(\overline{D}_{tr}{}' - \frac{1}{L}\right) \qquad (14.06)$$

Where $\overline{D}_{tr'}$ is obtained from one of the following equations:

i. For the Double Declining Balance method of liberalized depreciation and relatively small amount of net salvage:

$$\frac{1}{p}\left\{\left(\frac{2}{L}\right)\frac{r'+\overline{q}_{r'}}{r'+2/L}\left[1-\left(\frac{1-2/L}{1+r'}\right)^m\right]+\left[\frac{(1+r')^{L-m}-1}{(1+r')^L-1}\right]\times\left[\frac{(1-2/L)^m}{L-m}-\frac{1-p}{L-m}\right]\right\} \quad (14.07)$$

Where $\overline{q}_{r'}$ is $\dfrac{r'}{(1+r')^L-1}$ and can be obtained directly, or by interpolation from Table 18 for the given life expectancy and the specified effective earning rate r'. To determine at what optimum end of year m the change should be made from the Declining Balance to the Straight-Line method to recover all of the Original Cost less net salvage, the following equation must be solved:

$$2/L\,(1-2/L)^{m-1}=\frac{(1-2/L)^m}{L-m}-\frac{1-p}{L-m} \quad (14.08)$$

When p is 1, then m is $L/2+1$; (if L is even, m can also be equal to $\left(\dfrac{L}{2}+2\right)$.

When p is not equal to 1, then m must be determined by trial and error.

It is to be noted that under this method, depreciation annual rate is equal to $2/L$ which is the maximum allowed.

ii. For the Sum of Year's Digits method of liberalized depreciation:

$$\frac{2\left(r'+\overline{q}_{r'}-\dfrac{1}{L}\right)}{r'\,(L+1)} \quad (14.09)$$

Tables 22 and 23 provide computed values of $W_{r'}=\left(\overline{D}_{tr'}-\dfrac{1}{L}\right)$ for the Double Declining Balance method of liberalized depreciation under the optimum conversion to Straight-Line method, and for the Sum of Year's Digits method of such liberalized depreciation, respectively, for the condition of zero net salvage. The tables cover a wide range of life expectancies and for a number of annual effective earning rates, in steps of one-quarter of a percent ranging from 4 to 6-3/4 percent.

Under the above numerical assumptions $\left(\overline{D}_{tr'} - \dfrac{1}{L}\right)$ for the

Double Declining Balance method is interpolated from Table 22 at 0.49 percent, and for the Sum of Year's Digits method it is interpolated from Table 23 at 0.71 percent.

Thus, the incremental change, or adjustment, in levelized tax rate due to these two liberalized methods of depreciation for the tax computation become: for the Double Declining Balance method – 0.61 percent, and for the Sum of Year's Digits method – 0.89

4. *Tax adjustment* on account of difference in depreciable plant for tax purposes (largely because of interest during construction reflected in the book costs and eliminated for tax purposes) can be computed from the following equation:

$$\text{For Straight-Line Depreciation} = \frac{T}{(1 - T)} \, f \, \frac{1}{L} \quad (14.10)$$

and as an increment for liberalized depreciation $= \dfrac{T}{(1 - T)} \times$

$$f\left(\overline{D}_{tr'} - \frac{1}{L}\right) (14.11)$$

Where

f equals the ratio of eliminated items of Original Cost (such as interest during construction) to the Original Cost.

Assuming f is 0.06, and other values as reflected in the preceding statements, the tax adjustment for Straight-Line Depreciation becomes 0.19 percent; and the increment for liberalized depreciation 0.04 percent for the Double Declining Balance method, and 0.05 percent for the Sum of Year's Digits method.

Summary. Under the stated numerical example, the over-all levelized Carrying Charge rate (in percent of Original Cost) for the elements of the interdependent category can be summarized as shown in the following table:

TABLE 17. SUMMARY OF CARRYING CHARGE COMPUTATIONS

Return on invested capital:
  a. Basic   3.95 ⎫
  b. Additional for interim replacements   0.38 ⎬ 4.33
Straight-Line Depreciation   2.50
Taxes directly dependent on income:
  a. Reflecting Straight-Line Depreciation   3.38
  b. Adjustment for Double Declining method   −0.61
Tax adjustment a/c of difference in depreciation plant
    for tax purpose:
  a. Reflecting Straight-Line Depreciation   0.19
  b. Increment for Double Declining method   0.04

Total Carrying Charge rate for elements of the Inter-
    dependent Category   9.83

To complete the picture, other elements of the Carrying Charges which were designated as of the individual category, such as property taxes, insurance, and the like, depending upon individual conditions of utilities and of functional elements of the supply system to which they apply could increase the total rate to a level of around 12 percent.

Simplified Formulas. Although the information contained in Tables 18 to 23 in the Appendix permit the calculation of Carrying Charge rates with a high degree of accuracy and pursuant to the basic principles of the mathematical theory of true equivalency, which provides a sense of scientific and mathematical security, it must be noted that most of the factors to be used in the formulas, when solving practical problems of operational economics, must reflect someone's judgment, be that of the analyst or his boss or someone else whose job qualifies him to provide such data. I have found, therefore, that in many applications requiring the use of levelized Carrying Charge rates $\bar{f}$ for the elements of the interdependent category, their computation can be materially simplified, with little sacrifice in the over-all accuracy and, especially when a specific retirement dispersion pattern is not known, through the use of the following equations:

a) For conditions when taxes are computed using Straight-Line Depreciation:

$$\bar{f} = Kr + \frac{p}{L} + \frac{T}{1-T}\left(1 - \frac{ib}{r}\right)Kr \qquad (14.12)$$

and b) for conditions when taxes are computed using one of the acceptable methods of liberalized depreciation:

$$\bar{f} = Kr + \frac{p}{L} + \frac{T}{1-T} \left(1 - \frac{ib}{r}\right) Kr - \frac{Tp}{1-T} K' \quad (14.13)$$

Where the letters not previously defined are:

K = an empirical constant, to be established after consideration of all pertinent facts. Its general level can be gauged from a study of past and estimated future ratios of the magnitudes of the net depreciated plant to the total of its Original Cost. Ordinarily it will be found in the range between 0.7 and 0.8 for the bulk of average life expectancies and retirement dispersions of facilities used on electric utility systems, which range from 30 to 50 years

K' = an empirical constant which, for average life expectancies between 30 and 50 years and under present-day general financial practices of utility system's operations, can be taken at 0.009 for the Sum of Year's Digits method and at 0.006 for the Declining Balance method at optimum conditions of transferring to the Straight-Line method

Under the foregoing numerical assumptions, and using $K = 0.75$, the levelized Carrying Charge rate for the elements of the interdependent category are calculated under the simplified formula to be 9.76 percent for the Double Declining method of liberalized depreciation for tax purposes. From practical considerations of the underlying assumptions, this is sufficiently close to the rate computed through the use of the complete general formulas, as illustrated in the foregoing summary.

PRESENT WORTH

From the preceding paragraphs we have learned that levelized Carrying Charge rates, fully equivalent to the year-by-year varying rates, are developed through the application of the Present-Worth technique. The mathematical principles of it are well known, and it finds frequent application in the solution of numerous problems in the operational economics of electric utilities, especially as an aid to judgment in establishing an economic basis for decision on the choice between two or more alternative projects or courses of action. Frequently the alternatives involve differences as to the time the costs are incurred or the expenditures made, and this involves moving them (carrying charges and expenses) for each alternative through time to the present, to permit the selection of the least expensive alternative in terms of today's worth of money; and money cannot be moved through time without altering its value. This is one of the most important characteristics of the entire economic structure of our society. The present value of money is always greater than the identical amount in the future, because money can be used to advantage in the interim. This may be likened to the well-known proverb that "a bird in the hand is worth two in the bush." The controlling factor in the changing value of money through time is normally called "interest rate." But in operational economics of modern investor-owned electric utilities, it is the "effective earning rate" r' discussed in the preceding section of this chapter.

The Present Worth technique can be defined as the mathematical process by which different amounts of money are moved, either forward or backward, from one or more time levels to a single time level, by reflecting the changes in the value of this money because of its potential effective earning power during the interim periods. The word *present* does not necessarily mean the current date when the study is made. Present Worth can be determined as of any desired date. It is important, however, that the same Present Worth date must be used for all factors being compared.

The Present Worth of money moved forward in time by one year at an effective earning rate r' is expressed by the multiplying factor:

$$(1 + r') \tag{14.14}$$

and is known as the compounding process.

The Present Worth of money moved backward in time by one year at an effective earning rate r' is divided by the foregoing factor, thus becoming the following multiplier:

$$\frac{1}{(1 + r')} \tag{14.15}$$

and this is known as the process of discounting at a given effective earning rate r'

By extension, multiplying an amount of money by a particular

n^{th} power of the factor (14.15) carries it backward in time n number of years. For convenience, Table 24 provides, for a number of stated earning rates in steps of one-fourth of a percentage point, the resultant of this multiplier for a wide range of years of practical significance in the operational economics of electric utilities.

The Present Worth factors described in the foregoing paragraphs are sufficient to provide the needed economic information for a direct comparison between amounts of money available at various times. However, additional factors, known as Present Worth of *annuities* are frequently also useful. An *annuity* is a series of equal (i.e., level) payments extending over a period of years. Its Present Worth is expressed by the following general equation:

$$a_n = \frac{(1 + r')^n - 1}{r'(1 + r')^n} \tag{14.16}$$

and gives the Present Worth of a payment at the end of each year for n years, at a specified effective earning rate r' compounded annually. It is to be noted that the Present Worth in the foregoing equation is always *one year prior* to the first annuity payment.

Table 25 provides, for a number of stated effective earning rates, in steps of one-fourth of a percentage point, the resultant Present Worth of annuity per dollar paid in at the end of a year, for a wide range of years. When the values in this table are used as divisors, they in effect convert a single amount into equal annual payments. But it must be remembered that to convert a single amount into an annuity (i.e., level annual payment) the single amount must be adjusted to a point in time one year prior to the first annuity payment.

The information contained in these tables offers convenient means for application of the Present Worth technique for the evaluation of numerous problems encountered in operational economics which deal with making choices between alternative projects or courses of action. Details of its application can be found in many comprehensive texts on this subject.[6] It is im-

[6]See, John Charles Lounsbury Fish, *Engineering Economics, First Principles* (2d ed., New York, McGraw-Hill Book Company, Inc., 1923); E. L. Grant, *Principles of Engineering Economy* (3d ed., New York, The Ronald Press Company, 1950); and, Clarence E. Bullinger, *Engineering Economic Analysis* (2d ed., New York, McGraw-Hill Book Company, Inc., 1950).

portant to note, however, that most of these texts fail to inform the readers that for investor-owned enterprises in this country, under existing capital structures and income tax regulations, the discount rates to be used in these tables must be the effective values r', as defined by equation (14.02).

"BELOW-THE-LINE" ANALYSES

The term "below the line," employed in connection with economic analyses of electric utility operations, is a colloquial, but rather effective, expression frequently used to convey the desired end-result of an analysis; that is, to show the effects of an alternative action or of a change in environmental conditions on earnings available for dividends or for transfer to earned surplus. All such studies are fundamentally of a *comparative* nature; that is, they can only show estimated changes which are likely to take place under one or another course of action or under some expected changes in environmental conditions, in *comparison* with the performance under a stated *base* situation. Obviously, such base situations can be either the actual economic performance of the enterprise for one or more years in the past, or it can be an estimate of its future economic performance reflected in either a "standard" forecast for one or more years or in some other type of forecast whose basis is clearly defined.

From extensive experience in this form of economic analyses of electric utility operations, it is my considered judgment that analyses of the "below-the-line" effects of alternatives on future economic performance of a utility, should employ for comparison, whenever possible, a standard forecast for the base situation because the use of such base requires the least amount of explanatory definitions, is most effective in the promptness of providing the answers, and should be most certain to be devoid of bias or preconceived notions as to the significance of the alternatives under study. However, to provide confidence in the results, the standard forecast of utility's operations must be complete, current, built-up in detail from the "grass roots," and encompass data coverage for all pertinent elements of operational economics of the utility, not too dissimilar to that available in its actual performance for the past years. Considering the time lead necessary in many of the decisions confronting managements of electric utilities, it seems to me that standard forecasts of the type described should cover not less than five, and preferably one or two years more.

There are many aspects in the operations of a modern electric utility that require below-the-line analyses, and many result in queries from top managerial levels either for their enlightenment or for use by them as guides in policy decisions. Some of these queries can be answered with little effort. For example, the below-the-line effect of a new income tax rate can be quickly determined from the knowledge of the new and the existing rates and the total income tax liability reflected in the annual income statements. Other queries require more elaborate computations: for example, the below-the-line effect of a new price for fuel requires the knowledge of the new price, the old price, the quantity of fuel used, any of the possible effects of these changes on revenues which are subject to automatic fuel-adjustment clauses in rates, or which depend upon prices determined from periodic "bus bar cost" computations, and finally their effects on taxes dependent on revenue and on income. There are still other inquiries for information which require very lengthy computations involving a great many elements of cost data. As an example of these we can cite the below-the-line effects of postponing the installation of a major capacity addition of the production system with its concomitant deferral of installation of bulk transmission facilities applicable thereto. The answer to this inquiry requires complex computations, ranging over a wide field of information on the operational economics of the utility. They encompass data on the production capacities and peak loads of the system and its neighbors; of changes in construction expenditures and related capitalization of overheads, interest and taxes during construction and possible escalation in costs; changes in fuel costs, in costs of interchange transactions, in labor and maintenance and other expenditures, and of their effects on revenue through the automatic operations of fuel-adjustment clauses and in rates or charges based on "bus bar cost" computations in special contracts; changes in financing requirements and their effects on payments of interest on debt and of dividends on preferred and common stocks; changes in depreciation allowances for income statement and for tax purposes; changes in the credits to income of capitalized interest and taxes during construction;

changes in taxes which depend on payroll, on revenues and on taxable income; and last, but not least, the reflections of changes in some elements which interdependently change others, such as the requirement for the preservations of an established level of capitalization ratios, which is interrelated with financing and the amounts available to surplus.

It is believed that the foregoing provided a sufficient illustration, within the scope of this book, on the general features pertaining to the below-the-line analyses of electric utility operations. Notwithstanding the complexity of some of the problems encountered in such analyses, they can be solved effectively when basic data are available for their solution; and the quality of the answers will depend directly on the comprehensiveness of the available data. But the economic significance of the answers will depend also in no small measure on the skill and experience of the personnel making the analysis, on its knowledge of engineering, accounting and business principles and practices of the utility's operations, and, as in many other phases of operational economics, on the exercise of sound judgment in interpreting and applying them to the problem at hand.

CONCLUSION

In conclusion, the reader of this book must have received many impressions on the operational economics of electric utilities. It is apparent that it is a complex subject, that much conceptual imagination is required in its analyses, that much judgment is needed in the application of the analytical results in practice, and that the understanding of a major portion of cost behavior resides largely in the probability relationships between some of the more important of the parameters.

At first, it may seem hopeless either to obtain the necessary basic facts or to apply them in the practical solutions of day-to-day problems. But study, hard work, and experience will show that it can be mastered if there be the will to master it, and that it can be made an effective aid in the exercise of judgment needed in the multitude of decisions required in the successful conduct of policies and affairs of a modern electric utility enterprise, be it investor-owned or owned by either a municipal, state, or federal government. The basic principles and concepts are universally applicable to any type of electric utility; but the cost numbers will differ because of differences in the nature of capital structures, and in taxes which in this country represent heavy cost burdens on investor-owned enterprises but are practically nonexistent for the other types. In my opinion, this tax discrimination, especially at the federal level of taxation, is unjust and, therefore, should be eliminated, in one way or another, for the good of the American system of free enterprise.

Notwithstanding the difficulties involved, and the false claims made by some in and out of the industry to the futility of endeavors in the study and analysis of operational economics of electric utilities, it is my considered judgment that fully distributed cost-to-serve information is essential as an aid to judgment needed in establishing rates and rate structures which would provide an equitable carrying of the cost burdens by various classes of service, as well as over a wide range of service requirements within each of the classes. What is even more important, it seems to me, is the fact that the principles underlying a proper analysis of the underlying forces which determine these and other features of operational economics of modern electric utilities described in this book will reveal many aspects of that subject in plenty of time to permit taking remedial actions, if need be, toward enhancing the use of electricity, under the lowest possible rate levels consistent with the interest of consumers, investors, employees, and the public at large. No business-managed enterprise can survive successfully or serve the public well, over a period of time, if its price structure is so low for existing or new business as to cause a dissipation of existing and new capital, particularly with each increase in sales volume. But to know whether the price structure is low or high requires a thorough knowledge of costs, their incidence and their causation. Ignorance of facts creates fear and stifles progress; knowledge of them inspires confidence and guides to better accomplishments. My lengthy experience in the field of operational economics of electric utilities convinces me that facts revealed through the application of economic analyses such as described in this book will provide proper bases for policy decisions in taking actions and vigorous leadership for increasing the welfare of the people through the conveniences and advantages provided by all-electric living.

GLOSSARY

In setting forth the thoughts and concepts in this book, I have done my best to be lucid, using sparingly the lesser known technical terms, and only when I could not find another alternative to convey the true meaning. But since use had to be made of a number of special terms singularly fitted to the subject matter of this book, a glossary is provided with the hope that it will be helpful to the reader in grasping their significance, and will serve him as a convenient reference guide.

The source of the definition for each of the selected terms is shown in parentheses. The meaning of the letters in them is as follows: (EEI) stands for the Edison Electric Institute Statistical Committee; (FPC), for the Federal Power Commission; (AEIC), for the Association of Edison Illuminating Companies Load Research Committee; (BEA), for the British Electricity Authority; and (CWB), for the author.

AMPERE (EEI) The unit of measurement of electric current or quantity of electrons flowing, analogous to cubic feet per second of water. It is the current produced by one volt acting through a resistance of one ohm.

ANNUAL (AEIC) Pertaining to any 12 consecutive calendar months.

AVERAGE USE (CWB) (KILOWATTHOURS)

annual average use (AEIC) Annual average use per customer. Annual kilowatthour use divided by annual average number of customers.

average monthly use (AEIC) One-twelfth of the annual average use.

AVERAGE WEEKDAY (AEIC) The average weekday, as it relates to specific load characteristic data, is defined as the average of such data for Monday through Friday, excluding holidays.

CARRYING CHARGE (CWB) The component of revenue requirements which is needed to provide for the return of and on invested capital in plant and facilities, for the associated taxes, and for insurance premiums.

CIRCUIT (EEI) A circuit is a conducting part or a system of conducting parts through which an electric current is intended to flow.

CLASS OF SERVICE (CWB) The collective grouping of individual customers of electric service possessing properties or characteristics in common, the nature of which forms the distinguishing attribute of the grouping. For example, the basic determinants for the classification of the component parts of the total load of an electric utility used in this book are (a) the physical (voltage) character of service supply and (b) the general nature for which the service is used.

COINCIDENCE FACTOR (RECIPROCAL OF DIVERSITY FACTOR) (AEIC) The ratio of the maximum demand of a group, class, or system as a whole to the sum of the individual maximum demands of the several components of the group, class, or system. As defined, coincidence factor never can be greater than unity.

interclass coincidence factor (CWB) The ratio of the diversified maximum demand of two or more classes, which may constitute the system or a major geographical division thereof, to the sum of the maximum demands of those classes.

intraclass coincidence factor (AEIC) The ratio of the maximum demand of a class to the sum of the maximum demands of the individual customers in the class.

intergroup coincidence factor (CWB) The ratio of the diversified maximum demand of two or more groups to the sum .of the maximum demands of these groups.

intragroup coincidence factor (CWB) The ratio of the diversified maximum demand of a group of two or more customers to the sum of the maximum demands of those individual customers.

COINCIDENT (AEIC) Use only to express "occurring over the same time interval," as in "the demand coincident with...." Use the expression "diversified demand" instead of "coincident demand."

COST-TO-SERVE (CWB) The sum total of the monetary value of labor expended, wealth consumed, taxes incurred, and compensation to investors by an electric utility enterprise in the supply of electric service to its customers.

DEMAND (AEIC) The average rate at which energy is delivered during a specified continuous interval of time, such as 15, 30, or 60 minutes. It may be expressed in kilowatts, kilovolt-amperes, or other suitable units.

actual demand (FPC) The registered demand.

billing demand (FPC) The demand upon which the billing is based as specified in a rate schedule. The billing demand may be greater or less than the actual demand for the billing period.

class maximum demand (AEIC) The maximum demand of a class of customers.

demand charge (AEIC) A component part of a rate schedule which provides for a charge based upon the customer's demand or equivalent, without regard to the use of energy.

demand factor (FPC) The ratio of the maximum demand of a system, or part of a system, to the total connected load of the system, or part of the system, under consideration.

demand interval (EEI) The period of time during which the electric energy flow or load is averaged in determining effective demand, such as 15, 30, or 60 minutes.

diversified demand (AEIC) The simultaneous demands of a group of appliances or customers taken as a whole. Diversified demands are determined by direct measurement or by the addition of the load curves of the individual appliances or customers constituting the group.

diversified maximum demand (CWB) The maximum demand of a diversified nature, obtained either from direct measurement, by the addition, hour by hour, of the load curves of individual elements, or by the mathematical application of probability factors (such as of coincidence or of diversity) to the noncoincident maximum demands of individual components comprising the whole.

group demand (CWB) Also diversified demand.

individual customer's maximum demand (AEIC) The maximum rate at which a customer takes energy.

integrated demand (EEI) The average kilowatt demand determined by an integrating demand meter or by the averaging of a load curve, over an inteval of stated length. It is the average of the continuously varying instantaneous demands during the given interval. Demand intervals are commonly 15, 30, or 60 minutes in length.

kilovolt-ampere demand (FPC) The average kva demand over a specific interval of time.

kilowatt demand (AEIC) Demand expressed in kilowatts.

maximum demand (AEIC) The maximum demand is the greatest of all of the integrated demands of the load under consideration which has occurred during a specified period of time.
Duration: 15, 30, or 60 minutes
Period: daily, weekly, monthly, or annual
          appliance, individual customer, group, class or system

noncoincident maximum demand (AEIC) The maximum demand of any appliance, individual customer, group, class, or system within a specified period (e.g., daily, weekly, monthly, or annually), regardless of time of occurrence.

peak demand (AEIC) The maximum demand.

reactive kilovolt-ampere demand (CWB) The average $kvar$ demand over a specified interval of time.

system maximum demand (CWB) The maximum demand of the entire supply system under consideration. It is the diversified maximum demand of the combined classes of customers at the point of measurement of the system maximum demand.

system peak demand (CWB) Also system maximum demand.

EFFECTIVE EARNING RATE (CWB) The discount rate used in the computations involving present worth techniques which becomes equal to a specified return rate on invested capital minus the effect of tax exemption on that portion of such return rate which is represented by the interest requirement of the debt portion of such capital.

ENERGY (AEIC) The kilowatthours supplied to or used by an individual customer, a group of customers, or a class of customers. Energy use in kilowatthours is determined by measurement or by calculation.

energy loss (EEI) The kilowatthours of energy dissipated in the operation of an electric system, principally as unavoidable energy transformations (usually to waste heat) in electrical conductors or apparatus.

FAIR VALUE (CWB) A juridical-economic concept used in some regulatory jurisdictions in the United States for establishing, for rate-making purposes, the money measure of a utility's plant used and useful in rendering its service to the public. To arrive at this measure, consideration is given to, with appropriately weighting of, a number of dollar amounts, including the plant's Original Cost, its Trended Original Cost, its Reproduction Cost New, and the corresponding accrued depreciations.

FREQUENCY DISTRIBUTION (BEA) A tabular or graphic representation of the spread of the values of a variable, showing the number of percentage of times ("frequency" with which) the variable takes values lying between each of a set of specified limits covering the whole range of the variable.

KILOVOLT (CWB) One thousand volts. Abbreviated as *kv.*

KILOVOLT-AMPERE (CWB) One thousand volt-amperes of apparent power. Abbreviated as *kva.*

reactive kilovolt-ampere (CWB) One thousand volt-amperes of reactive power. Abbreviated as *kvar.*

KILOWATT (CWB) One thousand watts of power. Abbreviated as *kw.*

KILOWATTHOUR (CWB) One thousand watts lasting for one hour. Measure of electrical energy. Abbreviated as *kwh,* or as *kwhr.*

LOAD (FPC) The amount of power delivered or received at a given point at any instant. It may be applied to a generating plant, a transmission or distribution system, a whole power system, or a customer's requirements.

load characteristics (AEIC) Collectively, all or each of the features of the electric service rendered, including the quantity of energy supplied, the load or demand, the time of its occurrence, and derivable factors, such as coincidence factor, diversity factor, and load factor.

load curve (AEIC) A load curve, as applied to a customer, a group of customers, a class, or the system, is a curve of integrated kilowatts of demand vs time showing the value of the specific integrated demand consecutively for each unit of time in the period covered and related to the end of the time interval. The units of time may be 15, 30, or 60 minutes. Load curves may be expressed as a percentage of the maximum demand in a specific period.

load diversity (FPC) The difference between the sum of the peaks of two or more individual loads and the peak of the combined load.

load duration curve (FPC) A curve showing the total time within a specified period, during which the load equalled or exceeded the power values shown.

load factor (AEIC) The ratio of the average demand over a designated period of time to the maximum demand occurring in that period. Load factor, in percent, also may be derived by multiplying the kilowatthours in the period by 100 and dividing by the product of the maximum demand in kilowatts and the number of hours in the period. The term "load factor" can refer to a customer, a group of customers, a class of customers, or a system.
Period: daily, weekly, monthly, annual, or average
Kind: appliance, individual customer, group, class, or system

load occurrence curve (CWB) A curve showing the total energy (kilowatthours) within a specified period, which is cumulatively encompassed by all load values up to the specified load value (kilowatts) existing during the period.

load research (AEIC) Load research is an activity embracing the measurement and study of the characteristics of electric loads for the purpose of providing a thorough and reliable knowledge of trends in, and the general behavior of, the load characteristics of the more important electric services rendered by the electric utility industry. Such studies should serve as essential guides to aid company managements in the development of economically sound policies governing system planning and design, cost-of-service analyses, rate structures, and sales promotion programs.

load survey (AEIC) The various steps and processes generally used in making load tests; i.e., selecting loads to be studied, collecting and analyzing load data resulting from such tests, and presenting the load characteristics data in useful form.

peak load (AEIC) The maximum load used or produced by a unit or group of units in a stated period of time. It may be the instantaneous maximum load or the average maximum load over a designated interval of time (integrated). Average maximum load is used ordinarily. In commercial transactions involving peak load (peak power) it is taken as the average load (power) during a time interval of specified duration occurring within a given period of time, that time interval being selected during which the average power is greatest.

MANUFACTURING (AEIC)   A classification covering service for manufacturing uses.   These are: (Div. D, Major Group 19–39) manufacturing; (Div. I) such part of government services as are classified in the two digit classification, 19 through 39.*

MEGA BTU (CWB) One million British Thermal Units.

NONMANUFACTURING (AEIC) A classification covering service for nonmanufacturing uses. These are: (Div. A, Major Group 01–09) agriculture, forestry, and fisheries; (Div. B, Major Group 10–14) mining; (Div. C, Major Group 15–17) contract construction; (Div. E, Major Group 40–49) transportation, communication, electric, gas, and sanitary services; (Div. F, Major Group 50–59) wholesale and retail trade; (Div. G, Major Group 60–67) finance, insurance, and real estate; (Div. H, Major Group 70–89) services; (Div. I) such part of government services as are classified as nonmanufacturing in the two-digit classification, 01 through 89*; and (Div. J) nonclassifiable establishments.**

OUTPUT, SYSTEM (EEI) The net generation plus purchased power, plus or minus only net interchange energy.

POWER (CWB) The rate of doing work, i.e., the product of current and voltage, and with alternating-current electricity when both current and voltage are sinusoidal multiplied by the cosine of the angle which expresses the phase difference between current and voltage. It is commonly expressed in watts.

apparent power (CWB) Present in alternating-current only. The product of the total current and voltage. It is commonly expressed in volt-amperes.

power factor (CWB) The ratio of power to apparent power, i.e., watts to volt-amperes. When both current and voltage are sinusoidal, the power factor is the cosine of the angle which expresses the phase difference between them.

reactive power (CWB) Present in alternating-current only. When both current and voltage are sinusoidal, it is the product of the total current and voltage multiplied by the sine of the angle which expresses the phase difference between them. It is commonly expressed in reactive volt-amperes, abbreviated as *vars.*

SYSTEM (AEIC) The combination or assemblage of all physical or functional parts or elements which are interdependent and form the organic whole of an enterprise engaged in the production and delivery of electricity to the public.

USE (AEIC) Kilowatthours—hourly, daily, weekly, monthly, bimonthly, quarterly, and annual.

*Divisions and major group classifications are those listed under Part I, titles and descriptions of industries, standard industrial classification manual, executive office of the president, bureau of the budget, 1957.

**Nonclassifiable establishments are assumed to be classified as commercial in the commercial industrial classification complex, and as nonmanufacturing in the manufacturing-nonmanufacturing classification complex.

UTILITY RATE STRUCTURE (EEI) A utility's approved schedules
of charges to be made in billing for utility service rendered to
various classes of customers.

VOLT (AEIC) The unit of electromotive force which, if steadily applied to a conductor having a resistance of one ohm, will produce
a current of one ampere.

VOLTAGE OF A CIRCUIT (EEI) The voltage of a circuit in an electric system is the measure of electric pressure of the circuit,
which is analogous to water pressure in a water system. It is
generally a nominal rating based on the maximum effective difference of potential between any two conductors of the circuit
concerned.

WATT (EEI) The electrical unit of power or rate of doing work. In
its simplest terms it is the rate of energy transfer equivalent to
one ampere flowing under the pressure of one volt. It is analogous to horsepower or foot-pounds per minute of mechanical
power.

APPENDIX

The tables of numerical values, listed below, should be helpful in computations of Carrying Charge rates and in determination of Present Worth.

TABLE 18. SINKING FUND ANNUITY
Annual Year End Deposits That Will Grow to $1 at Future Date
(Under the specified effective annual earning rate r')

$$\bar{q}_r = \frac{r'}{(1+r')^n - 1}$$

Avg. Life in Yrs. L=n	4.0%	4¼%	4½%	4¾%	5.0%	5¼%	5½%	5¾%	6.0%	6¼%	6½%	6¾%	Avg. Life in Yrs. L=n
1	1.0000	1.0000	1.0000	1.0000	1.0000	1.0000	1.0000	1.0000	1.0000	1.0000	1.0000	1.0000	1
2	.4902	.4896	.4890	.4884	.4878	.4872	.4866	.4860	.4854	.4848	.4843	.4837	2
3	.3203	.3196	.3188	.3180	.3172	.3164	.3157	.3149	.3141	.3133	.3126	.3118	3
4	.2355	.2346	.2337	.2329	.2320	.2312	.2303	.2294	.2286	.2277	.2269	.2261	4
5	.1846	.1837	.1828	.1819	.1810	.1801	.1792	.1783	.1774	.1765	.1756	.1748	5
6	.1508	.1498	.1489	.1479	.1470	.1461	.1452	.1443	.1434	.1425	.1416	.1407	6
7	.1266	.1257	.1247	.1238	.1228	.1219	.1210	.1200	.1191	.1182	.1173	.1164	7
8	.1085	.1076	.1066	.1057	.1047	.1038	.1029	.1019	.1010	.1001	.0992	.0983	8
9	.0945	.0935	.0926	.0916	.0907	.0898	.0888	.0879	.0870	.0861	.0852	.0844	9
10	.0833	.0823	.0814	.0804	.0795	.0786	.0777	.0768	.0759	.0750	.0741	.0732	10
11	.0741	.0732	.0722	.0713	.0704	.0695	.0686	.0677	.0668	.0659	.0651	.0642	11
12	.0666	.0656	.0647	.0637	.0628	.0619	.0610	.0601	.0593	.0584	.0576	.0567	12
13	.0601	.0592	.0583	.0574	.0565	.0556	.0547	.0538	.0530	.0521	.0513	.0505	13
14	.0547	.0537	.0528	.0519	.0510	.0501	.0493	.0484	.0476	.0468	.0459	.0451	14
15	.0499	.0490	.0481	.0472	.0463	.0455	.0446	.0438	.0430	.0422	.0414	.0406	15
16	.0458	.0449	.0440	.0431	.0423	.0414	.0406	.0398	.0390	.0382	.0374	.0366	16
17	.0422	.0413	.0404	.0396	.0387	.0379	.0370	.0362	.0354	.0347	.0339	.0332	17
18	.0390	.0381	.0372	.0364	.0355	.0347	.0339	.0331	.0324	.0316	.0309	.0301	18
19	.0361	.0353	.0344	.0336	.0327	.0319	.0312	.0304	.0296	.0289	.0282	.0274	19
20	.0336	.0327	.0319	.0311	.0302	.0295	.0287	.0279	.0272	.0265	.0258	.0251	20
21	.0313	.0304	.0296	.0288	.0280	.0272	.0265	.0257	.0250	.0243	.0236	.0229	21
22	.0292	.0284	.0275	.0267	.0260	.0252	.0245	.0237	.0230	.0224	.0217	.0210	22
23	.0273	.0265	.0257	.0249	.0241	.0234	.0227	.0220	.0213	.0206	.0200	.0193	23
24	.0256	.0248	.0240	.0232	.0225	.0217	.0210	.0203	.0197	.0190	.0184	.0178	24
25	.0240	.0232	.0224	.0217	.0210	.0202	.0195	.0189	.0182	.0176	.0170	.0164	25
26	.0226	.0218	.0210	.0203	.0196	.0189	.0182	.0175	.0169	.0163	.0157	.0151	26

27	.0140	.0145	.0151	.0157	.0163	.0170	.0176	.0183	.0190	.0197	.0205	.0212	27
28	.0129	.0135	.0140	.0146	.0152	.0158	.0165	.0171	.0178	.0185	.0193	.0200	28
29	.0120	.0125	.0130	.0136	.0142	.0148	.0154	.0160	.0167	.0174	.0181	.0189	29
30	.0111	.0116	.0121	.0126	.0132	.0138	.0144	.0151	.0157	.0164	.0171	.0178	30
31	.0103	.0108	.0113	.0118	.0123	.0129	.0135	.0141	.0148	.0154	.0161	.0169	31
32	.0095	.0100	.0105	.0110	.0115	.0121	.0127	.0133	.0139	.0146	.0152	.0159	32
33	.0088	.0093	.0098	.0103	.0108	.0113	.0119	.0125	.0131	.0137	.0144	.0151	33
34	.0082	.0087	.0091	.0096	.0101	.0106	.0112	.0118	.0124	.0130	.0136	.0143	34
35	.0076	.0081	.0085	.0090	.0095	.0100	.0105	.0111	.0117	.0123	.0129	.0136	35
36	.0071	.0075	.0079	.0084	.0089	.0094	.0099	.0104	.0110	.0116	.0122	.0129	36
37	.0066	.0070	.0074	.0079	.0083	.0088	.0093	.0098	.0104	.0110	.0116	.0122	37
38	.0062	.0065	.0069	.0074	.0078	.0083	.0088	.0093	.0098	.0104	.0110	.0116	38
39	.0057	.0061	.0065	.0069	.0073	.0078	.0083	.0088	.0093	.0099	.0104	.0111	39
40	.0053	.0057	.0061	.0065	.0069	.0073	.0078	.0083	.0088	.0093	.0099	.0105	40
41	.0050	.0053	.0057	.0061	.0065	.0069	.0073	.0078	.0083	.0089	.0094	.0100	41
42	.0046	.0050	.0053	.0057	.0061	.0065	.0069	.0074	.0079	.0084	.0090	.0095	42
43	.0043	.0046	.0050	.0053	.0057	.0061	.0065	.0070	.0075	.0080	.0085	.0091	43
44	.0040	.0043	.0047	.0050	.0054	.0058	.0062	.0066	.0071	.0076	.0081	.0087	44
45	.0038	.0041	.0044	.0047	.0051	.0054	.0058	.0063	.0067	.0072	.0077	.0083	45
46	.0035	.0038	.0041	.0044	.0048	.0051	.0055	.0059	.0064	.0068	.0073	.0079	46
47	.0033	.0036	.0038	.0041	.0045	.0048	.0052	.0056	.0060	.0065	.0070	.0075	47
48	.0031	.0033	.0036	.0039	.0042	.0046	.0049	.0053	.0057	.0062	.0067	.0072	48
49	.0029	.0031	.0034	.0037	.0040	.0043	.0047	.0050	.0054	.0059	.0064	.0069	49
50	.0027	.0029	.0032	.0034	.0037	.0041	.0044	.0048	.0052	.0056	.0061	.0066	**50**
55	.0019	.0021	.0023	.0025	.0028	.0031	.0033	.0037	.0040	.0044	.0048	.0052	55
60	.0014	.0015	.0017	.0019	.0021	.0023	.0026	.0028	.0031	.0035	.0038	.0042	60
65	.0010	.0011	.0012	.0014	.0016	.0017	.0020	.0022	.0024	.0027	.0030	.0034	65
70	.0007	.0008	.0009	.0010	.0012	.0013	.0015	.0017	.0019	.0022	.0024	.0027	70
75	.0005	.0006	.0007	.0008	.0009	.0010	.0012	.0013	.0015	.0017	.0020	.0022	75
80	.0004	.0004	.0005	.0006	.0007	.0008	.0009	.0010	.0012	.0014	.0016	.0018	80
85	.0003	.0003	.0004	.0004	.0005	.0006	.0007	.0008	.0009	.0011	.0013	.0015	85
90	.0002	.0002	.0003	.0003	.0004	.0004	.0005	.0006	.0007	.0009	.0010	.0012	90
95	.0001	.0002	.0002	.0002	.0003	.0003	.0004	.0005	.0006	.0007	.0008	.0010	95
100	.0001	.0001	.0001	.0002	.0002	.0003	.0003	.0004	.0005	.0006	.0007	.0008	100
∞	.0000	.0000	.0000	.0000	.0000	.0000	.0000	.0000	.0000	.0000	.0000	.0000	∞

TABLE 19. ADDITIONAL SINKING FUND ANNUITY FOR INTERIM REPLACEMENTS WITH IOWA-TYPE SYMMETRICAL DISPERSIONS
(Under the specified effective annual earning rate r')

$$\bar{u}_{r'} = \bar{d}_{r'} - \bar{q}_{r'}$$

Avg. Life in Yrs.	Effec. Annual Earning Rate-% r'	SC	$S_{-\frac{1}{2}}$	S_0	$S_{\frac{1}{2}}$	S_1	$S_{1\frac{1}{2}}$	S_2	S_3	S_4	S_5	S_6	Effec. Annual Earning Rate-% r'	Avg. Life in Yrs.
5	5	.0088	.0073	.0058	.0048	.0039	.0032	.0025	.0016	.0008	.0004	.0002	5	5
	6	.0106	.0088	.0069	.0058	.0047	.0038	.0030	.0019	.0010	.0005	.0002	6	
	7	.0125	.0103	.0081	.0068	.0055	.0045	.0035	.0022	.0011	.0006	.0002	7	
6	5	.0088	.0073	.0058	.0048	.0039	.0032	.0025	.0016	.0008	.0004	.0002	5	6
	6	.0106	.0088	.0069	.0058	.0047	.0038	.0030	.0019	.0010	.0005	.0002	6	
	7	.0125	.0103	.0081	.0067	.0054	.0044	.0035	.0022	.0011	.0005	.0002	7	
7	5	.0088	.0073	.0058	.0048	.0039	.0032	.0025	.0015	.0008	.0004	.0002	5	7
	6	.0107	.0088	.0069	.0058	.0047	.0038	.0030	.0019	.0010	.0005	.0002	6	
	7	.0125	.0103	.0081	.0067	.0054	.0044	.0034	.0021	.0010	.0005	.0002	7	
8	5	.0088	.0073	.0058	.0048	.0039	.0032	.0025	.0015	.0008	.0004	.0002	5	8
	6	.0107	.0088	.0069	.0058	.0046	.0038	.0030	.0019	.0010	.0005	.0002	6	
	7	.0125	.0103	.0081	.0067	.0053	.0044	.0034	.0021	.0010	.0005	.0002	7	
9	5	.0088	.0073	.0058	.0048	.0038	.0031	.0024	.0015	.0008	.0004	.0002	5	9
	6	.0107	.0088	.0069	.0058	.0046	.0038	.0029	.0018	.0009	.0005	.0002	6	
	7	.0125	.0103	.0081	.0067	.0053	.0044	.0034	.0021	.0010	.0005	.0002	7	
10	5	.0089	.0073	.0058	.0048	.0038	.0031	.0024	.0015	.0008	.0004	.0002	5	10
	6	.0107	.0088	.0069	.0057	.0046	.0037	.0029	.0018	.0009	.0004	.0002	6	
	7	.0125	.0103	.0081	.0067	.0053	.0043	.0033	.0020	.0010	.0005	.0002	7	
11	5	.0089	.0073	.0058	.0048	.0038	.0031	.0024	.0015	.0008	.0004	.0002	5	11
	6	.0107	.0088	.0069	.0057	.0046	.0037	.0029	.0018	.0009	.0004	.0002	6	
	7	.0125	.0103	.0080	.0066	.0053	.0043	.0033	.0020	.0010	.0004	.0002	7	

	5,6,7												5,6,7	
12	5	.0089	.0074	.0058	.0048	.0038	.0031	.0024	.0015	.0008	.0004	.0002	5	12
	6	.0107	.0088	.0069	.0057	.0045	.0037	.0028	.0017	.0009	.0004	.0002	6	
	7	.0126	.0103	.0080	.0066	.0053	.0043	.0033	.0020	.0010	.0004	.0002	7	
13	5	.0089	.0074	.0058	.0048	.0038	.0031	.0024	.0015	.0008	.0004	.0002	5	13
	6	.0107	.0088	.0069	.0057	.0045	.0037	.0028	.0017	.0009	.0004	.0002	6	
	7	.0126	.0102	.0080	.0066	.0052	.0042	.0033	.0020	.0010	.0004	.0002	7	
14	5	.0090	.0074	.0058	.0048	.0038	.0031	.0024	.0015	.0008	.0004	.0002	5	14
	6	.0108	.0088	.0069	.0057	.0045	.0037	.0028	.0017	.0009	.0004	.0002	6	
	7	.0126	.0102	.0080	.0066	.0052	.0042	.0033	.0020	.0010	.0004	.0002	7	
15	5	.0090	.0074	.0058	.0048	.0038	.0031	.0024	.0015	.0008	.0004	.0002	5	15
	6	.0108	.0088	.0069	.0057	.0045	.0036	.0028	.0017	.0008	.0004	.0002	6	
	7	.0126	.0102	.0080	.0066	.0052	.0042	.0033	.0020	.0010	.0004	.0002	7	
16	5	.0090	.0074	.0057	.0048	.0038	.0031	.0024	.0015	.0008	.0004	.0002	5	16
	6	.0108	.0088	.0068	.0056	.0044	.0036	.0028	.0017	.0008	.0004	.0002	6	
	7	.0125	.0102	.0079	.0065	.0051	.0042	.0032	.0019	.0010	.0004	.0002	7	
17	5	.0090	.0074	.0057	.0048	.0038	.0031	.0024	.0015	.0008	.0004	.0002	5	17
	6	.0108	.0088	.0068	.0056	.0044	.0036	.0028	.0017	.0008	.0004	.0002	6	
	7	.0125	.0102	.0079	.0065	.0051	.0042	.0032	.0019	.0010	.0004	.0002	7	
18	5	.0090	.0074	.0057	.0048	.0038	.0031	.0024	.0015	.0008	.0004	.0002	5	18
	6	.0108	.0087	.0068	.0056	.0044	.0036	.0027	.0016	.0008	.0004	.0002	6	
	7	.0125	.0102	.0079	.0064	.0050	.0041	.0032	.0019	.0010	.0004	.0002	7	
19	5	.0090	.0074	.0057	.0048	.0038	.0031	.0024	.0015	.0008	.0004	.0002	5	19
	6	.0108	.0087	.0068	.0056	.0044	.0035	.0027	.0016	.0008	.0004	.0002	6	
	7	.0125	.0101	.0078	.0064	.0050	.0041	.0031	.0019	.0009	.0004	.0002	7	
20	5	.0090	.0074	.0057	.0048	.0038	.0031	.0024	.0015	.0008	.0004	.0002	5	20
	6	.0108	.0087	.0068	.0056	.0044	.0035	.0027	.0016	.0008	.0004	.0002	6	
	7	.0125	.0101	.0078	.0064	.0050	.0041	.0031	.0019	.0009	.0004	.0002	7	

TABLE 19 (Continued)

$$\bar{u}_r{}' = \bar{d}_r{}' - q_r{}'$$

Avg. Life in Yrs.	Effec. Annual Earning Rate-% r'	SC	$S_{-\frac{1}{2}}$	S_0	$S_{\frac{1}{2}}$	S_1	$S_{1\frac{1}{2}}$	S_2	S_3	S_4	S_5	S_6
21	5	.0090	.0073	.0057	.0047	.0037	.0030	.0023	.0014	.0007	.0003	.0001
	6	.0108	.0087	.0068	.0055	.0044	.0035	.0027	.0017	.0008	.0004	.0002
	7	.0124	.0100	.0077	.0063	.0050	.0040	.0031	.0018	.0009	.0004	.0002
22	5	.0090	.0073	.0057	.0046	.0037	.0030	.0023	.0014	.0007	.0003	.0001
	6	.0108	.0087	.0068	.0055	.0044	.0035	.0027	.0017	.0008	.0004	.0002
	7	.0124	.0100	.0077	.0063	.0049	.0040	.0030	.0018	.0009	.0004	.0002
23	5	.0090	.0073	.0057	.0046	.0037	.0030	.0023	.0014	.0007	.0003	.0001
	6	.0107	.0086	.0067	.0054	.0043	.0035	.0026	.0016	.0008	.0004	.0001
	7	.0123	.0099	.0076	.0062	.0049	.0039	.0030	.0018	.0009	.0004	.0002
24	5	.0089	.0072	.0056	.0046	.0036	.0029	.0022	.0014	.0007	.0003	.0001
	6	.0106	.0086	.0066	.0054	.0043	.0034	.0026	.0016	.0008	.0004	.0001
	7	.0122	.0098	.0075	.0061	.0048	.0039	.0029	.0018	.0009	.0004	.0001
25	5	.0089	.0072	.0056	.0046	.0036	.0029	.0022	.0013	.0007	.0003	.0001
	6	.0106	.0086	.0066	.0054	.0043	.0034	.0026	.0016	.0008	.0004	.0001
	7	.0122	.0098	.0075	.0061	.0048	.0038	.0029	.0018	.0009	.0004	.0001
26	5	.0089	.0072	.0056	.0046	.0036	.0029	.0022	.0013	.0007	.0003	.0001
	6	.0106	.0085	.0066	.0054	.0042	.0034	.0026	.0016	.0008	.0004	.0001
	7	.0121	.0097	.0074	.0060	.0047	.0038	.0029	.0017	.0008	.0004	.0001
27	5	.0089	.0072	.0056	.0046	.0036	.0029	.0022	.0013	.0007	.0003	.0001
	6	.0105	.0085	.0065	.0053	.0042	.0034	.0026	.0015	.0007	.0003	.0001
	7	.0121	.0097	.0074	.0060	.0047	.0038	.0029	.0017	.0008	.0004	.0001

28	5	.0001	.0003	.0007	.0013	.0022	.0029	.0036	.0046	.0056	.0072	.0089
	6	.0001	.0003	.0007	.0015	.0025	.0033	.0041	.0053	.0065	.0084	.0105
	7	.0001	.0004	.0008	.0017	.0028	.0037	.0046	.0059	.0073	.0095	.0119
29	5	.0001	.0003	.0007	.0013	.0022	.0029	.0036	.0046	.0056	.0072	.0089
	6	.0001	.0003	.0007	.0015	.0025	.0033	.0041	.0052	.0064	.0084	.0104
	7	.0001	.0004	.0008	.0017	.0028	.0037	.0046	.0059	.0073	.0095	.0119
30	5	.0001	.0003	.0006	.0013	.0021	.0028	.0035	.0044	.0055	.0071	.0088
	6	.0001	.0003	.0007	.0015	.0025	.0033	.0041	.0052	.0064	.0084	.0104
	7	.0001	.0003	.0008	.0016	.0027	.0036	.0045	.0058	.0071	.0094	.0118
31	5	.0001	.0003	.0006	.0013	.0021	.0028	.0035	.0044	.0055	.0071	.0088
	6	.0001	.0003	.0007	.0014	.0024	.0032	.0040	.0051	.0063	.0083	.0103
	7	.0001	.0003	.0008	.0016	.0027	.0035	.0044	.0057	.0070	.0093	.0117
32	5	.0001	.0003	.0006	.0013	.0021	.0028	.0035	.0044	.0054	.0070	.0088
	6	.0002	.0003	.0007	.0014	.0024	.0032	.0040	.0051	.0063	.0082	.0103
	7	.0001	.0003	.0007	.0015	.0026	.0035	.0043	.0056	.0069	.0092	.0116
33	5	.0001	.0003	.0006	.0013	.0021	.0028	.0034	.0044	.0054	.0070	.0087
	6	.0001	.0003	.0007	.0014	.0023	.0031	.0039	.0050	.0062	.0081	.0102
	7	.0001	.0003	.0007	.0015	.0026	.0034	.0043	.0056	.0069	.0091	.0115
34	5	.0001	.0002	.0006	.0012	.0021	.0027	.0034	.0043	.0053	.0070	.0087
	6	.0001	.0003	.0007	.0014	.0023	.0031	.0039	.0050	.0061	.0081	.0101
	7	.0001	.0003	.0007	.0015	.0025	.0034	.0042	.0055	.0068	.0090	.0114
35	5	.0001	.0002	.0006	.0012	.0021	.0027	.0034	.0043	.0053	.0069	.0087
	6	.0001	.0003	.0006	.0014	.0023	.0030	.0038	.0049	.0061	.0080	.0101
	7	.0001	.0003	.0007	.0015	.0025	.0033	.0042	.0055	.0068	.0090	.0113
36	5	.0001	.0002	.0006	.0012	.0021	.0027	.0034	.0043	.0053	.0069	.0087
	6	.0001	.0003	.0006	.0013	.0023	.0030	.0038	.0049	.0060	.0080	.0100
	7	.0001	.0003	.0007	.0014	.0024	.0033	.0041	.0053	.0066	.0089	.0112

TABLE 19 (Continued)

$$\bar{u}_r{}' = \bar{d}_r{}' - \bar{q}_r{}'$$

Avg. Life in Yrs.	Effec. Annual Earning Rate—% r'	SC	$S_{-\frac{1}{2}}$	$\dot{S}_0$	$S_{\frac{1}{2}}$	S_1	$S_{1\frac{1}{2}}$	S_2	S_3	S_4	S_5	S_6	Effec. Annual Earning Rate—% r'	Avg. Life in Yrs.
37	5	.0086	.0069	.0053	.0043	.0034	.0027	.0021	.0012	.0006	.0002	.0001	5	37
	6	.0099	.0079	.0059	.0048	.0037	.0029	.0022	.0013	.0006	.0002	.0001	6	
	7	.0111	.0088	.0066	.0053	.0041	.0032	.0024	.0014	.0007	.0003	.0001	7	
38	5	.0086	.0068	.0052	.0042	.0033	.0026	.0020	.0012	.0006	.0002	.0001	5	38
	6	.0098	.0078	.0058	.0047	.0037	.0029	.0022	.0013	.0006	.0002	.0001	6	
	7	.0110	.0086	.0064	.0052	.0040	.0031	.0023	.0014	.0006	.0003	.0001	7	
39	5	.0085	.0068	.0052	.0042	.0032	.0026	.0020	.0012	.0005	.0002	.0001	5	39
	6	.0098	.0078	.0058	.0047	.0036	.0029	.0022	.0013	.0006	.0002	.0001	6	
	7	.0109	.0086	.0063	.0051	.0039	.0031	.0023	.0013	.0006	.0003	.0001	7	
40	5	.0085	.0067	.0051	.0042	.0032	.0026	.0020	.0012	.0005	.0002	.0001	5	40
	6	.0097	.0077	.0057	.0046	.0036	.0028	.0021	.0012	.0006	.0002	.0001	6	
	7	.0108	.0085	.0063	.0050	.0038	.0031	.0023	.0013	.0006	.0003	.0001	7	
41	5	.0085	.0067	.0051	.0042	.0032	.0026	.0020	.0012	.0005	.0002	.0001	5	41
	6	.0096	.0076	.0057	.0046	.0035	.0028	.0021	.0012	.0006	.0002	.0001	6	
	7	.0106	.0083	.0062	.0049	.0037	.0030	.0022	.0013	.0006	.0003	.0001	7	
42	5	.0084	.0067	.0051	.0041	.0032	.0025	.0019	.0011	.0005	.0002	.0001	5	42
	6	.0096	.0075	.0056	.0046	.0035	.0028	.0021	.0012	.0006	.0002	.0001	6	
	7	.0106	.0083	.0061	.0049	.0037	.0030	.0022	.0013	.0006	.0003	.0001	7	
43	5	.0083	.0066	.0050	.0041	.0031	.0025	.0019	.0011	.0005	.0002	.0001	5	43
	6	.0095	.0075	.0056	.0045	.0035	.0028	.0021	.0012	.0006	.0002	.0001	6	
	7	.0105	.0082	.0060	.0048	.0037	.0029	.0022	.0013	.0006	.0003	.0001	7	

44	5	.0001	.0002	.0005	.0011	.0019	.0025	.0031	.0041	.0050	.0066	.0083
	6	.0001	.0002	.0006	.0012	.0020	.0027	.0034	.0045	.0055	.0074	.0094
	7	.0001	.0002	.0005	.0011	.0020	.0028	.0035	.0047	.0059	.0080	.0103
45	5	.0001	.0002	.0005	.0011	.0018	.0024	.0030	.0040	.0049	.0065	.0082
	6	.0001	.0002	.0006	.0012	.0020	.0027	.0034	.0044	.0055	.0074	.0093
	7	.0001	.0002	.0005	.0011	.0020	.0028	.0035	.0045	.0058	.0080	.0102
46	5	.0001	.0002	.0005	.0011	.0018	.0024	.0030	.0040	.0049	.0065	.0082
	6	.0001	.0002	.0006	.0011	.0020	.0026	.0033	.0044	.0054	.0073	.0093
	7	.0001	.0002	.0005	.0011	.0019	.0027	.0034	.0045	.0057	.0078	.0101
47	5	.0001	.0002	.0005	.0011	.0018	.0024	.0030	.0039	.0049	.0065	.0082
	6	.0001	.0002	.0006	.0011	.0020	.0026	.0033	.0043	.0054	.0073	.0092
	7	.0001	.0002	.0005	.0011	.0019	.0027	.0034	.0045	.0057	.0078	.0100
48	5	.0001	.0002	.0005	.0011	.0018	.0024	.0030	.0039	.0048	.0064	.0081
	6	.0001	.0002	.0006	.0011	.0019	.0025	.0032	.0042	.0053	.0072	.0091
	7	.0001	.0002	.0005	.0011	.0019	.0026	.0033	.0045	.0056	.0077	.0099
49	5	.0001	.0002	.0005	.0011	.0018	.0024	.0030	.0039	.0048	.0064	.0081
	6	.0001	.0002	.0005	.0010	.0019	.0025	.0031	.0041	.0052	.0070	.0090
	7	.0001	.0002	.0005	.0011	.0019	.0026	.0033	.0044	.0055	.0076	.0098
50	5	.0001	.0002	.0005	.0010	.0017	.0023	.0029	.0038	.0047	.0063	.0080
	6	.0001	.0002	.0005	.0010	.0019	.0025	.0032	.0041	.0052	.0070	.0090
	7	.0001	.0002	.0005	.0010	.0018	.0025	.0031	.0042	.0054	.0074	.0096
55	5	.0001	.0002	.0005	.0009	.0016	.0022	.0027	.0036	.0045	.0060	.0077
	6	.0001	.0002	.0005	.0010	.0017	.0023	.0029	.0039	.0049	.0067	.0086
	7	.0001	.0002	.0005	.0009	.0016	.0023	.0029	.0040	.0050	.0070	.0092
60	5	.0001	.0002	.0004	.0009	.0015	.0021	.0026	.0034	.0043	.0058	.0075
	6	.0001	.0001	.0005	.0008	.0015	.0020	.0026	.0035	.0045	.0062	.0081
	7	.0001	.0002	.0004	.0008	.0014	.0020	.0026	.0036	.0046	.0066	.0086

TABLE 20. ADDITIONAL SINKING FUND ANNUITY FOR INTERIM REPLACEMENTS WITH IOWA-TYPE LEFT-MODED DISPERSIONS

(Under the specified effective annual earning rate r')

$$\bar{u}_{r'} = \bar{d}_{r'} - \bar{q}_{r'}$$

Avg. Life in Yrs.	Effec. Annual Earning Rate-% r'	L_0	$L_{\frac{1}{2}}$	L_1	$L_{1\frac{1}{2}}$	L_2	L_3	L_4	L_5	Effec. Annual Earning Rate-% r'	Avg. Life in Yrs.
5	5	.0102	.0085	.0069	.0058	.0046	.0028	.0015	.0008	5	5
	6	.0123	.0102	.0083	.0069	.0056	.0034	.0017	.0007	6	
	7	.0143	.0119	.0096	.0080	.0065	.0040	.0020	.0009	7	
6	5	.0101	.0085	.0069	.0058	.0046	.0028	.0015	.0008	5	6
	6	.0122	.0102	.0083	.0069	.0055	.0033	.0017	.0008	6	
	7	.0142	.0119	.0096	.0080	.0064	.0039	.0020	.0010	7	
7	5	.0101	.0085	.0069	.0057	.0046	.0028	.0014	.0007	5	7
	6	.0122	.0102	.0083	.0069	.0055	.0033	.0017	.0009	6	
	7	.0141	.0118	.0096	.0079	.0063	.0038	.0019	.0009	7	
8	5	.0101	.0085	.0069	.0057	.0046	.0028	.0014	.0007	5	8
	6	.0121	.0102	.0082	.0069	.0055	.0033	.0017	.0009	6	
	7	.0140	.0117	.0095	.0079	.0063	.0038	.0019	.0009	7	
9	5	.0101	.0084	.0068	.0057	.0046	.0027	.0014	.0007	5	9
	6	.0121	.0101	.0082	.0068	.0055	.0033	.0016	.0008	6	
	7	.0140	.0117	.0095	.0079	.0063	.0038	.0019	.0009	7	
10	5	.0100	.0084	.0068	.0057	.0046	.0027	.0014	.0007	5	10
	6	.0119	.0100	.0081	.0067	.0054	.0032	.0016	.0008	6	
	7	.0139	.0116	.0094	.0078	.0062	.0037	.0019	.0009	7	
11	5	.0100	.0084	.0068	.0056	.0045	.0027	.0014	.0007	5	11
	6	.0119	.0100	.0081	.0067	.0054	.0032	.0016	.0008	6	
	7	.0139	.0116	.0094	.0078	.0062	.0037	.0018	.0009	7	

12	5	.0007	.0014	.0027	.0045	.0056	.0068	.0084	.0100
	6	.0007	.0016	.0032	.0053	.0067	.0081	.0100	.0119
	7	.0009	.0018	.0037	.0061	.0077	.0093	.0116	.0138
13	5	.0007	.0013	.0027	.0045	.0056	.0068	.0083	.0099
	6	.0007	.0015	.0031	.0052	.0066	.0080	.0099	.0118
	7	.0009	.0018	.0036	.0061	.0076	.0093	.0114	.0137
14	5	.0007	.0013	.0027	.0045	.0056	.0068	.0083	.0099
	6	.0007	.0015	.0031	.0052	.0066	.0080	.0099	.0118
	7	.0009	.0018	.0036	.0061	.0076	.0093	.0114	.0137
15	5	.0007	.0013	.0027	.0045	.0056	.0068	.0083	.0099
	6	.0007	.0015	.0031	.0052	.0065	.0079	.0098	.0117
	7	.0009	.0018	.0036	.0060	.0075	.0092	.0113	.0135
16	5	.0007	.0013	.0027	.0044	.0055	.0067	.0082	.0098
	6	.0007	.0015	.0031	.0052	.0065	.0079	.0097	.0117
	7	.0009	.0018	.0035	.0059	.0074	.0090	.0112	.0134
17	5	.0007	.0013	.0026	.0044	.0055	.0067	.0082	.0098
	6	.0007	.0015	.0031	.0052	.0065	.0079	.0097	.0117
	7	.0009	.0017	.0035	.0059	.0074	.0090	.0112	.0133
18	5	.0007	.0013	.0026	.0044	.0055	.0067	.0082	.0098
	6	.0007	.0015	.0030	.0051	.0064	.0078	.0096	.0115
	7	.0008	.0017	.0034	.0058	.0073	.0090	.0110	.0133
19	5	.0007	.0013	.0026	.0044	.0055	.0067	.0082	.0098
	6	.0007	.0015	.0030	.0051	.0064	.0078	.0096	.0115
	7	.0008	.0016	.0033	.0057	.0072	.0088	.0109	.0131
20	5	.0007	.0013	.0026	.0043	.0054	.0066	.0081	.0097
	6	.0007	.0015	.0029	.0050	.0063	.0077	.0095	.0114
	7	.0008	.0016	.0033	.0056	.0072	.0088	.0108	.0130

TABLE 20 (Continued)

$$\bar{u}_{r'} = \bar{d}_{r'} - \bar{q}_{r'}$$

Avg. Life in Yrs.	Effec. Annual Earning Rate–% r'	L_0	$L_{1/2}$	L_1	$L_{1\frac{1}{2}}$	L_2	L_3	L_4	L_5	Effec. Annual Earning Rate–% r'	Avg. Life in Yrs.
21	5	.0096	.0081	.0065	.0054	.0042	.0025	.0012	.0006	5	21
	6	.0113	.0095	.0076	.0063	.0049	.0029	.0015	.0007	6	
	7	.0129	.0107	.0086	.0071	.0056	.0033	.0016	.0008	7	
22	5	.0096	.0080	.0065	.0053	.0042	.0025	.0012	.0006	5	22
	6	.0113	.0094	.0076	.0063	.0049	.0029	.0015	.0007	6	
	7	.0128	.0107	.0086	.0070	.0055	.0032	.0016	.0008	7	
23	5	.0096	.0080	.0065	.0053	.0042	.0025	.0012	.0006	5	23
	6	.0112	.0093	.0075	.0061	.0048	.0028	.0014	.0007	6	
	7	.0127	.0105	.0085	.0069	.0054	.0032	.0016	.0008	7	
24	5	.0095	.0079	.0064	.0052	.0041	.0024	.0012	.0006	5	24
	6	.0111	.0092	.0074	.0061	.0048	.0028	.0014	.0007	6	
	7	.0125	.0104	.0084	.0068	.0053	.0031	.0015	.0007	7	
25	5	.0094	.0078	.0063	.0052	.0041	.0024	.0012	.0006	5	25
	6	.0110	.0092	.0074	.0061	.0047	.0028	.0014	.0007	6	
	7	.0124	.0103	.0083	.0067	.0053	.0031	.0015	.0007	7	
26	5	.0094	.0078	.0063	.0051	.0040	.0024	.0012	.0006	5	26
	6	.0109	.0091	.0073	.0060	.0047	.0028	.0014	.0007	6	
	7	.0122	.0101	.0081	.0066	.0051	.0030	.0015	.0007	7	
27	5	.0093	.0078	.0063	.0051	.0040	.0024	.0012	.0006	5	27
	6	.0108	.0090	.0072	.0059	.0046	.0027	.0013	.0006	6	
	7	.0121	.0101	.0081	.0066	.0051	.0030	.0015	.0007	7	

28	5	.0006	.0012	.0024	.0040	.0051	.0063	.0077	.0093
	6	.0006	.0013	.0027	.0045	.0058	.0072	.0089	.0107
	7	.0007	.0015	.0029	.0050	.0064	.0079	.0099	.0120
29	5	.0006	.0012	.0024	.0040	.0051	.0062	.0077	.0093
	6	.0006	.0013	.0026	.0045	.0058	.0071	.0088	.0106
	7	.0007	.0015	.0029	.0050	.0064	.0079	.0099	.0119
30	5	.0006	.0012	.0023	.0039	.0050	.0061	.0076	.0091
	6	.0006	.0013	.0026	.0045	.0058	.0071	.0088	.0106
	7	.0007	.0014	.0028	.0048	.0063	.0077	.0097	.0117
31	5	.0006	.0012	.0023	.0039	.0050	.0061	.0076	.0091
	6	.0006	.0013	.0025	.0044	.0056	.0069	.0086	.0104
	7	.0006	.0014	.0028	.0048	.0062	.0076	.0095	.0115
32	5	.0005	.0011	.0022	.0038	.0049	.0060	.0075	.0090
	6	.0006	.0012	.0025	.0043	.0056	.0069	.0086	.0103
	7	.0006	.0013	.0027	.0046	.0060	.0075	.0094	.0114
33	5	.0005	.0011	.0022	.0038	.0049	.0060	.0074	.0089
	6	.0006	.0012	.0025	.0042	.0055	.0068	.0084	.0102
	7	.0006	.0013	.0027	.0046	.0060	.0074	.0093	.0113
34	5	.0005	.0011	.0022	.0037	.0048	.0059	.0073	.0088
	6	.0006	.0012	.0024	.0042	.0054	.0067	.0084	.0101
	7	.0006	.0013	.0026	.0045	.0059	.0073	.0092	.0111
35	5	.0005	.0011	.0022	.0037	.0048	.0059	.0073	.0088
	6	.0006	.0012	.0024	.0041	.0053	.0066	.0083	.0100
	7	.0006	.0013	.0026	.0044	.0058	.0072	.0091	.0110
36	5	.0005	.0011	.0022	.0037	.0048	.0059	.0073	.0088
	6	.0006	.0012	.0024	.0041	.0053	.0065	.0082	.0099
	7	.0006	.0012	.0025	.0043	.0057	.0071	.0089	.0108

TABLE 20 (Continued)

$$\bar{u}_r' = \bar{d}_r' - \bar{q}_r'$$

Avg. Life in Yrs.	Effec. Annual Earning Rate-% r'	L_0	$L_{1/2}$	L_1	$L_{1½}$	L_2	L_3	L_4	L_5
37	5	.0087	.0072	.0058	.0047	.0037	.0022	.0011	.0005
	6	.0097	.0080	.0064	.0052	.0040	.0023	.0011	.0005
	7	.0107	.0088	.0070	.0056	.0043	.0025	.0012	.0006
38	5	.0086	.0071	.0057	.0046	.0036	.0021	.0010	.0005
	6	.0096	.0079	.0063	.0051	.0039	.0022	.0011	.0005
	7	.0105	.0086	.0068	.0055	.0042	.0024	.0012	.0005
39	5	.0085	.0070	.0056	.0046	.0035	.0020	.0010	.0005
	6	.0096	.0079	.0063	.0051	.0039	.0022	.0011	.0005
	7	.0104	.0085	.0067	.0054	.0041	.0023	.0011	.0005
40	5	.0084	.0070	.0056	.0045	.0035	.0020	.0010	.0005
	6	.0094	.0078	.0062	.0050	.0038	.0022	.0010	.0005
	7	.0102	.0082	.0067	.0053	.0040	.0023	.0011	.0005
41	5	.0084	.0070	.0056	.0045	.0035	.0020	.0010	.0005
	6	.0093	.0077	.0061	.0049	.0037	.0021	.0010	.0005
	7	.0101	.0082	.0065	.0052	.0039	.0022	.0011	.0005
42	5	.0083	.0069	.0055	.0044	.0034	.0020	.0010	.0005
	6	.0092	.0076	.0060	.0048	.0037	.0021	.0010	.0005
	7	.0100	.0082	.0065	.0051	.0039	.0022	.0011	.0005
43	5	.0082	.0068	.0054	.0044	.0034	.0020	.0010	.0005
	6	.0092	.0075	.0060	.0048	.0037	.0021	.0010	.0005
	7	.0098	.0080	.0063	.0050	.0038	.0022	.0011	.0005

44	5	.0005	.0010	.0020	.0034	.0044	.0054	.0068	.0082
	6	.0005	.0010	.0020	.0036	.0047	.0059	.0074	.0090
	7	.0004	.0010	.0020	.0036	.0049	.0061	.0079	.0096
45	5	.0005	.0009	.0019	.0033	.0043	.0053	.0066	.0081
	6	.0005	.0010	.0020	.0035	.0046	.0058	.0073	.0089
	7	.0004	.0010	.0020	.0036	.0048	.0061	.0078	.0095
46	5	.0005	.0009	.0019	.0033	.0043	.0053	.0066	.0080
	6	.0005	.0010	.0020	.0035	.0046	.0057	.0072	.0088
	7	.0004	.0009	.0020	.0035	.0047	.0059	.0076	.0093
47	5	.0004	.0009	.0019	.0032	.0042	.0052	.0066	.0080
	6	.0005	.0010	.0020	.0034	.0045	.0057	.0072	.0088
	7	.0004	.0009	.0020	.0035	.0047	.0059	.0076	.0093
48	5	.0004	.0009	.0018	.0032	.0042	.0052	.0065	.0079
	6	.0004	.0009	.0019	.0033	.0044	.0056	.0070	.0086
	7	.0004	.0009	.0019	.0034	.0046	.0058	.0074	.0091
49	5	.0004	.0009	.0018	.0032	.0041	.0051	.0065	.0078
	6	.0004	.0009	.0019	.0033	.0043	.0054	.0069	.0085
	7	.0004	.0009	.0019	.0033	.0045	.0057	.0073	.0090
50	5	.0004	.0008	.0017	.0031	.0040	.0050	.0063	.0077
	6	.0004	.0009	.0019	.0033	.0043	.0054	.0069	.0084
	7	.0004	.0008	.0017	.0032	.0043	.0055	.0071	.0088
55	5	.0004	.0008	.0016	.0028	.0038	.0047	.0060	.0073
	6	.0004	.0008	.0017	.0030	.0040	.0050	.0064	.0079
	7	.0004	.0008	.0016	.0029	.0040	.0051	.0066	.0082
60	5	.0004	.0008	.0015	.0027	.0036	.0045	.0057	.0070
	6	.0003	.0007	.0014	.0026	.0036	.0046	.0060	.0074
	7	.0003	.0007	.0014	.0026	.0036	.0046	.0061	.0076

TABLE 21. ADDITIONAL SINKING FUND ANNUITY
FOR INTERIM REPLACEMENTS WITH IOWA-TYPE RIGHT-MODED DISPERSIONS
(Under the specified effective annual earning rate r')

$$\bar{u}_r' = \bar{d}_r' - \bar{q}_r'$$

Avg. Life in Yrs.	Effec. Annual Earning Rate—% r'	$R_{\frac{1}{2}}$	R_1	$R_{1\frac{1}{2}}$	R_2	$R_{2\frac{1}{2}}$	R_3	R_4	R_5	Effec. Annual Earning Rate—% r'	Avg. Life in Yrs.
5	5	.0073	.0057	.0046	.0036	.0028	.0020	.0011	.0005	5	5
	6	.0088	.0069	.0056	.0044	.0034	.0025	.0014	.0007	6	
	7	.0103	.0081	.0066	.0051	.0039	.0029	.0016	.0008	7	
6	5	.0073	.0057	.0046	.0036	.0028	.0020	.0011	.0005	5	6
	6	.0088	.0069	.0056	.0043	.0034	.0024	.0014	.0006	6	
	7	.0103	.0081	.0066	.0050	.0039	.0028	.0015	.0007	7	
7	5	.0073	.0057	.0046	.0036	.0028	.0020	.0011	.0005	5	7
	6	.0088	.0069	.0056	.0043	.0034	.0024	.0014	.0006	6	
	7	.0103	.0081	.0065	.0050	.0039	.0028	.0015	.0006	7	
8	5	.0073	.0057	.0046	.0036	.0028	.0020	.0011	.0005	5	8
	6	.0088	.0069	.0056	.0043	.0034	.0024	.0014	.0006	6	
	7	.0103	.0081	.0065	.0050	.0039	.0028	.0015	.0006	7	
9	5	.0073	.0058	.0046	.0036	.0028	.0020	.0011	.0005	5	9
	6	.0088	.0069	.0056	.0043	.0034	.0024	.0013	.0006	6	
	7	.0103	.0081	.0065	.0050	.0039	.0028	.0015	.0006	7	
10	5	.0073	.0058	.0046	.0036	.0028	.0020	.0011	.0005	5	10
	6	.0088	.0069	.0056	.0043	.0033	.0024	.0013	.0005	6	
	7	.0103	.0081	.0065	.0050	.0039	.0028	.0015	.0006	7	
11	5	.0073	.0058	.0046	.0036	.0028	.0020	.0011	.0005	5	11
	6	.0088	.0069	.0056	.0043	.0033	.0024	.0013	.0005	6	
	7	.0103	.0081	.0065	.0050	.0039	.0028	.0014	.0006	7	

12	5	.0005	.0011	.0020	.0028	.0036	.0047	.0058	.0073	5	12
	6	.0005	.0013	.0024	.0033	.0042	.0056	.0069	.0088	6	
	7	.0006	.0014	.0028	.0039	.0050	.0065	.0081	.0103	7	
13	5	.0005	.0011	.0020	.0028	.0036	.0047	.0058	.0073	5	13
	6	.0005	.0013	.0024	.0033	.0042	.0056	.0069	.0088	6	
	7	.0006	.0014	.0027	.0038	.0050	.0065	.0081	.0103	7	
14	5	.0005	.0011	.0020	.0028	.0036	.0047	.0058	.0074	5	14
	6	.0005	.0012	.0024	.0033	.0042	.0056	.0069	.0088	6	
	7	.0006	.0014	.0027	.0038	.0050	.0065	.0081	.0103	7	
15	5	.0005	.0011	.0020	.0028	.0036	.0047	.0058	.0074	5	15
	6	.0005	.0012	.0023	.0033	.0042	.0055	.0069	.0088	6	
	7	.0006	.0014	.0027	.0038	.0050	.0065	.0081	.0103	7	
16	5	.0005	.0011	.0020	.0028	.0036	.0047	.0058	.0074	5	16
	6	.0005	.0012	.0023	.0033	.0042	.0055	.0069	.0088	6	
	7	.0006	.0014	.0027	.0038	.0049	.0065	.0081	.0103	7	
17	5	.0005	.0011	.0020	.0028	.0036	.0047	.0058	.0074	5	17
	6	.0005	.0012	.0023	.0033	.0042	.0055	.0069	.0088	6	
	7	.0006	.0014	.0027	.0038	.0049	.0065	.0081	.0103	7	
18	5	.0005	.0011	.0020	.0028	.0036	.0047	.0058	.0074	5	18
	6	.0005	.0012	.0023	.0033	.0042	.0055	.0069	.0088	6	
	7	.0006	.0014	.0027	.0038	.0049	.0065	.0081	.0103	7	
19	5	.0005	.0011	.0020	.0028	.0036	.0047	.0058	.0074	5	19
	6	.0005	.0012	.0023	.0033	.0042	.0055	.0069	.0088	6	
	7	.0006	.0014	.0026	.0037	.0049	.0064	.0080	.0102	7	
20	5	.0005	.0011	.0020	.0028	.0036	.0047	.0058	.0074	5	20
	6	.0005	.0012	.0023	.0033	.0042	.0055	.0069	.0088	6	
	7	.0006	.0014	.0026	.0037	.0049	.0064	.0080	.0102	7	

TABLE 21 (Continued)

$$\bar{u}_r' = \bar{d}_r' - \bar{q}_r'$$

Avg. Life in Yrs.	Effec. Annual Earning Rate—% r'	$R_{\frac{1}{2}}$	R_1	$R_{1\frac{1}{4}}$	R_2	$R_{2\frac{1}{2}}$	R_3	R_4	R_5
21	5	.0073	.0058	.0046	.0035	.0027	.0020	.0010	.0004
	6	.0088	.0069	.0055	.0042	.0033	.0023	.0012	.0005
	7	.0101	.0080	.0064	.0048	.0037	.0026	.0014	.0006
22	5	.0073	.0057	.0046	.0035	.0027	.0020	.0010	.0004
	6	.0088	.0069	.0055	.0042	.0033	.0023	.0012	.0005
	7	.0101	.0079	.0064	.0048	.0037	.0026	.0014	.0006
23	5	.0073	.0057	.0046	.0035	.0027	.0020	.0010	.0004
	6	.0087	.0068	.0055	.0042	.0032	.0023	.0012	.0005
	7	.0101	.0079	.0063	.0048	.0037	.0026	.0014	.0006
24	5	.0073	.0057	.0046	.0035	.0027	.0019	.0010	.0004
	6	.0087	.0068	.0055	.0041	.0032	.0023	.0012	.0005
	7	.0100	.0078	.0063	.0047	.0036	.0026	.0013	.0005
25	5	.0073	.0057	.0046	.0035	.0027	.0019	.0010	.0004
	6	.0087	.0068	.0055	.0041	.0032	.0023	.0012	.0005
	7	.0100	.0078	.0062	.0047	.0036	.0026	.0013	.0005
26	5	.0073	.0057	.0046	.0035	.0027	.0019	.0010	.0004
	6	.0086	.0068	.0054	.0041	.0032	.0022	.0012	.0005
	7	.0098	.0077	.0062	.0047	.0036	.0025	.0013	.0005
27	5	.0073	.0057	.0046	.0035	.0027	.0019	.0010	.0004
	6	.0086	.0067	.0054	.0041	.0031	.0022	.0012	.0005
	7	.0098	.0077	.0062	.0047	.0036	.0025	.0013	.0005

28	5	.0073	.0057	.0046	.0035	.0027	.0019	.0010	.0004
	6	.0086	.0067	.0054	.0041	.0031	.0022	.0011	.0004
	7	.0097	.0076	.0061	.0046	.0035	.0025	.0013	.0005
29	5	.0073	.0057	.0046	.0035	.0027	.0019	.0010	.0004
	6	.0085	.0067	.0053	.0040	.0031	.0022	.0011	.0004
	7	.0097	.0076	.0061	.0046	.0035	.0025	.0013	.0005
30	5	.0072	.0056	.0045	.0034	.0026	.0019	.0010	.0004
	6	.0085	.0067	.0053	.0040	.0031	.0022	.0011	.0004
	7	.0096	.0075	.0060	.0045	.0034	.0024	.0012	.0005
31	5	.0072	.0056	.0045	.0034	.0026	.0019	.0010	.0004
	6	.0085	.0066	.0053	.0040	.0031	.0022	.0011	.0004
	7	.0095	.0075	.0059	.0045	.0034	.0024	.0012	.0005
32	5	.0071	.0056	.0045	.0034	.0026	.0018	.0009	.0004
	6	.0084	.0066	.0052	.0040	.0030	.0021	.0011	.0004
	7	.0094	.0074	.0059	.0044	.0034	.0023	.0012	.0005
33	5	.0071	.0056	.0045	.0034	.0026	.0018	.0009	.0004
	6	.0083	.0065	.0052	.0039	.0030	.0021	.0011	.0004
	7	.0094	.0074	.0059	.0044	.0034	.0023	.0012	.0005
34	5	.0071	.0055	.0044	.0033	.0026	.0018	.0009	.0003
	6	.0083	.0065	.0052	.0039	.0030	.0021	.0011	.0004
	7	.0093	.0073	.0058	.0043	.0033	.0023	.0012	.0005
35	5	.0071	.0055	.0044	.0033	.0026	.0018	.0009	.0003
	6	.0082	.0064	.0051	.0038	.0029	.0020	.0010	.0004
	7	.0092	.0072	.0058	.0043	.0033	.0023	.0012	.0005
36	5	.0071	.0055	.0044	.0033	.0026	.0018	.0009	.0003
	6	.0082	.0064	.0051	.0038	.0029	.0020	.0010	.0004
	7	.0091	.0072	.0057	.0043	.0032	.0023	.0011	.0004

TABLE 21 (*Continued*)

$$\overline{u_r'} = \overline{d_r'} - \overline{q_r'}$$

Avg. Life in Yrs.	Effec. Annual Earning Rate—% r'	$R_{1/2}$	R_1	$R_{1\frac{1}{2}}$	R_2	$R_{2\frac{1}{2}}$	R_3	R_4	R_5	Effec. Annual Earning Rate—% r'	Avg. Life in Yrs.
37	5 6 7	.0071 .0081 .0091	.0055 .0063 .0071	.0044 .0050 .0056	.0033 .0038 .0042	.0026 .0029 .0032	.0018 .0020 .0022	.0009 .0010 .0011	.0003 .0004 .0004	5 6 7	37
38	5 6 7	.0070 .0080 .0089	.0055 .0063 .0070	.0044 .0050 .0055	.0033 .0037 .0041	.0025 .0028 .0031	.0018 .0020 .0022	.0009 .0010 .0011	.0003 .0003 .0004	5 6 7	38
39	5 6 7	.0069 .0080 .0089	.0054 .0063 .0069	.0043 .0050 .0055	.0033 .0037 .0041	.0025 .0028 .0031	.0017 .0020 .0021	.0009 .0010 .0010	.0003 .0003 .0004	5 6 7	39
40	5 6 7	.0069 .0079 .0088	.0054 .0062 .0069	.0043 .0049 .0054	.0032 .0037 .0041	.0025 .0028 .0031	.0017 .0019 .0021	.0009 .0009 .0010	.0003 .0003 .0004	5 6 7	40
41	5 6 7	.0069 .0078 .0086	.0054 .0061 .0067	.0043 .0048 .0053	.0032 .0036 .0040	.0025 .0028 .0030	.0017 .0019 .0020	.0009 .0009 .0010	.0003 .0003 .0004	5 6 7	41
42	5 6 7	.0068 .0078 .0086	.0054 .0061 .0067	.0043 .0048 .0053	.0032 .0036 .0040	.0025 .0027 .0030	.0017 .0019 .0020	.0009 .0009 .0010	.0003 .0003 .0004	5 6 7	42
43	5 6 7	.0068 .0078 .0085	.0053 .0061 .0067	.0042 .0048 .0053	.0032 .0036 .0039	.0024 .0027 .0030	.0017 .0019 .0020	.0009 .0009 .0010	.0003 .0003 .0004	5 6 7	43

44	5	.0068	.0053	.0042	.0032	.0024	.0017	.0009	.0003
	6	.0077	.0060	.0048	.0035	.0027	.0019	.0009	.0003
	7	.0084	.0065	.0051	.0038	.0029	.0019	.0009	.0003
45	5	.0067	.0052	.0042	.0031	.0024	.0017	.0008	.0003
	6	.0076	.0060	.0047	.0035	.0027	.0018	.0009	.0003
	7	.0083	.0065	.0051	.0038	.0029	.0019	.0009	.0003
46	5	.0067	.0052	.0042	.0031	.0024	.0017	.0008	.0003
	6	.0076	.0059	.0047	.0035	.0026	.0018	.0009	.0003
	7	.0082	.0064	.0050	.0037	.0028	.0019	.0009	.0003
47	5	.0066	.0052	.0041	.0031	.0024	.0017	.0008	.0003
	6	.0075	.0059	.0047	.0035	.0026	.0018	.0009	.0003
	7	.0082	.0064	.0050	.0037	.0028	.0019	.0009	.0003
48	5	.0066	.0052	.0041	.0031	.0024	.0016	.0008	.0003
	6	.0074	.0058	.0046	.0034	.0026	.0018	.0009	.0003
	7	.0081	.0063	.0050	.0037	.0028	.0019	.0009	.0003
49	5	.0066	.0052	.0041	.0031	.0024	.0016	.0008	.0003
	6	.0073	.0057	.0045	.0033	.0025	.0017	.0008	.0003
	7	.0080	.0062	.0049	.0036	.0027	.0018	.0009	.0003
50	5	.0065	.0051	.0040	.0030	.0023	.0016	.0008	.0003
	6	.0073	.0057	.0045	.0033	.0025	.0017	.0008	.0003
	7	.0078	.0061	.0048	.0035	.0026	.0017	.0008	.0003
55	5	.0062	.0049	.0039	.0029	.0022	.0015	.0007	.0002
	6	.0070	.0054	.0043	.0032	.0024	.0016	.0008	.0003
	7	.0074	.0058	.0045	.0033	.0025	.0016	.0008	.0003
60	5	.0061	.0047	.0038	.0028	.0021	.0015	.0007	.0002
	6	.0066	.0051	.0040	.0029	.0022	.0014	.0007	.0002
	7	.0070	.0054	.0042	.0031	.3023	.0015	.0007	.0002

TABLE 22. ADDITIONAL MAXIMUM LEVEL ANNUAL DEPRECIATION ACCRUAL DUE TO THE SUBSTITUTION OF DOUBLE DECLINING BALANCE METHOD UNDER OPTIMUM BASIS IN PLACE OF THE STRAIGHT LINE METHOD

(Additional level annual year end accrual for recovery in L years of an investment of $1 [zero net salvage] under the specified effective annual earning rate r')

$$\overline{W}_r' = (\overline{D}_{tr}' - 1/L)$$

Avg. Life in Yrs. L	4.0%	4¼%	4½%	4¾%	5.0%	5¼%	5½%	5¾%	6.0%	Avg. Life in Yrs. L
5	.0057	.0060	.0064	.0067	.0071	.0074	.0078	.0081	.0085	5
6	.0052	.0056	.0059	.0062	.0066	.0069	.0072	.0075	.0078	6
7	.0050	.0053	.0057	.0060	.0063	.0066	.0069	.0072	.0075	7
8	.0049	.0052	.0055	.0058	.0061	.0064	.0067	.0070	.0073	8
9	.0048	.0051	.0054	.0057	.0060	.0063	.0065	.0068	.0071	9
10	.0046	.0049	.0052	.0055	.0058	.0061	.0064	.0067	.0070	10
11	.0046	.0049	.0052	.0054	.0057	.0060	.0063	.0066	.0069	11
12	.0045	.0048	.0051	.0054	.0057	.0059	.0062	.0065	.0068	12
13	.0045	.0048	.0050	.0053	.0056	.0059	.0062	.0064	.0067	13
14	.0044	.0047	.0049	.0053	.0055	.0058	.0061	.0064	.0066	14
15	.0043	.0046	.0049	.0052	.0055	.0057	.0060	.0063	.0065	15
16	.0043	.0046	.0049	.0052	.0054	.0057	.0060	.0062	.0065	16
17	.0043	.0046	.0049	.0052	.0054	.0057	.0060	.0062	.0065	17
18	.0043	.0046	.0048	.0051	.0054	.0056	.0059	.0061	.0064	18
19	.0043	.0046	.0048	.0051	.0054	.0056	.0059	.0061	.0064	19
20	.0042	.0045	.0048	.0050	.0053	.0056	.0058	.0061	.0064	20
21	.0042	.0045	.0048	.0050	.0053	.0056	.0058	.0061	.0064	21
22	.0042	.0045	.0047	.0050	.0052	.0055	.0058	.0060	.0063	22
23	.0042	.0045	.0047	.0050	.0052	.0055	.0058	.0060	.0063	23
24	.0042	.0044	.0047	.0050	.0052	.0055	.0058	.0060	.0063	24
25	.0042	.0044	.0047	.0050	.0052	.0055	.0058	.0060	.0063	25

26	.0063	.0060	.0058	.0055	.0052	.0050	.0047	.0044	.0042
27	.0063	.0060	.0057	.0055	.0052	.0050	.0047	.0044	.0042
28	.0063	.0060	.0057	.0055	.0052	.0050	.0047	.0044	.0042
29	.0062	.0060	.0057	.0054	.0052	.0049	.0047	.0044	.0042
30	.0062	.0060	.0057	.0054	.0052	.0049	.0047	.0044	.0042
31	.0062	.0060	.0057	.0054	.0052	.0049	.0047	.0044	.0041
32	.0062	.0059	.0057	.0054	.0052	.0049	.0047	.0044	.0041
33	.0062	.0059	.0057	.0054	.0052	.0049	.0047	.0044	.0041
34	.0062	.0059	.0057	.0054	.0052	.0049	.0047	.0044	.0041
35	.0061	.0059	.0056	.0054	.0051	.0049	.0046	.0044	.0041
36	.0061	.0059	.0056	.0054	.0051	.0049	.0046	.0044	.0041
37	.0061	.0059	.0056	.0054	.0051	.0049	.0046	.0044	.0041
38	.0061	.0059	.0056	.0054	.0051	.0049	.0046	.0044	.0041
39	.0061	.0059	.0056	.0054	.0051	.0049	.0046	.0044	.0041
40	.0061	.0059	.0056	.0054	.0051	.0049	.0046	.0044	.0041
41	.0061	.0058	.0056	.0053	.0051	.0049	.0046	.0044	.0041
42	.0061	.0058	.0056	.0053	.0051	.0049	.0046	.0044	.0041
43	.0061	.0058	.0056	.0053	.0051	.0048	.0046	.0043	.0041
44	.0061	.0058	.0056	.0053	.0051	.0048	.0046	.0043	.0041
45	.0061	.0058	.0056	.0053	.0051	.0048	.0046	.0043	.0041
46	.0061	.0058	.0056	.0053	.0051	.0048	.0046	.0043	.0041
47	.0060	.0058	.0055	.0053	.0051	.0048	.0046	.0043	.0041
48	.0060	.0058	.0055	.0053	.0051	.0048	.0046	.0043	.0041
49	.0060	.0058	.0055	.0053	.0051	.0048	.0046	.0043	.0041
50	.0060	.0058	.0055	.0053	.0050	.0048	.0046	.0043	.0041
55	.0059	.0057	.0054	.0052	.0049	.0047	.0045	.0042	.0040
60	.0058	.0056	.0054	.0052	.0049	.0047	.0045	.0042	.0040
65	.0057	.0055	.0053	.0052	.0049	.0047	.0045	.0042	.0040
70	.0057	.0055	.0053	.0051	.0048	.0047	.0044	.0042	.0040
75	.0056	.0054	.0051	.0051	.0047	.0046	.0044	.0042	.0040
80	.0055	.0053	.0051	.0050	.0046	.0045	.0043	.0042	.0039
85	.0054	.0052	.0050	.0049	.0045	.0045	.0043	.0041	.0039
90	.0053	.0052	.0050	.0048	.0045	.0045	.0043	.0041	.0039
95	.0052	.0051	.0049	.0048	.0045	.0044	.0043	.0041	.0039
100	.0051	.0050	.0048	.0047	.0044	.0044	.0042	.0040	.0038
∞	.0000	.0000	.0000	.0000	.0000	.0000	.0000	.0000	.0000

TABLE 23. ADDITIONAL LEVEL ANNUAL DEPRECIATION ACCRUAL DUE TO THE SUBSTITUTION OF THE SUM-OF-YEARS DIGITS METHOD IN PLACE OF THE STRAIGHT LINE METHOD

(Additional level annual year end accrual for recovery in L years of an investment of $1 [zero net salvage] under the specified effective annual earning rate r")

$$\overline{W}_r' = (\overline{D}_{tr}' - 1/L)$$

Avg. Life in Yrs. L	4.0%	4¼%	4½%	4¾%	5.0%	5¼%	5½%	5¾%	6.0%	6¼%	6½%	6¾%	Avg. Life in Yrs. L
5	.0053	.0056	.0059	.0062	.0065	.0068	.0072	.0074	.0078	.0081	.0084	.0087	5
6	.0054	.0058	.0061	.0064	.0068	.0071	.0074	.0077	.0080	.0084	.0087	.0090	6
7	.0056	.0059	.0063	.0066	.0069	.0073	.0076	.0080	.0083	.0086	.0090	.0093	7
8	.0057	.0060	.0064	.0067	.0071	.0074	.0078	.0081	.0085	.0088	.0092	.0095	8
9	.0058	.0062	.0065	.0069	.0072	.0076	.0079	.0083	.0086	.0090	.0093	.0096	9
10	.0059	.0062	.0066	.0070	.0073	.0076	.0080	.0083	.0087	.0090	.0094	.0097	10
11	.0059	.0063	.0067	.0070	.0074	.0077	.0081	.0084	.0088	.0091	.0095	.0098	11
12	.0060	.0063	.0067	.0071	.0074	.0078	.0081	.0085	.0089	.0092	.0096	.0099	12
13	.0060	.0064	.0068	.0071	.0075	.0078	.0082	.0086	.0089	.0093	.0096	.0099	13
14	.0060	.0064	.0068	.0071	.0075	.0079	.0082	.0086	.0089	.0093	.0096	.0100	14
15	.0061	.0064	.0068	.0072	.0075	.0079	.0082	.0086	.0090	.0093	.0096	.0100	15
16	.0061	.0065	.0069	.0072	.0076	.0079	.0083	.0086	.0090	.0093	.0097	.0100	16
17	.0061	.0065	.0069	.0072	.0076	.0079	.0083	.0086	.0090	.0093	.0097	.0100	17
18	.0061	.0065	.0069	.0072	.0076	.0079	.0083	.0087	.0090	.0093	.0097	.0100	18
19	.0061	.0065	.0069	.0072	.0076	.0080	.0083	.0087	.0090	.0093	.0097	.0100	19
20	.0062	.0065	.0069	.0072	.0076	.0080	.0083	.0087	.0090	.0093	.0097	.0100	20
21	.0062	.0065	.0069	.0073	.0076	.0080	.0083	.0087	.0090	.0093	.0097	.0100	21
22	.0062	.0065	.0069	.0073	.0076	.0080	.0083	.0087	.0090	.0093	.0097	.0100	22
23	.0062	.0065	.0069	.0073	.0076	.0080	.0083	.0087	.0090	.0094	.0097	.0100	23
24	.0062	.0065	.0069	.0073	.0076	.0080	.0083	.0087	.0090	.0094	.0097	.0100	24
25	.0062	.0065	.0069	.0073	.0076	.0080	.0083	.0087	.0090	.0093	.0097	.0100	25

26	.0100	.0097	.0093	.0090	.0087	.0083	.0080	.0076	.0073	.0069	.0065	.0062
27	.0100	.0096	.0093	.0090	.0086	.0083	.0080	.0076	.0073	.0069	.0065	.0062
28	.0100	.0096	.0093	.0090	.0086	.0083	.0080	.0076	.0073	.0069	.0065	.0062
29	.0099	.0096	.0093	.0090	.0086	.0083	.0080	.0076	.0073	.0069	.0065	.0062
30	.0099	.0096	.0093	.0090	.0086	.0083	.0080	.0076	.0073	.0069	.0065	.0062
31	.0099	.0096	.0092	.0089	.0086	.0083	.0079	.0076	.0072	.0069	.0065	.0062
32	.0099	.0095	.0092	.0089	.0086	.0083	.0079	.0076	.0072	.0069	.0065	.0062
33	.0098	.0095	.0092	.0089	.0086	.0082	.0079	.0076	.0072	.0069	.0065	.0062
34	.0098	.0095	.0092	.0089	.0085	.0082	.0079	.0076	.0072	.0069	.0065	.0062
35	.0098	.0095	.0092	.0088	.0085	.0082	.0079	.0075	.0072	.0069	.0065	.0062
36	.0097	.0094	.0091	.0088	.0085	.0082	.0079	.0075	.0072	.0069	.0065	.0062
37	.0097	.0094	.0091	.0088	.0085	.0082	.0078	.0075	.0072	.0068	.0065	.0061
38	.0096	.0094	.0091	.0088	.0084	.0081	.0078	.0075	.0072	.0068	.0065	.0061
39	.0096	.0093	.0090	.0087	.0084	.0081	.0078	.0075	.0072	.0068	.0065	.0061
40	.0096	.0093	.0090	.0087	.0084	.0081	.0078	.0075	.0071	.0068	.0065	.0061
41	.0095	.0093	.0090	.0087	.0084	.0081	.0078	.0075	.0071	.0068	.0065	.0061
42	.0095	.0092	.0089	.0087	.0084	.0081	.0078	.0074	.0071	.0068	.0065	.0061
43	.0095	.0092	.0089	.0086	.0083	.0080	.0077	.0074	.0071	.0068	.0064	.0061
44	.0094	.0091	.0089	.0086	.0083	.0080	.0077	.0074	.0071	.0068	.0064	.0061
45	.0094	.0091	.0088	.0086	.0083	.0080	.0077	.0074	.0070	.0068	.0064	.0061
46	.0093	.0091	.0088	.0085	.0083	.0080	.0077	.0074	.0070	.0067	.0064	.0061
47	.0093	.0090	.0087	.0085	.0082	.0079	.0077	.0073	.0070	.0067	.0064	.0061
48	.0093	.0090	.0087	.0085	.0082	.0079	.0076	.0073	.0070	.0067	.0064	.0061
49	.0092	.0089	.0087	.0084	.0082	.0079	.0076	.0073	.0070	.0067	.0064	.0060
50	.0092	.0089	.0087	.0084	.0081	.0079	.0076	.0073	.0070	.0067	.0064	.0060
55	.0089	.0087	.0085	.0082	.0080	.0077	.0075	.0072	.0069	.0066	.0063	.0060
60	.0087	.0085	.0083	.0080	.0078	.0076	.0073	.0071	.0068	.0065	.0062	.0059
65	.0085	.0083	.0081	.0079	.0076	.0074	.0072	.0069	.0067	.0064	.0061	.0058
70	.0082	.0080	.0079	.0077	.0075	.0073	.0070	.0068	.0065	.0063	.0060	.0058
75	.0080	.0078	.0077	.0075	.0073	.0071	.0069	.0067	.0064	.0062	.0060	.0057
80	.0078	.0076	.0075	.0073	.0071	.0069	.0067	.0065	.0063	.0061	.0059	.0056
85	.0075	.0074	.0073	.0071	.0069	.0068	.0066	.0064	.0062	.0060	.0058	.0055
90	.0073	.0072	.0071	.0069	.0068	.0066	.0064	.0063	.0061	.0059	.0057	.0054
95	.0071	.0070	.0069	.0068	.0066	.0064	.0063	.0061	.0059	.0058	.0056	.0053
100	.0069	.0068	.0067	.0066	.0064	.0063	.0061	.0060	.0058	.0057	.0055	.0053
∞	.0000	.0000	.0000	.0000	.0000	.0000	.0000	.0000	.0000	.0000	.0000	.0000

TABLE 24. PRESENT WORTH OF $1
What $1 Due in the Future is Worth Today
(Under the specified effective annual earning rate r')

$$v^n = \frac{1}{(1+r')^n}$$

n in Yrs.	4.0%	4¼%	4½%	4¾%	5.0%	5¼%	5½%	5¾%	6.0%	6¼%	6½%	6¾%	n in Yrs.
1	.9615	.9592	.9569	.9547	.9524	.9501	.9479	.9456	.9434	.9412	.9390	.9368	1
2	.9246	.9201	.9157	.9114	.9070	.9027	.8985	.8942	.8900	.8858	.8817	.8775	2
3	.8890	.8826	.8763	.8700	.8638	.8577	.8516	.8456	.8396	.8337	.8278	.8220	3
4	.8548	.8466	.8386	.8306	.8227	.8149	.8072	.7996	.7921	.7847	.7773	.7701	4
5	.8219	.8121	.8025	.7929	.7835	.7743	.7651	.7561	.7473	.7385	.7299	.7214	5
6	.7903	.7790	.7679	.7570	.7462	.7356	.7252	.7150	.7050	.6951	.6853	.6758	6
7	.7599	.7473	.7348	.7226	.7107	.6989	.6874	.6761	.6651	.6542	.6435	.6330	7
8	.7307	.7168	.7032	.6899	.6768	.6641	.6516	.6394	.6274	.6157	.6042	.5930	8
9	.7026	.6876	.6729	.6586	.6446	.6310	.6176	.6046	.5919	.5795	.5674	.5555	9
10	.6756	.6595	.6439	.6287	.6139	.5995	.5854	.5717	.5584	.5454	.5327	.5204	10
11	.6496	.6326	.6162	.6002	.5847	.5696	.5549	.5406	.5268	.5133	.5002	.4875	11
12	.6246	.6069	.5897	.5730	.5568	.5412	.5260	.5113	.4970	.4831	.4697	.4567	12
13	.6006	.5821	.5643	.5470	.5303	.5142	.4986	.4835	.4688	.4547	.4410	.4278	13
14	.5775	.5584	.5400	.5222	.5051	.4885	.4726	.4572	.4423	.4280	.4141	.4007	14
15	.5553	.5356	.5167	.4985	.4810	.4642	.4479	.4323	.4173	.4028	.3888	.3754	15
16	.5339	.5138	.4945	.4759	.4581	.4410	.4246	.4088	.3936	.3791	.3651	.3517	16
17	.5134	.4928	.4732	.4543	.4363	.4190	.4024	.3866	.3714	.3568	.3428	.3294	17
18	.4936	.4727	.4528	.4337	.4155	.3981	.3815	.3656	.3503	.3358	.3219	.3086	18
19	.4746	.4535	.4333	.4141	.3957	.3783	.3616	.3457	.3305	.3160	.3022	.2891	19
20	.4564	.4350	.4146	.3952	.3769	.3594	.3427	.3269	.3118	.2975	.2838	.2708	20
21	.4388	.4173	.3968	.3774	.3589	.3415	.3249	.3091	.2942	.2800	.2665	.2537	21
22	.4220	.4002	.3797	.3603	.3418	.3244	.3079	.2923	.2775	.2635	.2502	.2376	22
23	.4057	.3839	.3634	.3439	.3256	.3082	.2919	.2764	.2618	.2480	.2349	.2226	23
24	.3901	.3683	.3477	.3283	.3101	.2929	.2767	.2614	.2470	.2334	.2206	.2085	24
25	.3751	.3533	.3327	.3134	.2953	.2783	.2622	.2472	.2330	.2197	.2071	.1953	25

26	.3607	.3389	.3184	.2992	.2812	.2644	.2486	.2337	.2198	.2068	.1945	.1830	26
27	.3468	.3250	.3047	.2857	.2678	.2512	.2356	.2210	.2074	.1946	.1826	.1714	27
28	.3335	.3118	.2916	.2727	.2551	.2387	.2233	.2090	.1956	.1831	.1715	.1606	28
29	.3207	.2991	.2790	.2603	.2429	.2268	.2117	.1976	.1846	.1724	.1610	.1504	29
30	.3083	.2869	.2670	.2485	.2314	.2154	.2006	.1869	.1741	.1622	.1512	.1409	30
31	.2965	.2752	.2555	.2373	.2204	.2047	.1902	.1767	.1643	.1527	.1420	.1320	31
32	.2851	.2640	.2445	.2265	.2099	.1945	.1809	.1671	.1550	.1457	.1333	.1237	32
33	.2741	.2532	.2340	.2162	.1999	.1848	.1709	.1580	.1462	.1353	.1252	.1158	33
34	.2636	.2429	.2239	.2064	.1904	.1756	.1620	.1494	.1379	.1273	.1175	.1085	34
35	.2534	.2330	.2143	.1971	.1813	.1668	.1535	.1413	.1301	.1198	.1103	.1017	35
36	.2437	.2235	.2050	.1881	.1727	.1585	.1455	.1336	.1227	.1128	.1036	.0952	36
37	.2343	.2144	.1962	.1796	.1644	.1506	.1379	.1264	.1158	.1061	.0973	.0892	37
38	.2253	.2056	.1878	.1715	.1566	.1431	.1307	.1195	.1092	.0999	.0914	.0836	38
39	.2166	.1973	.1797	.1637	.1491	.1359	.1239	.1130	.1031	.0940	.0858	.0783	39
40	.2083	.1892	.1719	.1563	.1420	.1292	.1175	.1069	.0972	.0885	.0805	.0733	40
41	.2003	.1815	.1645	.1492	.1353	.1227	.1113	.1010	.0917	.0833	.0756	.0687	41
42	.1926	.1741	.1574	.1424	.1288	.1166	.1055	.0955	.0865	.0784	.0710	.0644	42
43	.1852	.1670	.1507	.1359	.1227	.1108	.1000	.0904	.0816	.0738	.0667	.0603	43
44	.1780	.1602	.1442	.1298	.1169	.1053	.0948	.0854	.0770	.0694	.0626	.0565	44
45	.1712	.1537	.1380	.1239	.1113	.1000	.0899	.0808	.0727	.0653	.0588	.0529	45
46	.1646	.1474	.1320	.1183	.1060	.0950	.0852	.0764	.0685	.0615	.0552	.0496	46
47	.1583	.1414	.1263	.1129	.1009	.0903	.0807	.0722	.0647	.0579	.0518	.0464	47
48	.1522	.1356	.1209	.1078	.0961	.0858	.0765	.0683	.0610	.0545	.0487	.0435	48
49	.1463	.1301	.1157	.1029	.0916	.0815	.0725	.0646	.0575	.0513	.0457	.0407	49
50	.1407	.1248	.1107	.0982	.0872	.0774	.0688	.0611	.0543	.0483	.0429	.0382	50
55	.1157	.1013	.0888	.0779	.0683	.0599	.0526	.0462	.0406	.0356	.0313	.0275	55
60	.0951	.0823	.0713	.0618	.0535	.0464	.0403	.0349	.0303	.0263	.0229	.0199	60
65	.0781	.0668	.0572	.0490	.0419	.0359	.0308	.0264	.0227	.0194	.0167	.0143	65
70	.0642	.0543	.0459	.0388	.0329	.0278	.0236	.0200	.0169	.0144	.0122	.0103	70
75	.0528	.0441	.0368	.0308	.0258	.0215	.0180	.0151	.0126	.0106	.0089	.0075	75
80	.0434	.0358	.0296	.0244	.0202	.0167	.0138	.0114	.0095	.0078	.0065	.0054	80
85	.0357	.0293	.0237	.0194	.0158	.0129	.0106	.0086	.0071	.0058	.0047	.0039	85
90	.0293	.0241	.0190	.0154	.0124	.0100	.0081	.0065	.0053	.0043	.0035	.0028	90
95	.0241	.0198	.0153	.0122	.0097	.0077	.0062	.0049	.0039	.0032	.0025	.0020	95
100	.0198	.0156	.0123	.0097	.0076	.0060	.0047	.0037	.0029	.0023	.0018	.0015	100
∞	.0000	.0000	.0000	.0000	.0000	.0000	.0000	.0000	.0000	.0000	.0000	.0000	∞

TABLE 25. PRESENT WORTH OF $1 PER YEAR
What $1 Payable Annually at Each Year End is Worth Today
(Under the specified effective annual earning rate r')

$$a_n = \frac{(1+r')^n - 1}{r'(1+r')^n}$$

n in Yrs.	4.0%	4¼%	4½%	4¾%	5.0%	5¼%	5½%	5¾%	6.0%	6¼%	6½%	6¾%	n in Yrs.
1	0.962	0.959	0.957	0.955	0.952	0.950	0.948	0.946	0.943	0.941	0.939	0.937	1
2	1.886	1.879	1.873	1.866	1.859	1.855	1.846	1.840	1.833	1.827	1.821	1.814	2
3	2.775	2.762	2.749	2.736	2.723	2.711	2.698	2.685	2.673	2.661	2.648	2.636	3
4	3.630	3.609	3.588	3.567	3.546	3.525	3.505	3.485	3.465	3.445	3.426	3.406	4
5	4.452	4.421	4.390	4.360	4.329	4.300	4.270	4.241	4.212	4.184	4.156	4.128	5
6	5.242	5.200	5.158	5.117	5.076	5.035	4.996	4.956	4.917	4.879	4.841	4.804	6
7	6.002	5.947	5.893	5.839	5.786	5.734	5.683	5.632	5.582	5.533	5.485	5.437	7
8	6.733	6.664	6.596	6.529	6.463	6.398	6.335	6.272	6.210	6.149	6.089	6.030	8
9	7.435	7.351	7.269	7.188	7.108	7.029	6.952	6.876	6.802	6.728	6.656	6.585	9
10	8.111	8.011	7.913	7.816	7.722	7.629	7.538	7.448	7.360	7.274	7.189	7.105	10
11	8.760	8.644	8.529	8.417	8.306	8.198	8.093	7.989	7.887	7.787	7.689	7.593	11
12	9.385	9.250	9.119	8.990	8.863	8.740	8.619	8.500	8.384	8.270	8.159	8.050	12
13	9.986	9.833	9.683	9.537	9.394	9.254	9.117	8.983	8.853	8.725	8.600	8.477	13
14	10.563	10.391	10.223	10.059	9.899	9.742	9.590	9.441	9.295	9.153	9.014	8.878	14
15	11.118	10.927	10.740	10.557	10.380	10.206	10.038	9.873	9.712	9.556	9.403	9.253	15
16	11.652	11.440	11.234	11.033	10.838	10.647	10.462	10.282	10.106	9.935	9.768	9.605	16
17	12.166	11.933	11.707	11.488	11.274	11.066	10.865	10.668	10.477	10.291	10.111	9.935	17
18	12.659	12.406	12.160	11.921	11.690	11.465	11.246	11.034	10.828	10.627	10.432	10.243	18
19	13.134	12.859	12.593	12.335	12.085	11.843	11.608	11.379	11.158	10.943	10.735	10.532	19
20	13.590	13.294	13.008	12.731	12.462	12.202	11.950	11.706	11.470	11.241	11.019	10.803	20
21	14.029	13.712	13.405	13.108	12.821	12.544	12.275	12.015	11.764	11.521	11.285	11.057	21
22	14.451	14.112	13.784	13.468	13.163	12.868	12.583	12.308	12.042	11.784	11.535	11.294	22
23	14.857	14.496	14.148	13.812	13.489	13.176	12.875	12.584	12.303	12.032	11.770	11.517	23
24	15.247	14.864	14.495	14.141	13.799	13.469	13.152	12.846	12.550	12.266	11.991	11.725	24
25	15.622	15.217	14.828	14.454	14.094	13.747	13.414	13.093	12.783	12.485	12.198	11.921	25

n												
26	12.104	12.392	12.692	13.003	13.326	13.662	14.012	14.375	14.753	15.147	15.556	15.983
27	12.275	12.575	12.887	13.211	13.547	13.898	14.263	14.643	15.039	15.451	15.881	16.330
28	12.436	12.746	13.070	13.406	13.756	14.121	14.502	14.898	15.312	15.743	16.193	16.663
29	12.586	12.907	13.242	13.591	13.954	14.333	14.721	15.141	15.572	16.022	16.492	16.984
30	12.727	13.059	13.404	13.765	14.141	14.534	14.944	15.372	15.820	16.289	16.779	17.292
31	12.859	13.201	13.557	13.929	14.318	14.724	15.149	15.593	16.058	16.544	17.054	17.588
32	12.983	13.334	13.701	14.084	14.485	14.904	15.343	15.803	16.284	16.789	17.318	17.874
33	13.099	13.459	13.836	14.230	14.643	15.075	15.528	16.003	16.500	17.023	17.571	18.148
34	13.207	13.577	13.963	14.368	14.792	15.237	15.703	16.193	16.707	17.247	17.814	18.411
35	13.309	13.687	14.083	14.498	14.934	15.391	15.870	16.374	16.904	17.461	18.047	18.665
36	13.404	13.791	14.196	14.621	15.067	15.536	16.029	16.547	17.092	17.666	18.271	18.908
37	13.493	13.888	14.302	14.737	15.194	15.674	16.179	16.711	17.272	17.862	18.485	19.143
38	13.577	13.979	14.402	14.846	15.313	15.805	16.322	16.868	17.433	18.050	18.691	19.368
39	13.655	14.065	14.496	14.949	15.426	15.929	16.458	17.017	17.607	18.230	18.888	19.584
40	13.728	14.146	14.584	15.046	15.523	16.046	16.587	17.159	17.763	18.402	19.077	19.793
41	13.797	14.221	14.668	15.138	15.634	16.157	16.710	17.294	17.912	18.566	19.259	19.993
42	13.861	14.292	14.746	15.225	15.730	16.263	16.827	17.423	18.055	18.724	19.433	20.186
43	13.922	14.359	14.820	15.306	15.820	16.363	16.938	17.546	18.191	18.874	19.600	20.371
44	13.978	14.421	14.889	15.383	15.905	16.458	17.043	17.663	18.320	19.018	19.760	20.549
45	14.031	14.480	14.955	15.456	15.986	16.548	17.143	17.774	18.444	19.156	19.914	20.720
46	14.081	14.535	15.016	15.524	16.063	16.633	17.238	17.880	18.563	19.288	20.061	20.885
47	14.127	14.587	15.074	15.589	16.135	16.714	17.328	17.981	18.675	19.415	20.203	21.043
48	14.171	14.636	15.128	15.650	16.203	16.790	17.414	18.077	18.783	19.536	20.338	21.195
49	14.211	14.682	15.180	15.708	16.268	16.863	17.495	18.169	18.886	19.651	20.468	21.341
50	14.249	14.725	15.228	15.762	16.329	16.932	17.573	18.256	18.984	19.762	20.593	21.482
55	14.407	14.903	15.430	15.991	16.588	17.225	17.906	18.633	19.413	20.248	21.145	22.109
60	14.521	15.033	15.579	16.161	16.784	17.450	18.163	18.929	19.752	20.638	21.593	22.623
65	14.603	15.128	15.689	16.289	16.932	17.622	18.363	19.161	20.022	20.951	21.957	23.047
70	14.662	15.197	15.770	16.385	17.044	17.753	18.518	19.343	20.235	21.202	22.252	23.395
75	14.704	15.248	15.830	16.456	17.129	17.854	18.637	19.485	20.404	21.404	22.492	23.680
80	14.735	15.285	15.875	16.509	17.193	17.931	18.730	19.596	20.525	21.565	22.687	23.915
85	14.757	15.312	15.907	16.549	17.241	17.990	18.802	19.684	20.645	21.695	22.845	24.109
90	14.773	15.331	15.932	16.579	17.278	18.035	18.857	19.752	20.729	21.799	22.974	24.267
95	14.785	15.346	15.950	16.601	17.305	18.069	18.900	19.806	20.796	21.883	23.078	24.398
100	14.793	15.356	15.963	16.618	17.326	18.096	18.933	19.848	20.849	21.950	23.163	24.505
∞	14.815	15.385	16.000	16.667	17.391	18.182	19.048	20.000	21.053	22.222	23.529	25.000

INDEX

Absolute costs, 10

Accountants concerned with cost studies, 10

Accounting activities as factor in rates, 103

Accrued depreciation, *see* Depreciation

Aerial transmission: and bulk transmission, 148; and distribution, 149–50

Allocation ratios in cost assignment, 99, 100 (*equation*)

Alternative plans of operation, evaluation of, 9; capacity additions, 131; using Present Worth techniques, 167

American Institute of Electrical Engineers (AIEE), 39

American Power Conference, 42

Annual basis for cost and revenue data, 16

Annual class peaks, 74–75

Annual load duration curve, 47–48 (*fig.*)

Annual load factor trends and peaking capacity, 132

Annual load occurence curve, 47–48 (*fig.*)

Area coverage cost component: of primary voltage distribution, 31; of secondary voltage distribution, 31

Art of rate making, 7–8, 104

Association of Edison Illuminating Companies (AEIC), 39, 54; Special Committee on Load Studies of AEIC, 55; Load Research Committee of AEIC, 55

Automation, 151

Average costs, 10

Average weekday loads, 47 (*fig.*), 49–50 (*figs.*), 64, 68, 70, 71, 73, 74 (*fig.*)

Averages, ways of obtaining, 6–7

Balanced load building, 122–23

Bary, Constantine W., 42 n.1, 54 n.2, 55 n.3, 68 n.14, 126 n.3, 133 n.1, 157 n.1, 159 n.2, 162 n.5

Bary curve of load diversity, 55, 61 (*fig.*), 62–63 n.12, 65–67 n.13; 95

Base load capacity, 128–29, 139–43

"Below-the-line" analyses, 170–72

Billing of customers, 36; in Europe, 7

Billing demands, long-interval *vs.* short-interval, 113–15, 176

Billing, on monthly basis, 6, 16; as per cost model of supply system, 36

Block rate, 105–7 (*fig.*, *table*); residential rate in low use region, 117 (*fig.*)

Bolton, D. J., 58 n.9

Bonbright, James C., 8 n.2, 7–8, 59 n.10, 104 n.2

Branch portion of primary voltage circuits, 30